The Making
of the Labor
Bureaucrat

Warren R.
Van Tine

The Making of the Labor Bureaucrat

Union Leadership in the United States, 1870-1920

The University of Massachusetts Press Amherst 1973

To Howard H. Quint

Contents

Preface

Since World War II, there has been increased national concern over the activities of the labor bureaucrat. The growing awareness during the war of the power of leaders like John L. Lewis and Sidney Hillman, followed by the debates over the Taft-Hartley Act, the investigations of the McClellan Committee, the prosecution of Dave Beck and Jimmy Hoffa, and most recently the power struggle in the United Mine Workers between W. A. 'Tony' Boyle and the followers of the murdered Joseph Yablonsky have focused the attention of the general public, unionists, and the academic community on the modern labor leader and the related problem of internal union democracy.

One consequence of this increased interest has been the publication of a number of important studies on various aspects of union government. Written largely by sociologists, economists, and political scientists, these works provide valuable insights on the contemporary labor scene. Yet, with a few exceptions, they suffer from a general lack of historical perspective. Concerned with the modern labor leader and the organization he heads, many of these authors have dealt with their subject in static terms, unconcerned with the process of change and development. Lois MacDonald's *Leadership Dynamics and the Trade-Union Leader* (1959), for example, provided an extensive review of the literature on labor leadership and suggested areas for future research. She called for the psychologist, sociologist, economist, political scientist, and others in the social sciences to explore the dynamics of labor leadership, but never did she suggest that the historian could make any contribution to the subject. To be sure, several scholars of the labor movement, including C. Wright Mills, Eli Ginzberg, Will Herberg, and Richard Lester, have sought to give some historical dimensions to their studies. Yet in their concentration on the present, they did not linger long in the past. Usually they have fallen back on a romantic notion that in the beginning the labor movement was an innocent democracy which became corrupted in the years following the New Deal.

This study explores the historical development of labor leadership from 1870 to 1920. To explain the rise of trade union bureaucracy the study focuses on the varying social backgrounds of labor leaders, the changing ideology of unionism, the development of union-management relations, variations in rank-and-file attitudes, the evolution of union government, as well as the nature of the men who held office. Throughout the study, the terms "bureaucratic" and "bureaucrat" are used for their functional rather than pejorative connotations. While at times critical of the men who led labor, it is not the author's intent to condone or condemn but only to understand.

The study also reveals an important aspect of the increased bureaucratization of American life which occurred in the decades around the turn of the century, a subject which has received its broadest treatment in Robert Wiebe's *The Search for Order: 1877-1920* (1967). Wiebe and others have concentrated primarily on the impact which the rise of large-scale, bureaucratically structured organizations had on American society. The present study is concerned with the intricacies of organizational change during this period. Given the special conditions which unions faced, many of the conclusions of this study are applicable only to the labor movement. Yet many of the broader forces behind leadership development such as the members' values, prevailing social attitudes, and problems of basic organizational action were common to many of the emerging institutions of modern society. As the editor of the *United Mine Workers' Journal* trenchantly remarked in 1912: "The problem of leadership, one that is almost constantly before the public, is, after all, nothing more than the problem of mankind in all walks of life, in labor circles as well as others."

This book would not have been possible without the assistance of a number of institutions and individuals. I am indebted to the International Brotherhood of Teamsters for permission to use their papers. Moreau Chambers was particularly gracious in helping me use the archives at The Catholic University of America. The librarians of the University of Massachusetts, and particularly those manning the inter-library loan desk, worked tirelessly on my behalf. I am also grateful to the Labor Relations and Research Center at the University of Massachusetts, which provided me with microfilm and other services. The staffs at the Manuscript Division of the Library of Congress, the State Historical Society of Wisconsin, the Ohio Historical Society, and the Archives of Labor History and Urban Affairs at Wayne State University all offered me their full cooperation.

My understanding of the subject has been enriched by the wise counseling of others. I benefited from the learned advice of my colleagues at Ohio State University, among them Les Benedict, Peter Hoffer, and Austin Kerr. Likewise, Samuel Walker critically read the manuscript and offered valuable assistance. My wife, Anne, read the manuscript countless times while it was still in its primitive stages and caught many an error before it reached other eyes.

Two men deserve special thanks. Professor Melvyn Dubofsky first introduced me to the field of labor history and has become my friend as well as mentor. He suggested this topic for a dissertation and continued to work untiringly with me even after he left the University of Massachusetts. I was fortunate in having Professor Howard Quint take over the direction of my studies. In the spirit of scholarship and friendship, he made available to me his vast knowledge of history as well as his stylistic skills.

1.

The Traditional Labor Leader and the New Business Unionist

It does not do, therefore, to take the historian too seriously; at best he but weaves the warp of fancy into the woof of fact and gives us the web called history.

Terence V. Powderly[1]

I

Historians have long maintained that a fundamental turning point occurred in American labor history during the closing decade of the nineteenth century. On the one hand, the decline of the Knights of Labor marked the end of an era during which the labor movement had been strongly rural and middle class in orientation. The Knights had failed in their attempt to unite all producers into one big union, and to replace the wage system with an economy of cooperative associations. The rise of the American Federation of Labor, on the other hand, signified the beginning of a new era. Predominantly an urban skilled-workers' movement, the AFL advocated a new philosophy of "business unionism." Unlike the Knights, the Federation accepted the existence of industrial capitalism, abandoned all efforts to transform the workers into owners, and sought to advance the laborer's welfare by concentrating on the bread-and-butter issues of hours and wages.[2]

As part of this transition in the nature of the American labor movement, scholars have also perceived the emergence of a new type of union official. Selig Perlman, Philip Taft, Gerald Grob, Robert Wiebe, and a number of other historians have distinguished in their works between the old-school labor leader and the new business unionist. To a large extent, moreover, these scholars have seen the differences in outlook and attitude of the two phases of the labor movement as manifestations of the differing sociological backgrounds and behavioral patterns of the two types of leaders.[3] Such an approach is used by Gerald Grob to explain the origins of the Knights of Labor's "utopianism":

> The Knights, on the whole, were led by men who had been born and had grown to maturity during the eventful decades preceding the Civil War. The humanitarian crusades of the 1840's and 1850's had laid the foundation for an irrevocable hostility toward industrial society and the wage system. Belonging to an America where the develpment [sic] of an industrial economy had not yet overwhelmed a predominantly rural nation, these leaders did not think in terms of a permanent wage-earning class and its needs. Regarding the workers as the only legitimate members of the community, they sought to establish a co-operative society based upon a large number of small producers, for only under such conditions could the American democratic ideal be realized.[4]

John R. Commons similarly used environmentalism to reveal how men like Adolph Strasser and P. J. McGuire arrived at the philosophy of "business unionism." Unlike the old-school labor leaders, he maintained, these men did not regard "combination into trade unions as a mere stepping stone to self-employment. . . . At the same time their foreign birth and upbringing kept them from contact with the life of the great American middle class, the farmers and the small employers, the class which kept alive the philosophy of self-employment and voluntary co-operation."[5]

Descriptions found in secondary works of the characteristics of the old-school labor leaders and the new business unionists are for the most part highly generalized, frequently impressionistic, and often misleading. Even John R. Commons slighted the historical record to substantiate his impressions. P. J. McGuire, one of Commons's model new unionists, was, in fact, not of foreign origin and upbringing but born and raised in New York City's lower East Side. Yet scholars have freely borrowed conclusions from one another with the result that their portraits of the traditional and business unionists seldom differ. In effect, two stereotypes have been created. The characteristics of the old-school or traditional labor leader are the more delineated of the two types. He is seen as the product of a native American, middle-class, small town background. Quite probably his father was either a merchant, small manufacturer, farmer, or, at the least, a skilled craftsman. He received a respectable education, and perhaps even spent a year or two at a private academy. The traditional labor leader generally became associated with unionism through one of two paths. After leaving school he might have established a small business which, like so many such ventures during the Gilded Age, failed within a few years. Forced into the ranks of the wage-earners, he saw in the labor movement a means of regaining his lost status and also of combating the disruptive forces of industrialism. Another path into the labor movement was frequently taken by reformers, journalists, and politicians. Primarily desiring to advance their own careers and causes, such men would attach themselves to a fairly strong union in order to establish a base for their individual missions. As a product of the middle class, the old-school labor leader would inevitably misguide the union movement away from the "basic issues" of hours and wages and into such bourgeois causes as cooperatives, temperance, and particularly "antimonopolyism." He was active in politics, often a supporter of third-party movements, and frequently a candidate for political office himself. In his search for increasing status, he was a chronic joiner of middle-class fraternal organizations. Finally, if fortunate, the traditional labor leader eventually became a successful politician, lawyer, merchant, or journalist and would then lessen or completely break his ties with the labor movement.[6]

In *The Labor Movement in the United States, 1860-1895,* Norman Ware presents a description of an individual who he feels was representative of the traditional labor leader:

Charles Litchman, grand scribe of the Crispins, was made grand secretary of the Knights of Labor at its first convention in 1878. Litchman was a typical labor leader of the old school—trade unionist, reformer, politician, and publicist in one. He was born in Marblehead, Mass., April 8, 1849. His father was a shoe "manufacturer" and he went on the road as a salesman for the concern. He studied law and went into business but evidently failed, for in 1874 he was employed in a shoe factory. As a Republican he was twice defeated for the general court of Massachusetts. In 1878 he ran as an independent and supported Ben Butler for governor. He was elected by the Greenback-Labor Party and served one year in the lower house. In 1880 he went to Washington as a dele- to the conference which called the national convention of the Greenback-Labor Party, and he attended the Chicago convention as a delegate from Massachusetts. After holding office in the Knights of Labor off and on for fourteen years, he resigned in 1892 to return to his first love, the Republican Party.

> Litchman was a Mason; past grand and past chief patriarch, etc., of the Grand Encampment of Massachusetts I.O.O.F.; grand senior sagamore of the Great Council of the United States Improved Order of the Red Men; past regent of the Royal Arcanum; member of the American Legion of Honor and the Order of the Golden Cross. . . .[7]

The stereotype of the business unionist is far less developed than that of the traditional labor leader. Nor has any one individual been awarded the honor of serving as the new labor leaders' ideal representative. In the main, the business unionist has been described as being essentially those things which the traditional labor leader was not. Raised in an urban, working-class environment, he was quite probably a first or second generation immigrant. He received only a minimal education and went to work at an early age. His motive for joining the union was simply to advance his own welfare as a wage earner, and he had no visions of using the union as a base from which to attain self-employment or middle-class status. He rejected the notion that the promotion of his welfare depended on close cooperation with farmers, merchants, and small employers, and thus remained aloof from middle-class reform movements, fraternal societies, or political crusades. He sought the advancement of his cause solely through effective economic action, and thus was never a candidate for political office. In sum, the business unionist was a professional labor official primarily concerned with leading an efficient trade union in the drive simply to gain better hours and wages for its members.[8]

Although historians have widely accepted the above stereotypes, their creators and perpetuators have failed to present substantial documentation for their impressions. At best they have provided biographical information on one or two leaders as evidence to prove the case, while giving in some studies no concrete substantiation at all.[9] The reasons for this are several. As with most stereotypes, the image of the traditional labor leader and the business unionist appears, upon first examination, to contain enough truth to discourage closer scrutiny. As a result, no one has yet attempted a scholarly analysis of the evolution of labor union leadership from the Civil War to the death of Gompers. Information on particular labor leaders during this period, moreover, is unduly limited. Published scholarly biographies are available for only a few union officials, notably William Sylvis, Samuel Gompers, Andrew Furuseth, Eugene V. Debs, William D. Haywood, and Sidney Hillman. For the seventy nationally elected leaders of the Knights of Labor between 1878 and 1893, there are at the time of writing a handful of biographical sketches, two autobiographies, one dissertation, and no published scholarly biography. The sixty-eight national officers of the American Federation of Labor between 1881 and 1924 have fared somewhat better at the hands of historians, although we still know little about the majority of these men. Lacking the basic information from which such stereotypes should be constructed, scholars have arrived at the above-mentioned portraits by relying on highly impressionistic evidence. Such a methodology too easily yields historical accuracy to the forces of subconscious emotion and bias.

Preconceptions of historians were indeed a significant factor in shaping prevailing stereotypes. Under the inspiration of John. R. Commons, labor history in the United States came of age at the very time that the American Federation of Labor was rising to prominence. The early pioneers in the academic discipline encouraged the Federation's moderation and sympathized with its struggle for survival. Finding the AFL's outlook congenial to their own orientation, they tended to accept uncritically its analysis of its own ideology and sociological composition, as well as its critique of its opposition. Historians have consequently used such pejorative words as "reform-ist," "utopian," "unrealistic," and "anachronistic" to describe the Knights of Labor, while referring to the AFL as "pragmatic," "realis-tic," "mature," "bona fide," and "businesslike."[10]

Radical concepts also were important in shaping the stereotypes of union leadership. Samuel Gompers, who formulated many of the ideas later incorporated into the scholars' images, and Selig Perlman, who was a major figure in putting Gompers's ideas into academic form, were both Marxists in their youth.[11] John R. Commons was a Christian Socialist in the 1890s who studied Marx in order to refute charges that the labor movement as represented by the AFL was radical in approach.[12] While rejecting the ultimate conclusions of the Marxists, these men adhered to many of its radical concep-tions, including the nature of the ideal leader. The creators of the stereotypes agreed with many of their more radical critics that a good labor leader should avoid middle-class politics and reform movements and that he should not use the union as a stepping stone for self-advancement. Indeed, at times it seems that the de-bate between the Wisconsin School of Labor Studies and such Marxists as Philip Foner centers on the question of whether the business unionist was an ideal labor leader, rather than on what con-stitutes an ideal labor leader.[13]

Whereas the lack of adequate information has resulted in a dis-tortion in the stereotypes of union leadership, the preconceptions of historians have led to an insensitivity with the plight of the union official. There has been a tendency among scholars to pronounce hasty judgments on labor leaders in place of analyzing or under-standing the broader social environment in which they lived. Recent historians, most notably David Montgomery and Herbert Gutman, have attempted a more sophisticated approach.[14]

II

Through the use of statistical analysis, this chapter attempts to create more substantial portraits of the old-school labor leader and the new business unionist. Biographical sketches were developed on 150 traditional unionists and 200 new labor leaders.[15] To be included, an individual must have held an elective office in a national or international union, or national federation of labor. Leaders prominent primarily during the twenty-five years before 1895 were classified as traditional labor leaders, while those prominent largely from 1895 to 1920 were considered business unionists.

The year 1895 was chosen as the pivotal date, since historians have generally pointed to the mid-1890s as the period in which "business unionism" trimphed over "reform unionism."[16] Although the American Federation of Labor, founded in 1886, and its predecessor the Federation of Organized Trades and Labor Unions, founded in 1881, were the institutional representatives of the new philosophy of "pure and simple unionism," not all of their early members broke their ties with the past. During the 1880s and early 1890s a number of leaders and unions kept a foot in both camps. In 1883, for instance, Frank K. Foster served as both secretary of District Assembly 30, Knights of Labor and as a member of the Federation of Organized Trades and Labor Unions' executive board.[17] Similarly, Daniel McLaughlin spent a term on the governing bodies of both the Knights and the AFL.[18] Until the mid-1890s several unions, including the Mine Workers, Machinists, and Brewery Workers, maintained membership in both national federations.[19] Thus, in order to discern the emergence of a new type of labor leader, the 1895 date seemed the most judicious choice.

The final collection of sketches represents a good cross-section of the labor movement's leadership during this period. A total of seventy-four national or international labor bodies are included in the study. The Knights of Labor are represented by fifty-four national officers; the American Federation of Labor by forty-four. Among the various trade groups, the International Typographical Union, the International Association of Machinists, the United Mine Workers, and the International Ladies Garment Workers' Union have the largest representation, with over fifteen leaders each. The independent railroad brotherhoods account for nineteen officers. Excluding the Knights and the AFL, each union has an average of four leaders included.

Computations were made of the date and place of birth, educational attainment, father's occupation, political preferences, tenure in office, and other factors for the 350 individuals included in the sample. From this material, statistical portraits were constructed of the old-school labor leader and the new business unionist. The quantitative tools used in this study were the measures of central tendency, being the mean, median, and mode, plus such measures of distribution as percentile ranks and percentiles.

In a survey of this nature, the historian must be conscious of unavoidable bias in his material. Unlike the modern pollster or social scientist, he cannot freely construct a proper questionnaire or scientifically determine his sample. Rather he must work with the material at hand. The leaders used in this study, for instance, do not constitute a random sample of the universe of union officials during this period, but are those individuals on whom the most information is known. There were, of course, hundreds of other leaders meeting the criteria of this study, the details of whose lives have been forgotten. Similarly, humans have always been more fascinated by the unique than the typical, with the result that it has been easier to discover such oddities as which leaders supported the Socialist, Populist, Greenback, and other third parties than it has been to identify staunch Democrats and Republicans. Finally, one is confronted with the accuracy of the information itself, which is difficult to cross-check. Much of the data available on labor leaders originated with union officials or their supporters and was prepared as campaign literature or testimonials. In typically human fashion, men would distort facts to attain a desired image. Although difficult to prove, it seems likely that such men, living in a nation enamored with the "rags-to-riches" myth, would overdramatize their humble origins, lack of education, and commencement of work at an early age. As Eli Ginzberg suggests, labor leaders "who refer to their working-class origins do so boastfully. They desire to emphasize that they are thoroughly acquainted with the problems confronting the workers, since they themselves are workers."[20] Hopefully, through judicious interpretation of the data and by use of a large sample, such biases as these can be controlled. Nonetheless, the final statistics are not definitive but simply indicative of trends.[21]

III

The men who led labor during the last third of the nineteenth century represented a clear break with the pre–Civil War labor movement. With eighty-six percent of the traditional labor leaders born after 1830, and with 1844 as the median year of birth, the overwhelming majority were too young to have been active in the wave of unionism during the age of Jackson.[22] Indeed, out of a sample of 150, only two leaders are known to have been involved in the American labor movement of the 1840s and 1850s—William D. Robinson of the Locomotive Engineers and James L. Wright of the Knights of Labor. One other leader who was not included in the sample, Charles H. Rihl of the Bricklayers, was also active in the pre–Civil War labor movement. None of these men held major union posts during this time.[23]

Union offices during the Gilded Age were quite clearly reserved for white males of western European extraction. None of the leaders studied were Negro or Oriental, and only three were women— Leonora M. Barry of the Knights of Labor, Mary Burke of the Retail Clerks, and Augusta Lewis of the National Labor Union.[24] In terms of ethnic background, Irish Catholics were the most numerous group, accounting for nineteen of the seventy-eight leaders on whom information is known. The English were the next largest group with fifteen, while the Scots were third with nine. Scotch-Irish and Canadians each accounted for six; Germans and Welsh for five each; French for three; and Hungarians and Russian Jews for one each. Finally, eight of the leaders could distinctly be classified as being of Old American stock. Clearly, national labor union leadership during this period was dominated by individuals with ancestral roots in the British Isles. While certain ethnic groups such as the Germans were influential in the labor movement during these years, statistics suggest that their office holding was concentrated at the local level.

The religious backgrounds are known for only 49 of the 150 leaders in the sample. Of these, fifty percent were Catholic. Protestants accounted for forty-four percent, with Methodism, the faith most commonly associated with the English working class, constituting the largest single denomination. Four percent were Jews, and two percent were declared atheists. Actually, these proportions are probably more indicative of formal church attendance than of religious beliefs, for during the Gilded Age there was a tendency particularly among Protestant workingmen to disassociate themselves from the formal institution of the Church. A survey conducted by the Massachusetts Bureau of Labor Statistics in 1869 and 1870 revealed that most Protestant workingmen did not attend services. According to the labor politician Edward H. Rogers, "The church was very unsocial . . . poor people were not wanted."[25] The most significant statistic on religion, therefore, is that the faith, or lack of it, of two-thirds of these men is unknown. Perhaps a majority of them were vaguely Protestant, a third Catholic oriented, and the remainder undeclared agnostics and atheists. For such men, the sermons of the Social Gospelers and the encyclicals of the pope had little direct meaning.

Forty-eight percent of the old-school labor leaders studied were foreign born, with the vast majority coming from the British Isles. Roughly twenty-nine percent were born in England, twenty-three percent in Ireland, fifteen percent in Scotland, and eight percent in Wales. Outside the British Isles, Canada was the birthplace of the next largest group, totaling thirteen percent. Another ten percent were born in Germany. Only six percent of the foreign-born leaders came from countries other than those listed above.[26]

Thirty-eight percent of the foreign-born labor leaders immigrated to the United States while youths under the age of fourteen. The rest, sixty-two percent, came to America between their sixteenth and thirty-ninth birthdays, with the largest cluster of men, thirty-one percent, arriving while in their late twenties.[27] At least forty-three percent, and probably more, of the foreign-born leaders who were sixteen or older at immigration had been involved in union activities before reaching the United States. Among them were such notables as Thomas Phillips, John Siney, Richard Trevellick, Chris Evans, John Jarrett, and Adolf Strasser. While the largest proportion of these men were involved in mining, leaders with foreign trade union experience were influential in other industries as well.[28]

The evidence on the clear break between pre- and post-Civil War labor union leadership, the statistics on the ethnic backgrounds of the traditional leaders, plus the number of foreign born, their age at immigration, and their previous union activities all tend to support the conclusions of such scholars as Clifton Yearley and David Montgomery as to the predominant influence of British immigrants in the development of the American labor movement after the Civil War.[29] In his study of labor leadership between 1862 and 1872, Montgomery concludes that fifty-eight percent of his sample was foreign born, with forty-four percent coming from the British Isles.[30] Similarly, Yearley notes that "among the ten more important figures associated with the National Labor Union from 1862 to 1872, half were British. Of the twenty-five foremost leaders and organizers in the Knights of Labor at the peak of its power in 1886, eleven were English, Irish, Scotch or Welsh."[31]

Although foreign-born leaders proportionately decreased over time—from fifty-eight percent for the period 1862 to 1872, to forty-eight percent for the period 1870 to 1895—statistics on ethnic background plus individual biographical information suggest that their places were taken by the sons of immigrants, born in the United States and raised in a cultural environment which accepted unionism. While both John Brophy and Samuel Gompers were foreign born and of a later era, the attitudes toward unionism they absorbed during childhood were probably similar to those of many native-born sons of immigrants raised in the ethnic confines of a mining town or urban ghetto. "All my life," Gompers recalled, "I had been accustomed to the labor movement and accepted as a matter of course that every wage-earner should belong to the union of his trade. I did not yet [in 1864 when he joined the New York City English-speaking Cigarmakers' local] have a conscious appreciation of the labor movement. My awakening was to come later. However, I attended union meetings and observed union regulations."[32] Likewise, Brophy related, "Everybody belonged to unions, it was taken for granted as a normal part of life."[33] Brophy attributed a large part of his success in organizing a miners' union in South Fork, Pennsylvania "to the fact that the miners were almost all of British origin; very few were native Americans or from later immigration stock. The bulk were English, from Cornwall, Lancashire, or Staffordshire, with generous sprinklings of Welsh, Scottish, and Irish. . . . The British immigrants brought with them not only experience in British mines but also, like my father, the experience of British unions."[34] Native Americans, raised in community-centered societies which cherished the values of individualism and self-reliance, no doubt faced greater difficulty in accommodating their cultural heritage with the principles of unionism. Consequently they took longer in developing a sizable leadership group than many of the foreign born who brought this tradition with them and transmitted it to their children.

Most American-born labor leaders came from those regions of the country which experienced industrialism during the 1840s and 1850s. Forty-nine percent of the native unionists were born in the Middle Atlantic states of New York (twenty-five percent), Pennsylvania (twenty-one percent), and New Jersey (three percent). New England provided twenty-one percent of the leaders, two-thirds of whom were born in Massachusetts. The East-North-Central states were the birthplaces of fifteen percent, and the West-North-Central and South Atlantic states each contributed six percent. The remaining three percent came from the East-South-Central, the West-South-Central, the Mountain, and the Pacific regions of the country.[35]

The majority of traditional unionists were born in relatively highly populated urban centers. Seventy-nine percent of the native labor leaders were born in communities with populations over twenty-five hundred, the figure adopted by the United States Census in 1880 to define an urban area. In that year only 29.5 percent of the American people lived in communities of that size, and the percentage had been considerably lower thirty or forty years earlier when most of the labor leaders were growing up. Indeed, whereas only 12.5 percent of the nation's population lived in communities of eight thousand or more inhabitants in 1850, forty-one percent of the labor leaders were born in towns this size or larger. Approximately twenty-three percent of the leaders were born in cities with populations over a hundred thousand. Philadelphia, with a population of 340,000 in 1850, was the birthplace of more traditional labor leaders than any other single community.[36] The urban origins of union officials was further accented by the fact that a large percentage of the immigrant labor leaders were natives of such major cities as Liverpool, London, Glasgow, Belfast, Londonderry, and Toronto.

The industrial-urban orientation of the traditional unionists became even more marked once they began work. Upon their election to national office, seventy percent of the leaders came from the five industrial states of Massachusetts, New York, Pennsylvania, Ohio, and Illinois. In terms of regional breakdown, forty-one percent resided in the Middle Atlantic states, thirty percent in the East-North-Central states, eleven percent in New England, eight percent in the West-North-Central region, four percent in the South Atlantic area. The remaining six percent were distributed among the East-South-Central, West-South-Central, Mountain, and Pacific divisions of the nation. Ninety-one percent of the unionists resided in communities with a population of twenty-five hundred or more in 1880. Only 29.5 percent of the American population as a whole at this date lived in towns of this size or larger, indicating the extent to which the traditional labor leaders were atypical of the nation's populace. Twenty-eight percent lived in cities with a population between ten thousand and one hundred thousand; forty-three percent lived in cities with one hundred thousand to one million inhabitants; and ten percent lived in New York City, excluding Brooklyn, which had a population of 1,206,299.[37]

Fathers of the old-school unionists were for the most part laborers in an emerging industrial society. Only a handful of leaders had fathers identifiable as professional men or businessmen, among these a sea captain, a soldier, a minister, a physician, two shoe manufacturers, and a publisher. A slightly larger group had fathers who were farmers or tenant farmers. Such exceptions notwithstanding, the substantial majority of fathers were craftsmen or industrial workers, with approximately one-third being skilled workers, including miners, shawl makers, stonecutters, and coopers. From this breakdown it is evident that a majority of the traditional unionists came from working-class families.

As might be expected of children from such a background, the large majority of the men studied obtained a sixth grade education or less and began work by age fourteen. Almost one-fourth of the leaders, however, did extend their formal education beyond primary school. Some went to night school, twenty are known to have attended high school, seven were enrolled in institutions labeled "colleges," and four were involved in special training in law or theology. But for the most part, the traditional unionist left school early in his teens and, if lucky, attained further education through the apprenticeship system.

Only a small fraction of the future leaders, eight percent, went into business before or during their union careers. These men were mostly of three types. A few were frustrated entrepreneurs like P. M. Arthur of the Locomotive Engineers, who as a young man started a cartage business, or Thomas Talbot of the Machinists, who unsuccessfully attempted to open his own shop. Others resembled John James of the Miners' National Association and Frederick Turner of the Knights of Labor, both of whom had been blacklisted for union activities and forced to open stationery or grocery stores to earn a living. The Philadelphia Knights, in fact, provided initial financing for Turner's store so the Order might continue to have his services. The largest group, particularly among those in business while in office, were men like Frank Foster and Joseph Buchanan, who edited labor papers. Yet as noted previously, the vast majority of leaders remained wage-earners prior to running for union office.[38]

Starting work while still a youth, the typical old-school labor leader was also quite young when he attained his first national union office. Fifty percent of the leaders were elected to national positions before age thirty-five, and eighty-eight percent attained their posts by age forty-five. John Fehrenbatch was twenty-six when elected president of the International Machinists and Blacksmiths' Union; William Blair Prescott was twenty-eight when he became head of the International Typographical Union; and T. V. Powderly was chosen grand master workman of the Knights of Labor at age thirty.[39]

A number of factors help explain why so many young men rose to leadership positions during the formative years of American trade unionism. Early leaders usually obtained their start in the labor movement during a membership drive or strike, and these struggles were hard. The activists ran the risk of dismissal from their jobs, the blacklist, and frequently bodily harm. Consequently, older men, burdened with families, thought twice before taking prominent parts in labor struggles. Young men had less to lose. If the union won, they might have a new career open to them; if it lost, they could move on and find other jobs. Moreover, once these men began in union affairs they encountered few barriers. As Eli Ginzberg points out, "Unlike a bishop or a general, the labor leader did not have to complete a lengthy course of formal instruction. What he had to know about his fellow workers and employers he was able to acquire during the first ten years on the job. At twenty-five, he had a decade of experience under his belt."[40] Young men faced little opposition in gaining office. The risks and sufferings of the job—long hours, low pay, little security, and social ostracism—frequently resulted in the number of union positions exceeding the number of candidates. As Jonathan Grossman points out in regard to the early Molders' Union, offices often went begging "for weeks at a time until someone was flattered, cajoled or browbeaten into accepting."[41]

The unattractiveness of union office, plus the short lifespan of many of the early national organizations, contributed to making most careers in the labor movement of short duration. The average official gained his highest office within the union a year after attaining a position of national leadership, and his tenure at this post was relatively short. The typical leader held his highest post for a year and a half; eighty-two percent for five years or less. Their total tenure in national office was only slightly longer, with fifty percent in office for just over two years, and seventy-eight percent in positions of national leadership for five years or less. The longest total tenure was John W. Hayes's thirty-two years with the Knights of Labor, the larger proportion of which occurred after it became an inactive organization.

Although precise information is not available, it seems that a clear majority of the old-school labor leaders divided equally in political allegiance between the Democratic and Republican parties. But at least twenty-four percent of the traditional unionists displayed third-party proclivities at some time or other. Ten were staunch supporters of the Socialist Labor party. The remainder were distributed among the Greenbackers, Populists, and various other groups. Like the statistics on religion, the figures on party affiliation appear more indicative of political involvement than of political preference. It is revealing, therefore, that the affiliation of two-thirds of the sample is unknown, suggesting that politics was not of vital interest to most of these men.

Nonetheless, at least 38—or 25 percent—of our 150 traditional leaders were political activists. Nine were mainly involved in party affairs—three for the Greenback-Labor party, three for the Populists, and three for the Socialist Laborites. A few individuals held positions of party leadership. Philip Van Patten of the Knights of Labor was national secretary of the Socialist Labor party, while Robert Schilling of the Coopers' International Union had been one of the two laboring men at the founding convention of the Greenback party. Schilling also served as chairman of the central committee of the Wisconsin People's party in 1894.[42]

The other twenty-nine leaders were active primarily as political candidates. Including those who sought more than one post, ten ran for local positions, twenty were candidates for state posts, and six sought election to national offices. About half ran on third-party tickets; one-third as Democrats; and only a handful as Republicans. Ultimately, about half of the candidates were elected to some public office, although many ran several times before achieving victory. In general, success seemed directly proportional to the homogeneity of the constituency and inversely proportional to the size of the electorate. Eighty percent of those seeking some local office eventually won, although only fifty percent of those who coveted mayoralties were victorious. On the state level, ten of seventeen leaders who campaigned for district seats in various legislatures were successful, but none of the candidates running for state-wide executive offices ever won. Of eight candidates seeking election from various districts to Congress, three were successful. Eugene Debs, needless to say, never attained the presidency. Among the more notable political victors were Congressman Martin Foran of the International Coopers' Union, and Terence Powderly of the Knights of Labor, who in 1878 was elected mayor of Scranton, Pennsylvania, a city of 45,000. Finally, nine of twenty-nine leaders active as political candidates were semiprofessional or professional politicians, having run for office three or more times.[43]

A small minority of traditional labor leaders, approximately twelve percent, held appointive posts in government. Most of these appointments seem to have been made in light of the union official's expertise in industrial affairs; fifteen of the eighteen men were given posts concerned with labor problems. Robert Watchorn of the United Mine Workers was chief factory inspector of Pennsylvania; James R. Sovereign of the Knights of Labor was commissioner of labor statistics for Iowa; and John McBride of the Mine Workers held a similar post in Ohio. Other leaders worked in various state labor bureaus and served on state and federal investigatory commissions. The United States Immigration Service was the particular sphere of influence for the trade unions. A sizable number of former union men worked for the service, and two prominent leaders served as commissioner-general of immigration—Terence V. Powderly and Frank P. Sargent of the Brotherhood of Locomotive Firemen. In the final analysis, however, the proportion of labor leaders appointed to governmental posts, like the number active in politics, was small.[44]

Relatively few traditional unionists attempted to establish themselves in business or the professions after leaving union office. Of those in our sample, thirty-one, or twenty percent, followed this path. Not all of them were attempting to escape from the working class and its problems, as proved by the eleven who became editors of labor journals. Six of eleven who started small businesses did so because their reputations as champions of the workingman made it impossible to get jobs in their respective trades. Six other leaders, mainly among miners and typographers, accepted management positions in pro-union firms from which, they rationalized, they could promote better labor relations. Two of the three men who became lawyers, Martin Foran and Terence Powderly (who claimed he could not get a job at his trade after leaving the Knights), continued to work for labor's betterment.[45] About a third of those who went into business did attempt to become successful businessmen without working-class connections. Only one, however, actually achieved this goal. Combining luck with talent, Robert Watchorn went from trapper boy in a Derbyshire mine at the age of eleven, to secretary-treasurer of the United Mine Workers in 1890, to chief factory inspector for Pennsylvania in 1891, to an official in the Immigration Service from 1895 to 1908, to vice-president of the Union Oil Company. He was a major benefactor of the University of the Redlands at the time of his death in 1944. Such success, however, was entirely foreign to the overwhelming majority of old-school labor leaders, who spent their entire lives in the ranks of the wage-earners.[46]

Information on the social clubs and reform organizations to which the old-school unionists belonged is available for only sixteen percent of the sample. Lack of data on this point illustrates the weak foundation on which the accepted stereotype of the traditional labor leader has been built.[47] Quite clearly no meaningful conclusions can be made from available information. At best it can only be pointed out that the twenty-four leaders under consideration were members of six fraternal organizations, the Masons being the most popular. The reform groups to which these men gravitated included the Henry George Club, the National Citizens Alliance, and the Irish National Land League. The most prominent reform was the temperance movement, to which five leaders devoted some of their time.

The foregoing statistical analysis suggests a portrait of the old-school labor leaders which stands in sharp contrast to the traditional stereotype. The middle-class origins, third-party proclivities, and other characteristics by which such scholars as Gerald Grob, Selig Perlman, and Norman Ware have identified the traditional labor leaders are seen in perspective to be rather the attributes of a few exceptional unionists. Instead of having been an advocate of a passing rural, middle-class America, the average old-school union official appears as a working-class pioneer in an emerging urban-industrial society.

In sum, the model traditional labor leader was born in 1844 to parents of Irish-Catholic or English origins. He was raised in New England or the Middle Atlantic states in a town of five thousand. From a working-class family, he was only able to attend school until age fourteen and then began his life's labor. Joining the union of his trade, he rose quickly through the ranks and became a national officer before age thirty-five. His stay in office was usually only for one or two years. Once his term was over, he returned to the rank-and-file and his previous activities as a laborer. His life, then, was neither glamorous nor bizarre, and except for his brief period in union office, marked by few distinctions.

IV

Eighty-two percent of the business unionists studied were born during the twenty-five year period from 1855 to 1880, with 1869 representing the median year. Like the traditional labor leaders, they were overwhelmingly white males of western European extraction.

Only five of 200 leaders studied were women, and only two were black. Of the 120 leaders whose ethnic backgrounds are known, over half had ancestors in the British Isles. Thirty-three were Irish-Catholic, nineteen were English, ten Scotch, five Welsh, and five more Scotch-Irish. No doubt a majority of the six Canadians also had ancestors in Great Britain. Seven leaders were of German parentage; another six were Scandinavian, including two from Iceland; five were Italian, and one Dutch. The most significant new ethnic group to appear in the ranks of union leadership was that of the east European Jews, whose activities were concentrated in the needle trades.

In terms of religious background, fifty percent of the leaders were Catholic, about thirty-five percent were Protestant, ten percent Jewish, and the remaining five percent confirmed nonbelievers. These proportions were arrived at by inference, since, as in the case of the traditional unionists, the actual statistics seem more illustrative of active church participation than of religious belief. Following this assumption, about half of the leaders were active churchgoers. While this proportion would hardly please priests or parsons, it does signify increased church activity, since only a third of the old-school labor leaders seemed to have had institutional religious ties. The cause of such growth in religious devotion and participation stemmed in large part from the activities of Father Peter Dietz, the Militia of Christ for Social Service, and the Knights of Columbus, since it occurred primarily within the Church of Rome. During the Gilded Age, the Protestants and Catholics were about equal in the number of church activists, but in the Progressive era Catholics outnumbered Protestants in participation by almost three to one.[48]

As was true of the traditional labor leaders, the majority of business unionists were American born. Approximately forty-two percent, however, were immigrants. Of the seventy-one foreign-born leaders whose countries of birth are known, forty-three percent came from the British Isles. England accounted for fifteen leaders, Ireland nine, Scotland six, and Wales one. The British colonies contributed another fifteen percent of the leaders, ten having been born in Canada and one in New Zealand. Six leaders were born in Scandinavia, four in Italy, three in Austria-Hungary, and one each in

Germany and Luxembourg. Again fourteen of the leaders in the garment industry were immigrants from the eastern European countries of Russia, Poland, and Lithuania.

Unlike the foreign-born traditional labor leaders, immigrant business unionists tended to come to America while still in their teens. Of the fifty-four persons whose ages at immigration are known, fifty percent arrived in the United States by age sixteen, and seventy-eight percent by their twenty-first birthday. On the other hand, fifty percent of their earlier counterparts were over twenty when they arrived in the United States. Immigration at an early age meant that few of the foreign-born business unionists were active in the labor movements of their home countries. Only twelve of the seventy-one men are known to have had such experience, five of them in the miners' unions of the British Isles.

The majority of the business unionists were native born, and like the majority of traditional labor leaders grew up in the more industrial states east of the Mississippi River and north of the Mason-Dixon line. The four leading industrial states of New York, Pennsylvania, Ohio, and Illinois were the birthplace of fifty-four percent of the American-born business unionists. In terms of regional distribution, the Middle Atlantic and East-North-Central states each accounted for thirty-two percent of the leaders, while the West-North Central and South Atlantic states each accounted for twelve percent. The East-South-Central area was the birthplace of seven percent and New England of four percent. The remaining one percent came from the Mountain region.

Business unionists tended to be born in the same general urban environment as their earlier counterparts. Whereas only a quarter of the American people lived in towns of twenty-five hundred or more in 1870, sixty-six percent of the leaders were born in communities of this size or larger. Forty-one percent had birthplaces with populations greater than ten thousand; twenty-two percent greater than one hundred thousand; and seven percent were born in New York City, including Brooklyn, with a population of over one million. The statistically average leader was born in a town of six thousand. Many of those born in places with fewer inhabitants still came from industrial environments. This was particularly true of those who came from small mining communities in Pennsylvania, Illinois, and

Ohio. Finally, the majority of immigrant labor leaders also appear to have been born in major population centers.[49]

Raised in the more urban and industrial areas of the nation, the ment who led labor during the Progressive era, like their earlier counterparts, came from predominantly working-class families. The occupations of 107 fathers are known. Five percent were professional men, mostly lawyers and ministers, and eleven percent owned their own business. The majority were petty entrepreneurs—saloon keepers, grocers, small manufacturers—but one, the father of Max Zaritsky, was a businessman of considerable stature.[50] Another twenty percent were farmers, including the fathers of such prominent leaders as Warren Stone of the Locomotive Engineers, Arthur Wharton of the Machinists, and James Patrick Noonan of the Electrical Workers.[51] The remaining sixty-four percent of the sample were wage-earners, with over two-thirds of these being skilled or semiskilled workers.

Like the traditional labor leader, the typical business unionist attended school until the age of thirteen or fourteen. The majority of the new leaders received a sixth grade education or less before entering the mines and factories of industrial America. A significant minority of at least thirty-five percent, however, achieved more than a primary education. Fifty leaders attained some high school education, including John L. Lewis, who unlike most miners of the period was able to finish all but his senior year.[52] Twenty leaders graduated from high school and attended more specialized institutions. Thomas Rickert of the United Garment Workers and William Doak of the Trainmen were enrolled in business colleges where they mastered skills useful in union administration.[53] Law schools attracted to their doors a number of leaders including Matthew Woll and Frank Morrison of the AFL, both of whom attended Lake Forest University's law school, where they gained knowledge valuable in shaping the unions' internal rules as well as in meeting the unions' ever increasing legal obligations with government and business.[54] And a few of the future labor leaders received liberal arts educations. John Brown Lennon of the Journeymen Tailors' Union and treasurer of the AFL for eighteen years spent a year at Oberlin College, while Ben H. Williams of the Industrial Workers of the World was an "all-American boy" while at Tabor College—center on the football team, editor of the campus magazine, president of the Phi Delta Literary Society, and winner of several debating and oratorical awards.[55] Although men with more than a sixth grade education were the exception among business unionists, their advanced education did enable them to cope better with problems that their unions faced in an increasingly complex industrial society.

With a significant minority of business unionists coming from non-working-class backgrounds and attaining more than a primary school education, it is surprising that so few are known to have attempted self-employment before gaining union office. Evidence of independent business participation before assuming union office is available for only three percent of the sample. This fact does not indicate absence of entrepreneurial drive among the leaders, as will be seen later in discussing their business activities during and after office. Rather it suggests four phenomena. First, as was pointed out earlier, two-thirds of the business unionists were of working-class backgrounds, received only a minimum of schooling, and went to work while in their early teens. Thus they rarely, if ever, had the education or capital to start out on their own. Secondly, even those with better schooling and non-working-class backgrounds found it increasingly more costly and less appealing to start a small business in an age in which large firms were pushing under their smaller competitors. Closely related to this was the mounting evidence that through the union movement one could increase his status and eventually move into a managerial position with a good business firm, accept a comfortable governmental job, or even transform the union into a quasi-corporation which not only took part in labor relations but also managed banks, insurance companies, holding companies, and other ventures. As early as 1900, AFL president Samuel Gompers felt compelled to warn his followers that "with this marvelous growth of the trade union movement, a few persons here and there have endeavored to foist themselves upon our organization, and, without using a harsher term, the purpose sought by them is not calculated to promote the welfare of the cause for which organized labor stands. Self-seekers, political hucksters, and financial charlatans have sought to fasten their fangs upon some organizations, and particularly upon those newly formed."[56] Finally, and not to be underestimated, was the sincere desire of many business unionists simply to devote their lives to the advancement of the working class.

At the time of their election to national office, eighty-two percent of the business unionists were living in towns which had populations of over eight thousand in 1910. Proportionally, this was more than twice the national average of urban concentration. Sixty percent, moreover, lived in cities of over one hundred thousand inhabitants, and thirty-one percent resided in the metropolises of New York, Chicago, and Philadelphia.[57] As the statistics on place of residence suggest, a significant majority of the leaders—sixty-two percent—lived in the five most urbanized and industrialized states: New York, Ohio, Illinois, Pennsylvania, and Massachusetts. The actual geographical distribution of the leaders at the time of their elections, however, reveals to some extent the westward advance of industrialism. The East-North-Central states, which had ranked second to the Middle Atlantic area as place of residence of traditional labor leaders, now attained top honors, thirty-two percent to thirty percent. The West-South-Central area, moreover, tied New England for third place, each with ten percent. The South Atlantic and Mountain states were each the home of five percent of the leaders; the Pacific region of four percent; and the East-South-Central and West-South-Central areas of two percent.[58]

Surprisingly, business unionists were a few years younger than their earlier counterparts when they won election to their first national post. Whereas the average age of the traditional unionist at the time of his first election to national office was thirty-five, and eighty-eight percent were in office by the age of forty-five, the average age of the new labor leader was thirty-three, and ninety-two percent were at their posts by age forty-five. This slight decrease in the age of the union leaders seems to result primarily from the changing dynamics of the labor movement. It is almost axiomatic that new unions are founded by young blood, and the last decade of the nineteenth century and the first two decades of the twentieth witnessed a virtual organizational revolution. In 1870 there were only twenty-nine national trade unions. By 1920 the number had increased to 163. The majority of these unions, moreover, were formed in the years after 1890. As more unions were founded, more young men became national labor leaders.[59]

If the average business unionist was younger than the traditional labor leader upon assuming national office, he was also older than his counterpart when attaining his highest national office. The traditional unionist had generally reached his highest post in the union hierarchy a year after joining the national administration. The new generation, however, spent an average of five years moving up the ladder of power. This longer time period suggests both an increase in the number of career labor leaders and an increased rigidity in the union structure.

Also indicative of these trends are the statistics on the length of time in office. As observed above, the average old-school labor leader held his highest post in the union for only one and a half years and had a total tenure in national offices of just over two years. The situation for the business unionist was drastically different, for the typical new labor leader held his highest post for twelve years and experienced a total tenure in national offices of a decade and a half. Indeed, seventy-one percent had union careers of over five years, and a few individuals such as Matthew Woll of the AFL, William Mahan of the Street Railway Employees, and Harry Herman Cook of the Flint Glass Workers spent over a half-century in positions of authority in the labor movement.[60]

Attaining office while still relatively young and subsequently enjoying a lengthy tenure in office, the majority of the new generation of labor leaders remained in the labor movement all their lives. Less than ten percent actually left the labor movement to engage in private business. Yet this does not mean that the majority of them were aloof from the desire to gain wealth through the capitalist system. Lack of adequate records makes it difficult to know how many of them invested in stocks, bonds, and real estate, but the number seems to have been quite significant. At the time of his death in 1924, Samuel Gompers had developed an estate of $40,000 through such investments.[61] Emmet C. Davison, who became general secretary-treasurer of the Machinists in 1917, was also vice-president of the Mt. Vernon Savings Bank, vice-president of the District Securities Company, secretary-treasurer of the Hampton Road Ship Repair Corporation, president of the Potomac Holding Company, and a member of the board of directors of the Commercial National Bank.[62] Similarly, George L. Berry of the Printing Pressmen was a stockholder in the Clinchfield Hydro Electric Company, president of the International Playing Card and Label Company, owner and publisher of the Rogersville, Tennessee *Review*, and chairman of the board of directors of the Citizens' Union Bank of Rogersville.[63]

The spirit of such enterprise was expressed by John Mitchell, president of the United Mine Workers, when he advised his friend W. D. Ryan that "if we could organize a company of three or four, with a capital stock of five or six thousand dollars, we would clean up a handsome little stake each year."[64] By following his own counsel, Mitchell was able to accumulate an estate worth $244,295 upon his death twenty years later. Among his assets were bonds of Armour and Company, the Baltimore and Ohio Railroad, and the New York Central, all firms hardly friendly toward unionism.[65]

Several leaders, particularly those in office in the 1920s and beyond, became corporate executives within the union structure as various organizations began their own enterprises. The pioneer in these endeavors was Warren Stone of the Brotherhood of Locomotive Engineers. On his recommendation, a thirteen-story building was erected in Cleveland in 1910 which paid for itself within ten years and thereafter was listed as a $3 million asset. So successful was this project that the union built a second structure in 1925. Stone also launched the first labor bank, the Brotherhood of Locomotive Engineers Cooperative Bank of Cleveland, in November, 1920 with a capital of $1 million and a surplus also of $1 million. It was followed by other banks in New York, Philadelphia, Boston, Minneapolis, and elsewhere. The union also incorporated the Brotherhood Holding Company with a capital of $1 million and the Brotherhood Investment Company with a capital of $10 million and then acquired a controlling interest in the Empire Trust Company of New York. Other investments were made under Stone's direction so that, by the time of his death in 1925, the resources of the Locomotive Engineers had reached $145 million.[66] Other unions followed the path blazed by the Brotherhood, and before long men like Albert Berres of the Pattern Makers, Edward Manion of the Telegraphers, Edwin Weeks of the Railway Carmen, John L. Lewis of the Miners, and Anzuino Marimpietri of the Amalgamated Clothing Workers were directing the affairs of banks, insurance companies, and other business endeavors.[67] Indicative of the new activities of union officials was the identification of Warren Stone in *Who Was Who* as "labor leader and banker" and the *National Cyclopedia's* characterization of Matthew Woll as "labor leader and insurance executive."[68]

The majority of business unionists, like the majority of traditional labor leaders, supported the two established political parties. The actual statistics, however, are more revealing of strong political commitment than of the party preference of the group as a whole, for information of this nature is unknown for a majority of the officials. Some of these men concealed their political affiliations to prevent tensions within their unions, while others simply lacked political consciousness.[69] Among those whose party allegiances are known, there was a discernable preference for the Democrats. Forty-six percent supported the party of Wilson and Bryan while thirty-five percent championed the Republican cause. This bias appears to have been both a cause and a result of the AFL's increasing friendliness with the Democrats after 1908.[70] At least nineteen percent of the business unionists displayed third-party sympathies. Two-thirds of these were supporters of the Socialist and Socialist Labor parties, while the rest at one time or other backed the Populist, Bull Moose, or La Follette Progressive parties.

A minority of twenty-three percent of the business unionists were actively involved in politics. Approximately one-third were Democrats, one-third Republicans, and one-third supporters of minor parties, with half of these being Socialists. Fifteen of the men studied were primarily party activists, ranging from the Longshoremen's Richard Butler, who was a Tammany Hall leader, to the Carpenters' William L. Hutcheson, who managed the Labor Division of the Republican party in 1932.[71] Thirty other leaders were at some time political candidates, running for a total of thirty-nine offices and succeeding about half the time. Among these was the future president of the American Federation of Labor, William Green, who was elected as a Democrat to the Ohio legislature in 1911 and 1913.[72] William B. Wilson (D., Pa.) of the United Mine Workers, Frank J. McNulty (D., N.J.) of the International Brotherhood of Electrical Workers, John J. Casey (D., Pa.) of the Plumbers, and Frank Buchanan (D., Ill.) of the Bridge and Structural Iron Workers were all elected to the United States Congress.[73] Finally, nine business unionists were professional or semiprofessional politicians, running for office more than twice.

Before America's entrance into World War I, approximately thirteen percent of the business unionists received appointments to various governmental posts and commissions. As had been the case with the traditional labor leaders, their positions were generally concerned with labor problems. At the local level unionists served as factory inspectors and street railway commissioners. Several leaders were associated with state commissions of labor and one was a justice of the Michigan Court of Arbitration. Concomitantly, a significant proportion of business unionists were appointed to positions in the national government. Three were members of the 1913 United States Industrial Relations Commission, while two more served with the Bureau of Immigration. One former union official, William B. Wilson, became the nation's first secretary of labor in 1913, and another, William Doak, would fill this post during the Hoover administration.

Once the country began to mobilize in 1916 to meet the German threat, the number of labor leaders receiving government appointments increased dramatically. At the national level alone, 122 positions were established on war boards and commisions for representatives of labor. These posts were filled by sixty-five leaders, a third of whom were on more than one board, and one, John R. Alpine, serving on five. Twenty-three labor leaders were also delegates on various missions to Europe "to acquaint the working people of the war ridden countries of the stand taken by Labor in the United States."[74] Finally, an unknown number of leaders served on various state and local councils of defense and other war-related bodies.

Business unionists displayed a propensity to join social clubs and reform groups. The eighty-four leaders on whom information is available belonged to a total of fifty-nine organizations. On the average, each leader was a member of at least two groups. The reform bodies were basically of four types. The most prominent were organizations such as the National Civic Federation and the Foundation for the Promotion of Industrial Peace which were designed to promote improved labor relations. Second, there were religiously oriented groups such as the Militia of Christ for Social Service and the Federal Council of Churches. Third, societies established to promote world harmony. Among them was the National Arbitration and Peace Congress, which in its 1907 proceedings listed Samuel Gompers as a vice-president and twenty-two other unionists as delegates.[75] Finally, although less significant, there was the cause of temperance with at least five supporters including John B. Lennon, the AFL treasurer, who wrote several pamphlets for the Anti-Saloon League.[76]

In perspective, the number of leaders who belonged to reform groups was far less than the number belonging to social clubs. Indeed, the fraternal connections of such labor leaders as Martin Lawlor, James Lynch, or William P. Clarke would put Sinclair Lewis's Babbitt to shame.[77] The most extensive fraternal ties were those of Geroge L. Berry of the Pressmen, who belonged to the Masons, Elks, Odd Fellows, Shriners, Rotary, and the Lambs' Club. He was also a founder and national vice-commander of the American Legion.[78] The Masons and Elks were the most popular groups, each with twenty-seven leaders. Other organizations such as the Moose, Eagles, and Knights of Columbus drew their fair share of union officials, but the most significant indicator of the development of labor union leadership was the fact that the business unionists were entering the more exclusive social groups. Three had gained entrance into athletic associations, six were members of the budding country club set, and ten of various city clubs.

The cumulative portrait of the typical business unionist which emerges from the above statistical analysis is somewhat different from the accepted stereotype. As scholars have correctly pointed out, the working-class origins, urban-industrial background, long tenures in office, and lack of political involvement of the new unionists suggest a professional labor leader whose primary concern is with his union. Where they have erred has been in neglecting certain characteristics such as club membership and business activities which are indicative of middle-class aspirations and the increased status of a professional.

V

When the statistical portraits of the traditional labor leader and the business unionist are compared, it becomes evident that they do not represent two distinct types, as maintained by earlier historians, but rather different but continuous phases in the evolution of union leadership. The most outstanding comparisons between the old-school unionist and the new labor leader are the similarities which they shared, rather than the differences which divided them. Moreover, the differences that do exist are either the result of the professionalization of union leadership, or are simply minor differences of degree rather than of kind.

Sociologically, the traditional and the business unionists were quite similar. Of the full 350 leaders analyzed in this study, less than one-half percent were black and only two percent female. Moreover, more than ninety percent were of western European extraction with a majority of each group having ancestors in the British Isles. Over the sixty-year period from the 1860s to the 1920s there was a gradual decrease in the number of foreign-born leaders, but until the end of World War I, immigrants accounted for over forty percent of the samples. The native traditional and business unionists, who constituted a majority of both groups, were born in roughly the same size urban communities and resided in comparable cities at the time of their elections to national offices. Finally, the overwhelming proportion of leaders of both groups were from working-class families.

A number of important behavioral patterns of the old-school labor leaders and the business unionists are also comparable. By the age of fourteen the majority of both groups had dropped out of school and begun work. Moreover, at least half of the leaders in each period were elected to their first national union office by age thirty-five. Except for an increase in Jews, the religious affiliations of the leaders were roughly similar, with over half of each sample apparently having very loose church ties. Likewise, a majority of both groups were little concerned with politics. Although the number of Democrats increased during the Progressive era, third-party supporters represented less than twenty-five percent of each group, and political activists were also less than a fourth. Before the outbreak of World War I at least, only twelve percent of the traditional labor leaders and thirteen percent of the business unionists were appointed to governmental posts or commissions.

The differences that did exist between the two groups were primarily the result of the institutionalization of the union, and the simultaneous professionalization of union leadership. Most indicative of the rise of careerism are the statistics on tenure in office. The labor leaders of the Progressive era spent much longer moving up the union hierarchy than did their predecessors, and upon attaining their highest office remained there for considerably more time. Whereas fifty percent of the traditional leaders were in office for barely over two years, half of the new unionists held their posts for fifteen years or more. The longer tenures in offices were to a large extent proportional to the length of time the union had been in existence. In the Brotherhood of Railroad Trainmen, founded in 1883, the first president served for less than a year, the next four were in office for one year each, the sixth president served for ten years, the seventh for thirteen, and the eighth for nineteen years. Accompanying their longer tenures were higher salaries appropriate for professionals. As will be demonstrated later, the financial rewards for union work rose from at best a token fee in the 1870s to salaries of eight, nine, and ten thousand dollars in 1920. Allegedly shocked by some of the incomes union officials reportedly received at the latter date, *Literary Digest* ran an article "Labor Pays Its Leaders Capitalist Wages," the title of which contained at least a grain of truth.[79]

The rise of professionalism is indirectly suggested in other statistics. As union leadership assumed more of the features of an occupation, business unionists rejected some of the behaviorial patterns of traditional labor leaders and adopted new ones. While concerning only a minority of both groups, it is significant that the number of leaders with business career interests outside the union dropped from twenty percent of the old-school unionists to ten percent of the new leaders. The number of leaders belonging to social clubs, on the other hand, increased markedly. This development is suggestive of the greater status labor leaders began to enjoy as unionism became a more accepted part of American society.

The rise of professionalism was a phenomenon noticed by observers both inside and outside the union movement. Reporting to the Thirty-Fifth Annual Convention in 1915, the AFL Executive Council observed that "it was not so many years ago that an organizer for the labor movement was regarded as a dangerous man in a community. He was a marked man, blacklisted, denied opportunities for any kind of work, starved and persecuted, but since the labor movement has grown in power, and has been recognized as a movement for humanity, it now is regarded as a great constructive agency in the community. . . . Formerly one of the indispensable qualities of an organizer was ability for physical self-defense and protection." But, the council went on to point out, things have changed over the years. "Where industrial statemanship has been developed to a degree that co-operation with the organized labor movement is sought, there the work of the organizer of the labor movement becomes largely administrative and education."[80]

Discussing the labor leader of 1920, *Literary Digest* noticed a similar trend:

> The offices where these men hold forth, we are told, by no means resemble the labor headquarters of yore, which often were dark and dingy and smelled of stale beer and tobacco. The head office of a labor organization of today is equipped with good desks, the latest in filing cases, and other modern office devices, and it is manned by alert clerks and stenographers. The entire establishment bears the stamp of high-power business efficiency, and this it seems, is the principal characteristic of the man in charge.[81]

The pioneers in labor history also perceived the rise of professionalism in trade union leadership as one of the characteristics of the stereotype business unionist which distinguished him from the traditional labor leader. Yet these scholars never fully understood nor explored the development of careerism in the labor movement. Instead, the "business unionist" and his earlier counterpart became casualties in the ideological warfare between the Wisconsin School of Labor Studies and the more radical students of unionism. They were transformed from tools of historical understanding to issues of debate which in many ways were divorced from reality.[82]

Hopefully avoiding this tempting pitfall, the pages which follow are an attempt to analyze the rise of professionalism in the labor movement. In particular, they are concerned with certain basic questions which have been too long overlooked or lightly handled by scholars.[83] Why, for instance, did professionalism develop? What form did it take? And what were the consequences both for the labor movement and American society?

2.

Four Images of Unions

I

Labor leaders were not generally pensive men and spent little time or ink evaluating their roles. However, in their speeches and writings they used numerous similes, metaphors, and references to describe their unions, their followers, and themselves. Many of these rhetorical devices were intended simply for audience appeal in an age of oratory. But four images—the union as a fraternity, a democracy, an army, and a business—had singular import. They were repeated constantly by a great number of leaders and thus became part of many labor leaders' informal as well as formal tools of reference. Time and again, the leaders in outlining policies tried to transform the four images into reality. By studying the content of the four primary images which labor leaders used to describe the unions, it may be possible to understand how these men perceived their roles, the roles of the rank and file, and the nature of their organizations.

These images were nebulous entities. In part, they were idealized views of what their creators thought reality was or should be. Moreover, they were incomplete descriptions. The concept of the union as a democracy, for instance, excluded politics. Nor did the idea of the union as a business suggest the estrangement of the executive from the stockholders, a phenomenon associated with the modern corporation. Indeed, at the suggestion that such alienation was occurring, the leaders would deny it by reverting to the concept of the union as a democracy, thus revealing that the images were in fact interchangeable and functional.[1]

Over the period from Reconstruction to the end of World War I the content of the images as well as the dominance of one image over the others changed, directly reflecting the leaders' own changing perceptions. To a large extent, the particular imagery used at a certain time and place was related to the realities of the union's internal and external environment. The concept of the union as an army, for example, was most often voiced when the organization felt threatened; the union as a business emerged when the organization developed a sense of security and a degree of acceptance from business, government, and the external community. In the main, the notion of the union as a fraternity was most frequently advanced in the years before 1895, while the image of the union as a business was most often expressed after that date. The concepts of the union as a democracy and the union as an army appeared throughout the period from 1870 to 1920, but the content of these images tended to change over time.

The role of the images in the development of labor union leadership remained complex. As suggested above, the particular image which was dominant at a certain time mirrored the stage of union evolution. At the same time, labor leaders, by conforming to certain images, contributed to the development of unionism and leadership along certain lines. A leader viewing his union as a business, for instance, acted and established policies which reinforced his own businesslike behavior. In short, imagery both reflected the evolution of labor union leadership and also contributed to determining the course of that evolution. But given the nebulous nature of imagery, it is impossible to measure the extent of such contributions.

II

The image of the union as a fraternity was alluded to throughout the years from Reconstruction to the end of World War I. In 1920, as had been true many years earlier, it was standard practice to refer to a fellow unionist as "brother" and to sign labor correspondence with "fraternally yours." Yet, it was in the decades before the turn of the century that the image of the union as a fraternity was most pronounced and had actual substance. During the Gilded Age, the founders of many unions consciously sought to incorporate in the names of their new organizations words which would suggest the fraternal qualities of fellowship, righteousness, and nobility—thus, the Sons of Vulcan, the Knights of St. Crispin, the Industrial Brotherhood, and the Sovereigns of Industry. Founders of unions in later years, not as influenced by fraternal imagery, settled for words with fewer emotional and more structural implications such as "amalgamated," "association," "united" (meaning amalgamation rather than solidarity), "federated," and simply "union."

The union as a fraternity was to an extent an artificial creation. Early leaders such as Terence V. Powderly, Uriah S. Stephens, Frederick J. Turner, and Charles H. Litchman spent long hours developing symbols and rituals which would give their labor bodies the aura of fraternal organizations.[2] In part, fraternalism was used as a means of attracting and holding members when more immediate gains of better hours, wages, and working conditions were slow in coming, much in the way later unions would use death and relief funds.[3]

The appeal of fraternalism to unionists in the decades following the Civil War was rooted to a large extent in their extreme consciousness not only of their declining economic status, but also of their deteriorating social standing. The "hopeless degradation of the toiling masses" was a theme which appeared in the preambles of numerous labor organizations.[4] In the ritual of the Industrial Brotherhood, the head of the lodge instructed newly initiated members to the effect that "the great aim and object of our organization is to secure for the industrial classes that position in the world and in society to which they are entitled as the producers of the necessities and comforts of life."[5] Reflecting on the meaning of the machine and the factory to the previously self-employed craftsmen, Terence Powderly bemoaned the fact that the artisans "no longer carried the keys of the workshop, for workshops, tools and keys belonged not to them, but to their masters. . . . They saw that they were no longer engaged in that competition which is 'the life of the trade,' they realized that it was a competition which ultimately meant death to manhood and independence, unless through some means it became directed into a different channel."[6]

The process of industrialism, undercutting as it did craft skills, also enabled individuals of dubious social character to enter previously esteemed trades. "It may not be generally known to the public at large," related Chief Peter M. Arthur of the Locomotive Engineers, "that railroad men in the early days, speaking of them as a whole, were given to habits of dissipation and vice. Intoxication was quite general; habits were bad, which finally led to the formation of this brotherhood for the purpose of bettering the conditions of the men. That was the primary object."[7]

The desire to improve the moral quality and character of the worker, which originally was "the great mission of the Brotherhood," constituted an important factor in the founding of other labor bodies during this era.[8] One of the goals of the Sovereigns of Industry was "elevating the character" of its members. "The Order will aim," its constitution stated, "to cultivate in its members generous sympathies, soundness of thought, comprehensiveness of policy and a supreme respect for the rights of others, with an inflexible determination to maintain their own, while for labor it will seek to secure full and free opportunities."[9] The Preamble of the Industrial Brotherhood and numerous documents of the Knights of Labor expressed similar sentiments.

The ethos of fraternity was ideally suited for promoting a feeling of dignity, morality, and character among workers. Membership in fraternally oriented unions was open only to those whose lives were above reproach. The early Brotherhood of Locomotive Engineers, for example, required those admitted into its fellowship to be of high moral character and to be locomotive engineers of good standing with at least one year's experience.[10] And while the Knights of Labor proclaimed that its doors were open to all producers, it established an elaborate system of blackballing undesirables and, at one time or another, explicitly forbade the membership of such allegedly "degraded" types as lawyers, doctors, bankers, professional gamblers, stockbrokers, and those who sold liquor or made a living by its sale.[11] Moreover, the Industrial Brotherhood, the Knights of Labor, and other such organizations had strict rules of conduct and procedures for disciplining or expelling any member who by word or deed showed his character unworthy of fellowship. In the mid 1860s, the Brotherhood of Locomotive Engineers expelled its former grand chief, William D. Robinson, for deserting his wife and refusing to support his family.[12]

Leaders also designed other aspects of union rituals and laws to promote a feeling of dignity and fellowship among members. Upon entering the Sanctuary of the Noble and Holy Order, a Knight of Labor had to write his name on a card. Among the reasons given for this practice in the Knights' *Secret Circular:*

> The first is pride, for on entering the Sanctuary he desires to do so on an equal footing with his fellow member who can write his name. The second cause is that his eyes are opened, for the first time, maybe, to the fact that he is inferior to other men who can write, and a determination seizes him to emulate the example thus set before him, and which other men practice.[13]

The rhetoric of the fraternally oriented unions also served to instil in the members a sense of dignity. As Charles Madison observed, the grandiose thinking of the Knights of Labor's founder, Uriah S. Stephens, "may have been over the heads of many members, but none failed to appreciate his glorification of labor. And workers were then in need of such comfort."[14] Speeches and rituals constantly reminded the workers that they were fulfilling God's will. "The work to which this fraternity addresses itself," proclaimed one leader,

> is one of the greatest magnitude ever attempted in the history of the world. . . . It builds upon the immutable basis of the Fatherhood of God, and the logical principles of the Brotherhood of Man. . . . Inspired by these lofty principles, it moves majestically forward to elevate the race to a higher plane of existence,— a truer, nobler development of its capacities and power, and a realization of the greatest good possible within the limit of the law.[15]

Fraternity was important primarily for the ethos it gave early unions. In terms of suggesting organizational structure and the internal distribution of power, it was vague and contained conflicting elements. In this sense, the image differed from the concepts of the union as a democracy, an army, or a business, for they not only involved an outlook, but they implied particular power relations and structural forms.

In some ways, the fraternal tradition promoted a democratic spirit. All members were to be of equal standing. The requirement that each Knight of Labor sign his name served to remind participants that they were equal. Within the Sanctuary, moreover, "all members, whether they hold positions or not, occupy the same level." According to the *Secret Circular:*

> This is to indicate that there are no degree of rank, no upper or lower class—all men are admitted on an equal footing. By this lesson the member is encouraged to work in harmony with his fellow member; he feels that to him all are the same, and in our dealings with each other this idea must be carried out so far as is consistent with our teachings.[16]

Other rituals and symbols of fraternal unionism, however, supported a more authoritarian spirit. The pompous appellations given officers of these organizations struck many observers as undemocratic. Writing to B. F. Gordon of the Brotherhood of Railway Shop Employees, Samuel Gompers observed:

> I am free to say that in my judgment these high sounding titles of grand master and grand chief are both un-American and by all means not conducive to the best interests of organized labor. It tends to the belief as well as the practice that one man is to be looked up to as a saviour as well as the all-absorbing officer of the organization. It surrounds him with strange notions and necessarily develops a feeling of impotency as well as destroys sovereignty and manhood among the rank and file, nor do these high sounding titles ennoble men. Plain men with plain titles with officers and men having distinct duties to perform, instills manhood, intelligence and self-reliance as well as interdependence, and finally results in fraternity and solidarity.[17]

Apparently Terence Powderly felt the same way, for he took pains to point out in his autobiography that "when the General Assembly of the K. of L. was instituted we designated our officers as 'Grand

Officers.' Five years after in our General Assembly [of 1883] we decided that the word grand smacked too much of aristocracy and we changed it to general and since then our officers are known as General Officers."[18] In another instance, he requested of his fellow Knights that "in addressing letters to me, or in introducing me as a speaker, or addressing me in any way, to drop the HON. I detest titles; it is disgusting to notice how men, who should strive to level all distinctions will make use of these flummeries—plain Tom, Dick, and Harry, is good enough for any man."[19]

The authoritarian impulse went beyond mere titles and was embodied in a strict code of obedience. Workers seeking membership in the Knights of Labor, as was the case for most organizations of this nature, promised "strictly to obey all laws, regulations, solemn injunctions, and legal summons that may be sent, said or handed" to him by officers of the Order.[20] Their sworn duty was "Obedience to the 'officers of their choice.'"[21] Such submissiveness was not seen as being in conflict with individual values and opinions, for all members of the brotherhood accepted common principles and goals. Major ideological differences were not conceivable within the fraternal spirit. In the eyes of Powderly and many others, the fraternal labor organization was on a single-minded mission:

> and in that crusade we have burned the bridges behind us; we
> have stricken from our vocabulary the word fail; we aim at es-
> tablishing the complete rights of man throughout the world; we
> take as our guide no precedent ever set by mortal man unless it
> be right; we tolerate no dissension, and will have no disbanding
> save as ordained by the Great Master Workman when He calls
> from our ranks each individual member and bids him join that
> silent majority. . . .[22]

Despite the demand for obedience, the role of the labor leader was not one of a tyrant, but preeminently that of a teacher. The fraternal labor unions put great stress on education as a means of social change. The first plank in the platform of the Industrial Brotherhood, for instance, dedicated the organization to "making knowledge a standpoint of action."[23] Similarly, Powderly constantly reiterated that "the chief aim of the Knights of Labor is to educate. . . ."[24] As head of the Order, he longed to stand before great crowds, instructing the workers in the ways to a better world. He was constantly pushing for larger expenditures for educational work and was always bemoaning the fact that so much of his time was taken up answering trivial correspondence.[25]

This idea of the leader as teacher put a premium on oratorical and literary skills. Biographical sketches of labor leaders prominent before the turn of the century emphasized their rhetorical abilities, whereas sketches appearing in labor journals at a later date stressed special skills such as knowledge of the trade or finances. It was not uncommon to find a leader described as "one of the readiest impromptu speakers," whose powers of oratory were so great that even his opponents "cannot resist the temptation of going to hear him."[26] Another leader might be criticized for his "thinness of voice."[27] The role of the leader as an educator also placed a premium on journalistic skills, in part accounting for the greater number of labor editors who held union office before 1895. Administrative abilities, on the other hand, were considered less important. Reflecting the general dislike for such work, Uriah Stephens advised a local master workman "to call to his assistance as many light-footed and competent brothers as will be necessary to execute trifling duties."[28]

III

Whereas the image of the union as a fraternity was to some extent an artificial creation, it was natural that labor adopt the image of the union as a democracy. Most union members were native born or from the British Isles and shared a cultural heritage which sanctioned democracy as the only just form of government. Viewing unions in terms of this ideal was compatible with their social values. Moreover, immigrant unionists from cultures lacking in democratic traditions often proved avid democrats as they zealously protected their newly gained freedom. The Yiddish emigrés from Tsarist Russia who founded the United Cloth Hat and Cap Makers' Union in 1901, to cite just one of many cases, refused to designate a president, viewing such a position as tending to authoritarianism.[29]

Democratic imagery was also a natural corollary to American labor's interpretation of its historic mission to extend the meaning of the Declaration of Independence. "Civil and religious liberty and theoretical equality before the law we already have in America," explained Uriah Stephens in 1871.

> That was achieved for us by our revolutionary forefathers, and bequeathed by them as a sacred legacy to us, their descendants and successors. But an accursed slavery, a heaven-denounced tyranny, a degrading atheistical idolatry remains, has grown upon us, which it becomes our duty to ourselves, to our posterity, and to God and humanity, to destroy and utterly annihilate.[30]

Virtually every labor leader expressed similar sentiments, and beginning in the mid-1880s these became embodied in the concept of "industrial democracy."[31] Concerned primarily with gaining for labor a voice in the government of industry, the values of industrial democracy nonetheless were carried over to the internal polity of the unions. "There is something in the spirit of labor organizations," observed Henry White of the United Garment Workers, "that brings out the democratic instinct. Whether this instinct be given practical expression or not, it is at least seriously attempted. This democracy is perhaps identical with the striving for industrial equality and the revolt against authority from above, which is the mainspring of unionism."[32]

Most references to democracy in labor journals and in speeches of labor leaders focused on the role of the union within the larger community. While of secondary importance, the idea of the democratic nature of the union in its internal affairs received significant airing. At such times the union was pictured not simply as being democratic, but as "democracy in its purest and best sense. . . ."[33] "The labor movement," proclaimed the *United Mine Workers' Journal,* "is democratic through and through and no organization on earth is doing as much good work as organized labor is doing for the betterment of humanity for justice, equality and fraternity."[34] "In fact," a "Miner's Wife" declared, "if anything on this earth can or should partake of the natural and infinite justice it should be that institution whose foundation stone is a blending of both, viz. a labor organization."[35] "The world over," concurred the *Garment*

Worker, "trade unions are the foremost defenders and champions of democracy in all its forms."[36]

The leading booster of democratic imagery was, predictably, Samuel Gompers. "Our trade unions," he proudly wrote, "are democratic in character and recognize the sovereignty of the members and a federation of trade unions such as the A.F. of L. is, must depend for its success upon the good-will of every member in the ranks."[37] Although Adolph Strasser, president of the Cigar Makers, was nicknamed "the Prussian" because of his autocratic methods, Gompers upheld the union as "one of the most democratically conducted bodies to be found anywhere."[38] In his eyes, the AFL conventions were "the freest forum in the world,"[39] and its system of voting "the fairest devised by any legislative body in existence."[40] "It is at the numerous annual conventions of the international trade unions and the annual conventions of the American Federation of Labor that the spirit, genius, intentions, and tactics of the organized workers of America are clearly set forth by democratic methods. Indeed in no institution on earth is the controlling power so completely in the hands of the rank and file."[41]

This theme of the sovereignty of the membership was the basic premise upon which the role of leadership was developed. "There are no leaders—no dictators among us," declared William Sylvis of the National Labor Union, "and none can occupy a position unless by the clearly expressed will of the majority."[42] A half-century later, James Duncan of the Granite Cutters expressed the same sentiment: "No officer controls or commands. He, in turn, is commanded. The rank and file do the ordering."[43] "The term 'leader' is tabooed in union circles," observed Henry White of the Garment Workers. "However such a person may be recognized on the outside he has no existence inside. The officials are just 'servants' and the will of the mass presumably alone leads."[44]

In replying to criticism from the *Denver Evening Post,* Samuel Gompers elaborated on the role of the leader:

> You say that if I value my position as 'leader' of the common people I should lead them now. This betrays what a poor conception you have of the fundamental principles of our labor movement. Your idea seems to be that an executive officer of an organization should be their 'leader.' You do not seem to understand

that a leader implies followers, and that where there are leaders
and followers, there are dupers and duped. You do not know that
our movement is based upon the recognition of the sovereignty
of the workers; that when they declare for a purpose, they're pre-
sumed to mean what they say, and to act in accordance with it;
that they require their executive officer, not to lead them, but to
execute their will.[45]

Responding to similar criticism, John Mitchell of the UMW wrote:

Now, I know you will think that as president i ought to do
something more than i do, or in other words, i ought to take a
stand and have them come up to it.

But, Sir, let me say our organization is conducted along the
lines of Initiate [sic] and Referendum.

I, while head, can only sugest but must be referred back to
the rank and file for adoption or rejection.[46]

In this idealized view, labor union democracy was government
without politics. " 'Wire Pulling, electioneering,' and other methods
paculiar [sic] to the politician must not, *will not,* be practiced in
our order," insisted Powderly.[47] An unidentified miner agreed: "We
as sensible, practical men do not want men who stoop to humor
their constitutents merely to hold their office," he wrote. "We want
men who will do their duty and stand by the dogmas of a constitution
framed by us—the lawmakers."[48] Another miner, W. S. Glasgow,
also advised his fellow unionists to "keep politics out. . . . Let the
office seek the man and not the man the office," he argued, "and
two to one he will do us double service."[49]

Sensitive to such feelings, union officials constantly sought to
create the belief that they were beyond politics. Typical of many
labor leaders, Samuel Gompers proclaimed:

I never was an aspirant for any office in my life, in the labor movement or fraternity or other body—never. Office came to me always, I never went after it. In all my life I have never asked any
man either to nominate me for office or vote for me. Neither
directly nor indirectly have I made any request or suggestion or
even entered a caucus of any kind in furtherance of any office
for which I was a candidate.[50]

Completing the ritual, leaders were expected to swear, as John Mitchell did, that "When I have finished my term of office I shall return to Illinois and take up my pick among you."[51] Coming from the people, they returned to the people after doing the job which the people asked them to do. This complete ordeal was in part intended to buttress the democratic belief that labor leaders were "very much like the rest of us," and bore "a marked resemblance to other folk."[52]

The union as a democracy had several functional purposes. Desiring to win broad public support, labor leaders and journalists used the concept for propaganda purposes. It was presented most frequently and in most unconditional form in those publications intended to reach a wide, nonlabor audience. Counteracting frequent accusations by anti-unionists that labor leaders were unrepresentative of the workers and were out for personal gains, union officials reiterated the democratic theme over and over to assure middle-class supporters that their organizations were liberal vehicles in the crusade "against these twin monsters, tyranny and monopoly."[53] Moreover, the image was often presented in such a form as to convince genteel reformers that organized labor was a vital force in meeting challenges to the "American way of life" to which their audience was particularly sensitive. The *Textile Worker* argued, for instance:

> The real melting pot in which the nationalities who seek asylum on our shores are fused and purified into citizenship, is trade unions. The alien, first securing membership in a union, there gains his initial ideas of freedom and independence, learns that he controls himself, that without fear of king or potentate he may voice not only his protests, but his ideals and his aspirations, and, what is equally important, he learns to express his civic ideas in an orderly and responsible way.[54]

Such sentiments no doubt struck a responsive chord among many Americans who feared the rise of the masses and sought some means of social control. Charles Beard, for one, fully accepted the image of the union as a democracy. "When the full story of self-government in America is written . . . ," he wrote somewhat overzealously, "pages on the cellular growth of local craft unions will be placed beside the records of town meetings; while chapters on the formation of national labor structures will complement the sections on the origin and development of the federal Constitution."[55]

The image of the union as a democracy was also useful in managing internal union affairs. Policies which labor leaders either wanted or opposed could be condoned or condemned in terms of their democratic character. Plans for reorganizing the management of the *United Mine Workers' Journal,* for instance, were praised as having "the genuine ring of popular government. . . ."[56] On the other hand, the 1911 convention of the AFL rejected a proposal requiring that one of their eight vice-presidents be a representative of the federal unions, "the convention not deeming it advisable to make class distinctions when selecting members of the Executive Council."[57] In reality, this decision totally ignored the fact that class distinctions existed within the system of representation, so limiting the federal unions' strength as to curtail their abilities to elect a member of the council outright.

The image of the union as a democracy enabled labor leaders to save face in times of trouble. The concept of the sovereignty of the rank and file, Henry White of the Garment Workers observed from his own experience, "is encouraged by the union heads who at all times wish the members to feel that they merely execute their wishes, especially so when the results are not fortunate." Union officers, he continued, "encouraged the democratic sentiment in order to make things surer for themselves. By securing the apparent approval of the body of members, they could dodge blame for any ill conceived move."[58]

The democratic facade provided an argument for discrediting and suppressing dissension. By pointing to their own election to office, labor leaders could dismiss critics as small, undemocratic cliques unwilling to abide by the will of the majority. To the *Typographical Journal* such dissenters were "demagogues and charlatans who seek little less than their own preferment and advantage."[59] "A majority of the martyrs (?) for union who now protest against the policies of the different organizations," the miners' *Journal* ridiculed, "are men who didn't get office."[60] More important than such calumny was an underlying tendency to treat the right of dissent as having no justifiable place within the union. Typical of many labor leaders, a perplexed William Sylvis

> could never discover a single reason why there should be bickering or contention among workingmen. There are no leaders-no dictators among us; and none can occupy a position unless by the clearly expressed will of the majority. While such perform their duties faithfully, they should have their hands strengthened. If they neglect them, the *masses* have the power to remove them.
>
> Now, with this plain, democratic system to govern us, why should we encounter such drawbacks as discord, jarring, and unjust criticism?[61]

Expressing a similar view, a leader of the miners maintained

> that within this organization there is no room for strongly defined parties or partisans. When the verdict of the majority has been ascertained and announced it becomes the duty of all the members of our great union to give their active support to those who have been elected to fill the positions of trust and responsibility; for without such unanimous support no official can deliver the best that is possible.[62]

While the union as a democracy could serve practical functions, it was not basically a deception used by labor leaders. The image did have an essence of its own. Most labor leaders truly believed that their organizations were democratic, and when forced to resist the will of the majority, they maintained in all honesty that "it has been proven by experience that to give Democracy a fair chance of success it must to some extent be kept in check by a conservative power. . . ."[63] "Leadership is not inconsistent with democracy," insisted the *Mine Workers' Journal*. "In fact, it promotes democracy. In times of crisis the mass can not get the breadth of view that those at the head can. It can not know its own limitations or see the obstacles to be overcome or the strength of the opposition, and when quick action is required the mass is not competent to direct itself."[64]

The annals of labor contain numerous incidents in which labor leaders attempted to behave in accordance with democratic precepts. Uriah S. Stephens firmly opposed having the delegates to the General Assembly of the Knights of Labor chosen from district assemblies rather than from the membership at large, viewing such a practice as "Un-democratic an [sic] Oligarchy."[65] Powderly, when asked to make a decision on a grievance, replied: "Hear both sides, then judge, is my motto. I therefore return your letter with the request that you send a copy of it to your assembly to be read, and ask of them to send me, under seal, the other side of the case. If you do this I will be better prepared to decide impartially."[66] Gompers stood firmly for religious liberty in the labor movement. "Tolerance of religious belief, or non-belief is inherent in the Unions," he insisted, "and we have no right to permit the conscience of any man being shocked either for or against religion in the meetings of our Unions."[67] And accepting the full consequences of democracy, William Blair Prescott campaigned for the popular election of officers during his seven years as head of the International Typographical Union, only to be defeated for reelection the first time the referendum was put into practice.[68]

Yet, while democracy was meaningful, unions were never fully free to shape policy in its spirit. A sense of security, political scientists generally agree, is vital for the development and flowering of democracy in a body politic.[69] During the years 1870 to 1920, labor unions generally lacked such security, facing attacks from government, business, competing labor organizations, and other groups. Moreover, despite the commitment of union founders to the democratic tradition, they had come together, as Robert Hoxie observed, "not primarily to establish and vindicate a form of organization—the organization is merely means to end—but to establish and maintain certain conditions of living."[70] In striving for these goals, genuine democracy—embodying as it does two grave defects, a lack of stability and difficulty in mobilization—was frequently abandoned in the hope of attaining practical results. Finally, as the German sociologist Robert Michels demonstrated in his classic study, *Political Parties,* modern democratic organizations generate within themselves overbearing oligarchic tendencies. Those tendencies as they existed in the American labor movement are a major theme of the present study.

IV

While insecurity widened the gap between the ideal and the practice of democracy, it made the image of the union as an army more realistic. Participating in the most violent system of labor relations in any industrial nation, labor leaders naturally gravitated toward martial allusions.[71] "The struggle which organized labor is carrying on," the *American Federationist* pointed out, "resembles in some respects the campaign of an army. There are organizations, officials, and encounters with an opposing force."[72] Within union circles it was common practice to refer to the rank and file as "the army of labor" or the "organized army of discontent" and to label famous episodes in labor history "wars," "battles," and "massacres."[73]

The military theme was prevalent throughout the period 1870 to 1920. Many of the symbols of the Noble and Holy Order, for instance, had martial implications. The very name "Knights" drew a parallel with the crusaders of old, while "the lance which confronted the member who knocked for admittance on the Inner Veil signified 'defence'."[74] "Our order is like a military organization," wrote Powderly. "We require and must exact the strictest discipline and as a consequence our trials must be the same as Court Martials, hence the existence in our laws of such an officer as Judge Advocate."[75] Later unions tended to update the image by making references to trenches, general orders, the draft, and other aspects of modern warfare. "These are stern days in the struggles of the workers," declared the *Textile Worker* in 1916. "They are days that call for supreme alertness, endurance and endeavor. The trenches must be guarded and enlarged and extended. The line of march must be steady, intelligent and determined. Organization! That's the word."[76] To the *American Federationist,* the principles of unionism "should be promulgated as 'general orders' and our army made to obey, for we need a unionism of 'Industrial Discipline'."[77] This spirit was captured in a poem by Mrs. H. W. Brown. Written in 1916 and entitled "A Voice From the Ranks," it resembled the enlistment literature which was soon to encourage young men to go forth and fight the Huns:

> Join your brother—get into your union,
> Stand by him loyal and true.

He's fighting your battle unaided—
Wake up, man—fight with him too!
Be a volunteer soldier of labor,
Don't wait till they draft you to come!
Get into the ranks with your brother
And the battle is bound to be won.[78]

Unlike the other images, the implications of the union as a military unit in terms of power and authority were quite direct: the officers were to command; the rank and file were to obey. "He who would be a good soldier," declared a typical editorial,

must not only join the army, but must obey without question every command given him; must perform faithfully every task to which he is assigned, and discharge his duty thoroughly. He who would be a good union man must not be content to simply have his name on the roster of a local: he must attend the meetings, take a part in every movement for the advancement of the brotherhood. He should be ready when the call of forward is given to go; should be ready to retrace his steps if the retreat is sounded. In fact, he could follow the example set by the soldier in many ways, and he will profit thereby.[79]

President J. B. Rae of the coal miners expressed a similar sentiment in an essay revealingly entitled "The Ideal Organization":

The lack of discipline in the ranks of labor is also a hindrance, and indeed it is a real danger. To command confidence and secure compliance, plans have to be disclosed before the time for action has come. Such unfolding of plans makes it more difficult, if not impossible, to carry them out. . . . A general understanding as to what is going to be done is proper, but the plan of action and the time to move should be kept secret, and the rank and file, like the army in the field, should be prepared to move without question when the time for action has come. . . .[80]

The nonferrous metal miners were of the same opinion:

If the Western Federation of Miners is to live and go forward in the battle for justice, the membership must stand as a solid

phalanx against the encroaching power of the known enemy
that is sparing no effort to exterminate organized labor. Quib-
bling on frivolities relative to the constitution and the laws which
govern the organization will scarcely halt the known enemy on
its invasion into the very citadel of the labor movement.[81]

Within the image of the union as an army, then, the leader was a
general. He possessed special abilities and only he and his general
staff knew the full battle plan. To obtain glory, however, he had to
have strict obedience from his troops. "It ought to be inscribed, in
mammoth characters, on every miner's mind," declared the *United
Mine Workers' Journal,* "that the most efficient weapon in this fight
is peace and quietude, coupled with unanimity. If we remain united
and firm now, for a short time, the battle will be ours ere long, with
very little trouble."[82] "The greater the confidence of the rank and file
in its officials," concurred the AFL's official organ, "the more highly
probable is it that a union will win its victories."[83] The martial spirit
in the union, as in real armies, focused on the duty of the foot
soldiers to obey rather than the responsibilities of the generals in
leading. Simple and direct, the image had tremendous influence.

V

During the 1870s and 1880s spokesmen for labor alluded only occasionally to the union as a business. Far less pronounced than the
concepts of the union as a fraternity, a democracy, or an army, the
allusions to the union as a business initially called forth visions of
early industrial and commercial institutions. Uriah Stephens related
a local assembly of the Knights of Labor, for instance, to "a 'business
firm,' every member an equal partner, as much so as a bank, a commercial house, or a manufacturing establishment." As a partner,
every member was "duty bound to put in his equal share of *money
and time.*" Within the image, distinctions between leaders and followers faded away. " 'As ye sow so shall ye also reap,' fits exactly
here as much so as it does in the mercantile house, the factory or
the bank," he declared. "There can be no 'silent partners' in this
business. . . ."[84]

In the years after 1895 the image of the union as a business became far more pronounced. Countless editorials in the labor press argued "that up-to-date business methods should be adopted by trade unions,"[85] and delegates to the AFL convention in 1905 expressed belief that, "In its capacity as a labor exchange, the trade union cannot exempt itself from the necessity of compliance with sound business principles."[86] In 1909 the *Journal* of the locomotive engineers argued that the union was organized solely on a business basis, and four years later the Typographical Union proclaimed itself to be "A Large Business Institution."[87] "Trade Unions," observed the Atlantic City *Union Herald* in 1901, "are more and more being based on business principles, and are more and more being managed by business-minded leaders who operate according to business methods."[88]

The reasons for the increased attraction of the business image after 1895 were related to several interacting factors. In part, it was a direct outcome of the growing acceptance of the AFL's philosophy of "pure and simple unionism." Gompers's approach to the labor question, rejecting as it did broad social goals for concrete agreements with employers on hours, wages, and working conditions, put a premium on internal union discipline and proper administration. "We had developed discipline as an essential of trade unionism," the AFL leader wrote in his autobiography:

> With discipline the movement emerged from confusion of thinking and practice to a definite trade union philosophy. A practical business administrative system within unions had provided offices, salaried officials, and the beginning of systematic labor records. All these things were necessary to sustain contractual relations with employers.[89]

Equally important, an increase in union membership and an expansion of union activities contributed to the adoption of the businesslike image. From 1899 to 1903 total membership in the AFL rose from 349,000 to 1,465,000.[90] The United Mine Workers, who pushed their roster from a mere ten thousand members in 1897 to two hundred thousand five years later, stimulated much of this growth.[91] But the unionizing impulse was felt far beyond the coal fields. In Connecticut, to cite just one case, the number of labor organizations increased from 214 in 1899 to 591 in 1903.[92] With the expansion of union membership, administrative problems became more complex. Organizations had more records to keep, larger funds to manage, and additional services to provide. In 1909, Daniel Tobin of the Teamsters described his union as "a set institution having regular standing monthly expenses that cannot be avoided and must be paid, amounting to at least three thousand dollars per month. I refer to office rent, salary of help, salary of officers, per capita tax to American Federation of Labor, monthly publication of the Journal &c."[93] Similarly, a writer outlining those features which made the printers' union a business establishment emphasized that its executive council had just invested six hundred thousand dollars of the union's reserve funds in bonds that would net about four percent. He further pointed out that "with its increasing membership, its Printers Home in Colorado Springs, its old age pension fund, its school for apprentices, not to mention other union activities, the International Typographical Union has grown to be a great institution requiring a high degree of business ability in its management."[94] The imperatives of running large organizations was one of the main factors which historian John Laslett sees as forcing left-wing unions to become more conservative.[95]

Another force which contributed to the increasing use of the image of the union as a business was the emergence of a new system of values in American society around the turn of the century. Championed by groups which Robert Wiebe views as "a new middle class" (among whom were labor leaders), the new ideas "were bureaucratic ones, peculiarly suited to the fluidity and impersonality of an urban-industrial world. . . . Instead of liking society to a clock's simple gears in perpetual motion," Wiebe observed, "men were now thinking in terms of a complex social technology, of a mechanized and systematized factory."[96] Efficiency became a guide to action, expertise a necessity for the solution of social problems, and regulation and structure a requirement for social order and stability. Labor leaders found the image of the union as a business in harmony with the new social ethos.

In both outlook and practice, unions accepted the values of modern corporate enterprises. "There is not an investment known," declared the *Textile Worker,* "that has paid dividends equal to that which has been earned by unionism."[97] The *Garment Worker* de-

veloped the theme that labor as well as capital was working toward
a basic end, "namely: To regulate the production and distribution of
wealth."[98] Decisions whether to organize an area or not began to
be expressed in terms of profitability. "It will cost a barrel of money
and we cannot see any way of getting it back," commented Daniel
Tobin on the prospects of unionizing the New York City mail driv-
ers.[99]

The gospel of efficiency became a major influence in the labor
movement. In 1898 the Brotherhood of Locomotive Engineers, introducing more businesslike methods, ended its practice of destroying the year's accumulation of correspondence after each
convention.[100] Form letters began to constitute more and more of
the correspondence of labor unions. Long tenures in office and
higher pay for labor leaders were accepted on the ground of promoting efficiency and expertise, while the referendum system of
union government came under attack for its inefficiency.[101] From
1915 to 1918, the *Typographical Journal* published a long debate
on ways to transform the printers' annual meeting from a pleasure
outing to a business convention.[102] Reflecting the trend, the delegates to the 1912 convention of the AFL first decided "that the president should have the power to appoint convention committees, as
their election would take up considerable of the time of the convention and accomplish nothing of benefit to the labor movement,"
and secondly refused to elect permanent general organizers,
"declaring a convention less qualified to pass on qualifications and
especial fitness for certain work than the Executive Council."[103]

Labor leaders, like their corporate counterparts, were viewed as
having special abilities and character. As defined by the *United
Mine Workers' Journal,* union officers were "men who are making
a study of organized labor and know how to advise the lay member."[104] They were "trained in the school of experience" and able
to present the workers' side of every controversy "convincingly and
with national, yes, and international scope." They were also "able
enough to cope with the best brains that can be procured by the
employers. . . ."[105] A spokesman for the printers agreed: "There
is not a single corporation in the United States or Canada, that
requires as high an order of ability, and that has anywhere the
amount of business to be transacted as the International Typo-

graphical Union. . . ."[106] Under such circumstances, another printer maintained, the position of leadership called "for men possessing qualifications acquired only by specialization."[107] "What the American workman most needs to-day," concluded the *American Federationist,* "is a leadership which in point of mental endowment and moral stamina, surpasses the capitalist leaders. Intellectual strength always subdues inferiority, and moral worth will, in the long run, win the staunchest following."[108]

Mirroring this development, biographical sketches in union journals put emphasis on the leaders' education and training in industrial affairs, rather than the oratorical ability stressed ten or twenty years earlier. In 1892, for instance, the *United Mine Workers' Journal* described a leader as an eloquent speaker who "caused the tears to trickle down the cheeks of men whose nature is not such as to be wheedled into rapturous joy by mere sophisticated jargon. . . ."[109] The same paper in 1910 said of another officer that he not only possessed "a wide knowledge of men and human character, but is considered a walking budget of matters pertaining to the coal industry. . . . In addition he has a very good technical knowledge of coal mining, and taught evening classes for six years, many of his pupils qualifying for positions as mine managers."[110]

The image of the union as a business was leadership oriented. Extended references to the rank and file were seldom. The latter were the stockholders who willingly transferred control of their institution to a board of managers. Once having selected their executives, the membership was to refrain from activities which would upset the operations of the union and follow the directives of the officers in order to attain maximum efficiency and benefit from the organization. Reflecting the emerging bureaucratic order, Samuel Gompers wrote to the Brewery Workers' secretary:

> . . . if there is any hope entertained for the success and permanency of the trade union movement in our country, it must be by the individual member yielding his judgment to the decision of the local union of his trade, the local union yielding to the international union, and the international union in turn complying with the decisions of the highest tribunal of American organized labor—the American Federation of Labor.[111]

Only occasionally would labor leaders refer to members as their employers, particularly when they wanted more rank-and-file responsibility, salary increases, or some other program like the establishment of "a pension system for those who had given their life service" to the labor movement.[112] For the most part the members were treated as silent partners, a view far removed from Uriah Stephens's early concept.

VI

Within the four images of the union existed two interrelated thematic conflicts, the ultimate outcome of which had major implications for the nature of union government and the development of labor leadership. The first conflict was between the concept of the leader as "one of the gang" and the leader as unique and superior to the rank and file. As has been pointed out, the images of the union as a fraternity and a democracy had several elements in them which tended to treat the leader as one among equals. Moreover, the early view of the union as a business was of a partnership rather than a professionally managed corporation. On the other hand, the pretentious titles of fraternal unionism and the concept of an elect within democratic unionism tended to elevate the leader above the membership. And elitism was fundamental to the images of the union as an army and a business, both of which explicitly viewed organizational structure as hierarchical.

Closely related to this problem was the second thematic conflict— between individual freedom and discipline. Again, the images of the union as a fraternity and particularly the concept of the union as a democracy contained aspects promoting individual freedom. Yet they also had undertones demanding members to sacrifice personal desires for the good of the whole. This theme of obedience and conformity was even more forcefully expressed in the image of the union as a business and was at the heart of the union as an army.

Given the inconsistencies inherent in our four images, it was extremely significant that by the end of World War I the concepts of the union as an army and the union as a business were far more prominent and influential than the ideas of the union as a fraternity or a democracy. In effect, it meant that by 1920 labor leaders and their followers most fully related to those images which put a premium on the leader as unique and the need for rank-and-file discipline. Such attitudes both reflected and continued to shape the nature of labor union leadership.

3.

Unions, Management, and Leadership

I am not suggesting that the leadership has played a wholly passive role in the process of acquiring power or that it has not sought to add to that which was dictated by market forces. However, it seems to me that the personal ambitions of leaders have been far less significant in the building of their power than the market factors over which they had no control . . . .

Emanuel Stein[1]

I

From 1870 to 1920, American labor devoted the bulk of its energy to direct economic action. Concern for "bread and butter" issues characterized the "business unions" of the American Federation of Labor as well as most other unions. To be sure, during the formative years of unionism, some workingmen united primarily to advance the moral character of their class and provide mutual assistance. Unable markedly to improve the living standards of their members by these methods, such organizations either lost their following and faded from the scene or altered their focus to include direct economic action. Likewise, unions advocating replacement of the wage system in reality exerted most of their effort toward improving the laborer's welfare under the existing economic arrangement.[2] Even organized labor's extensive involvement in the political field was secondary to economic action. The AFL continually placed political agitation in a subordinate role, and "reformist" organizations like the Knights of Labor had extensive union-management relations, an aspect of the Order which scholars have unjustly ignored.[3]

The evolution of industrial relations from 1870 to 1920 strongly influenced the institutional structure of unions as well as their ideological outlook. The continuous efforts of unionized workers to improve their lot tended to transform their organizations from loose conglomerates of semi-autonomous locals into centralized bodies in which the national office commanded obedience from its subdivisions, performed a multitude of functions, and managed sizable funds. More important, economic action helped forge professional labor leadership. By 1920, the pattern of union-management relations was increasingly confined to interaction between employers and the leadership of labor.

The story of industrial relations during this era resists simplification. A multitude of unions confronted a variety of employers, market situations, skill requirements, and technological innovations. No two unions faced identical environments, and even for an individual union conflicting conditions often prevailed simultaneously. During the first decade of the twentieth century, for example, the Iron Molders' Union negotiated with the Stove Founders' Association at the same time that it was in bitter conflict with the National Founders' Association.[4] To any generalization about the development of union-management relations, therefore, exceptions abound. But a pattern of change emerges, and by focusing on significant events, clarity and order can be derived from confusion.

II

Labor relations from the Civil War to the 1890s were primarily localized and marked by a spontaneity edging on anarchy. Throughout the era, industrial conflict raged. According to the Federal Bureau of Labor, 9,668 strikes and lockouts occurred between 1881 and

1890. In the year 1886, the climax of labor's "Great Upheaval," 1,432 strikes and 140 lockouts threw 610,024 employees out of work.[5] Most of these struggles were confined to local communities—the Hocking Valley of Ohio, the three anthracite fields of Pennsylvania, the textile mills of Fall River, Massachusetts—and pitted local workers against local management.[6] Rebellions against the few large, nation-wide companies were generally directed against a local branch. Strikes of national or regional dimensions were largely confined to the railroads, and these were often the simultaneous outbreak of a number of local conflicts with little central coordination. As the committee established by the Pennsylvania legislature to investigate the "Railroad Riot of 1877" reported: "each strike was independent of those on other roads, each having a local cause particularly its own."[7] The large number of nonunion conflicts reflected the spontaneity of labor unrest. In 1881 and again in 1882, approximately fifty-two percent of the struggles were not initiated by labor organizations. During the 1880s the figure slowly declined, yet it averaged thirty-nine percent for the decade.[8]

Although the industrial disputes of the Gilded Age grew out of several issues, the primary question was that of wages—the resistance to wage cuts, the desire to reestablish previously reduced wage rates, or the demand for increased compensation. Of the 1881 strikes which can be traced to a single issue, seventy-three percent concerned wages, six percent focused on union recognition and union rules, and only three percent related to the hours of labor. For the entire decade of the 1880s remuneration was at issue in approximately sixty percent of the single cause conflicts.[9] Preoccupation with immediate economic returns rather than union recognition in part reflected the large proportion of nonunion strikes and also the local orientation of union-management affairs. As will be pointed out subsequently, the issue of union recognition was of greater concern to the national leadership.

While wages were the primary issue in dispute, the cause of industrial strife generally stemmed from the manner in which labor relations were conducted. The practice of collective bargaining was in its infancy. A few unions attained written agreements, including the iron workers of 1866 and the anthracite coal miners in 1869. Yet these contracts were generally shortlived and represented the exception rather than the rule. Likewise, although a number of unions including the Knights of Labor called for arbitration of industrial disputes, this was an unusual procedure for the age.[10]

The more customary practice was for labor or management to establish labor standards unilaterally. On the one hand, management would boldly announce that on a certain date new conditions would prevail. Faced with the decree, employees had few alternatives. If the boss agreed to meet with the workers to discuss the change, he would most likely insist that they approach him individually or that they select representatives from within the firm's work force. In either case, management had the upper hand through control of the jobs. When such pleading failed, employees could either submit, leave the firm on an individual basis and seek work elsewhere, or band together and strike.

On the other hand, workers also took the initiative in unilateral action. The standard practice was for employees to meet together and determine under what terms they would labor. The final decision was held as nonnegotiable and presented to the employer. If he accepted, all was well; but if he turned down labor's proposal, the workers had either to submit or go on strike. If they took the latter course, the chances of success were roughly fifty-fifty, and usually victory was achieved at great cost in human suffering and loss of wages.[11] Defeat not only multiplied personal grief, but frequently resulted in the demise of the union and dismissal from employment of its most active supporters.

The local orientation of labor relations following the Civil War mirrored existing economic conditions. As economist Emanuel Stein observed, "the locus of power within a union is going to be found at the point where the collective bargaining takes place, and this in turn is determined by market considerations."[12] Despite trends to the contrary, the nation's market system in the 1860s and 1870s remained localized. Economically, as well as socially and politically, America was a country of "island communities."[13] This was particularly true in some industries where strong local unions were developing—printing, bricklaying, carpentry. By 1890, however, technological developments had fundamentally altered the situation by encouraging a national market network. Yet localized labor relations persisted into the latter period, demonstrating the lag between environmental change and institutional response. The business history of the era was in large measure the story of efforts to cope with change in the size of the market and new forces of technology. Not until the 1890s were acceptable solutions found in the form of trusts, finance capital, large corporations, and employers' associations to deal with labor.

In a similar manner, organized labor reluctantly adapted to change. Originally, craftsmen had banded together to protect their interests in the immediate economic community. Over time, however, they became aware that their efforts were being thwarted by outside competition. In some instances products made in other towns by workers laboring at lower wages found their way into the local community, where they sold for lower prices. Local manufacturers were impelled to cut wages and reduce prices in order to compete. In other instances workers who had mastered their trade elsewhere moved into the community and accepted employment below the prevailing wage, thus forcing down the standards of the local workers. In order to meet the problems posed by an expanded product market and increased labor mobility, the local unionists sought alliances with organized workers in other communities. Out of these efforts emerged the national labor unions.[14]

Thus, the majority of national labor organizations during this era grew from the bottom up (as opposed to organization from the top down characteristic of many CIO unions). And in joining together into a larger association, the local bodies, like the thirteen colonies uniting under the Articles of Confederation, hesitated to surrender too much sovereignty. This was due in part to the desire of the local power elite to maintain control, in part to fear of allowing outsiders lacking knowledge of local conditions to interfere in their affairs, and in part to a belief that the problems did not warrant centralized control. As a result, most early national unions were loose federations of local bodies, much like America of the 1780s.

Duties of the early national officers under this arrangement were limited and routine, which helps explain why the secretary was often the first paid functionary.[15] The primarily clerical tasks assigned to the Bricklayers' executives led President White to report to the 1867 convention that his job "for the past year has not been very severe, owing to our worthy Secretary, who has always been willing to do my correspondence, and relieve me all that lay in his power."[16] Presidents of the International Association of Journeymen Plumbers were primarily responsible for managing the union's cooperative shops in Milwaukee, a task they so mishandled as to cause the failure of both the businesses and the union.[17] Some constitutions did grant national officers more extensive duties, but the reluctance and niggardliness of the locals frequently prevented their fulfillment. The chief executive of the Bricklayers was instructed "to visit subordinate Unions, and inspect their proceedings, either personally or by deputy," but the convention delegates continuously refused to provide sufficient money, either in salary or traveling funds, to allow compliance.[18] For similar reasons, Thomas Phillips, president of the Boot and Shoe Workers, was unable to accomplish his constitutional obligations.[19] Even if funds were available, the influence a national leader could exert on autonomy-minded locals was limited. In 1874, President John Siney of the Miners' National Association issued a general circular advising against strikes. Later he learned that several local officers had collected all circulars sent to their territory and incinerated them before they could reach the rank and file.[20]

The national executives' lack of power was particularly marked in union-management relations. Officers of the International Typographical Union, founded in 1852, played no role in calling strikes until the establishment of a defense fund in 1885. Likewise, the Cigar Makers, who organized a general union in 1864, rejected centralized strike control until 1879. Up to then the executive board was obliged to sanction without question all strikes except those for wage increases.[21] Lack of discretionary authority caused the secretary of the Miners' Association of Western Pennsylvania to complain in 1880 of the "iron jacket orders from convention."[22] For several years after its formation in 1859, locals of the Iron Molders' Union remained largely autonomous. Finally, in 1863, the Molders made the initiation of strikes subject to approval through a general referendum. This practice at least gave the national officers a chance to persuade the membership. Yet their influence remained limited. Union rules required the president to present all the facts in his possession when issuing strike circulars. The information, however, was attained from the local which wanted to go out and frequently displayed bias. Moreover, locals would approve each others' strike requests in anticipation of the day when they would want reciprocal support. Not until 1882, twenty-four years after the establishment of the national union, did the chief executive attain absolute control over strikes and lockouts.[23] The typographers, cigar makers, and iron molders were part of the labor vanguard; they were among the first to organize as well as to establish strike funds and some centralized authority. For most organizations, the process of enlarging the national officers' power in union-management affairs did not begin until the 1890s and after.

With power concentrated at the local level, it was here that the first professional labor leaders in the modern sense developed. While national leaders, denied a critical role in industrial relations, concentrated on broad labor reforms, local leaders were developing skills in union-management negotiations. Among the Carpenters, for instance, P. J. McGuire, partly of his own choice and partly due to the locals' desire to preserve their autonomy, guided the national administration toward broad reformist ends with organize-agitate-educate means. Concomitantly, salaried business agents emerged at the local level. Concerned with day-to-day relations of labor and management, they developed characteristics similar to those of the national union official of today.[24] A similar development occurred among the Knights of Labor, where national leaders devoted the greater portion of their time, after administrative work, to the broad issues of labor reform. Meanwhile, specialists in labor-management affairs were in the making, particularly in assemblies of skilled craftsmen. In 1879, for example, local assembly 322 of Pittsburgh glass blowers passed the following resolution:

> Whereas we believe the time has come when we should have an officer vested with power to settle all difficulties and to give his whole time for the advancement of the trade, Therefore be it resolved, that this Assembly elect a President with power to chose four counselors of the Assembly. The duty of the President shall be to take charge of all correspondence and when any difficulty arises between the employees and employers it shall be his duty to proceed to the place of contention and shall order such action as he may deem proper and in such cases of emergency the orders of the President shall be law. He shall keep him

self posted in the market so as to know when to ask for an advance or accept a reduction and keep himself posted in everything that will tend to the advancement of the trade. He shall be the organizer and Initiator for the Assembly and his term of office shall be one year. His salary shall be $15.00 per week and expenses. The Assembly reserves the right to impeach the President for violation of pledge taken, incompetency or for any other good or sufficient cause or dispense with the office if deamed necessary by a two-third vote.[25]

A corps of professional labor leaders failed to emerge, however, within most union locals or assemblies of the Knights of Labor. The administration of the labor movement during this era remained chaotic, due in large part to the inability of subordinate officials properly to perform their obligations. The labor demagogue often triumphed over the strategist. For the rank and file considering a strike, an early student of the labor movement observed:

the appeal of the cause rather than the prospect of success has been their chief consideration. The meetings called to decide whether or not to declare a strike are often influenced by emotionalism, enthusiasm, and excitement. Fiery orators declaim about the wrongs of labor, and declare that the threatened reduction in wages must be resisted since the union can never retreat, or that the principle of the closed shop is the backbone of trade unionism and must be upheld at any sacrifice. Questions of expediency, such as the amount of money in the treasury, the prosperity of the industry, or the number unemployed, have been too frequently overlooked.[26]

The fate of the Miners' National Association revealed the ultimate consequence of loose national control and local precipitancy. Founded in 1873, the union established a strike fund which allowed national officers little discretion in granting benefits. Aid was almost automatically granted when locals went out—a course they followed imprudently. Vigor and gallantry characterized the strikes at Johnstown, Pennsylvania and in the Hocking Valley of Ohio in 1874, as well as the 1875 struggles in Brazil, Indiana, the Shenango Valley of Pennsylvania, and the Mahoning and Tuscarawas Valley of

Ohio. Yet the depression of 1873 had thrown out of work hundreds of miners who were eager to replace those who struck. Failure to consider prevailing conditions resulted not only in the loss of the strikes but also in the bankruptcy and demise of the union.[27]

To prevent similar destruction, a number of conscientious unionists sought to stabilize their organizations by centralizing control. As noted earlier, a few unions including the Cigar Makers and the Molders eventually gave the top officers control over strike funds. The practice, however, was not widespread during this period. More significant was the informal extension of the leaders' influence. Although unauthorized by the Iron Molders' constitution, William Sylvis set out on a tour of the locals in the early 1860s. Heads of other unions soon followed suit, and distressed locals welcomed the aid which such perambulating officers could give.[28] Local workers felt an understandable insecurity when dealing with management. As John Mitchell observed, "The employer knows the state of the market both for his goods and for the labor which he wishes to purchase, and he . . . has probably made a practical study of the art of bargaining for labor, whereas the unorganized workman, unaccustomed to haggling or bargaining, is consequently at a disadvantage."[29]

To offset their vulnerability, local unionists increasingly requested assistance from national officers. The rising demand for the executives' services increased their influence and work load. Reporting to the Railway Conductors, President Austin Garretson pointed out that "a much greater amount of time is consumed in the settlement of difficulties than was formerly the case and on account of this development the staff of officers has not been large enough to meet the demands made upon it."[30] Eventually the responsibility of the officers to travel and aid subordinate bodies was embodied in various union constitutions. In 1876, over a decade after Sylvis had begun the practice, the Molders officially granted their chief executive the "power to visit subordinate Unions, and inspect their proceedings, either personally or by deputy."[31] The authority of the president in union-management affairs, however, was not explicit. He could advise and influence, but apparently the spirit of local autonomy still prevailed.

III

Early efforts to strengthen the powers of the national executives served as a foundation for the surge in union centralization which occurred around the turn of the century. From 1890 to 1905 numerous labor organizations transferred authority in union-management affairs, as well as in internal matters, from local bodies to national headquarters. Suggestive of the change was the redistribution of power among the top leaders. In the early days of unionism, when the duties of the central office were primarily clerical, the secretary-treasurer was often the central figure, as with the Carpenters and Bricklayers. In other organizations, such as the Iron Molders and the Glass Bottle Blowers, the president was more prominent but performed mostly secretarial duties. Increased involvement of the national office in union-management affairs reoriented the officers' roles. The burden of administrative work kept the secretary-treasurer tied down to his desk at headquarters. Meanwhile, the president assumed the responsibilities of visiting, organizing, and guiding locals, directing negotiations and conflicts with employers, and establishing the policy priorities of the union. An increasing staff of organizers further expanded his influence over subordinate bodies. In short, he became the focal point of union activity, and as such his power and prestige grew.[32]

For most unions, the impetus toward centralization derived from the changing economic and technological environment. By the turn of the century the localized market system of the Civil War era had been transformed into a nationwide network. Workers had to be far more conscious of labor standards in other areas of the country. In industries such as coal, clothing, and textiles, bitter competition between numerous firms operating in an enlarged market undermined hours and wages. In such an environment, it was imperative that a strong, national organization be established with power to standardize labor conditions and remove them as an item of competition between companies.[33]

The growth of large firms with a number of divisions characterized other industries such as steel and tobacco. To cope effectively with such enterprises, all plants had to be unionized and the locals made to act in concert. Otherwise, if one plant were struck, another would

continue production and offset any loss to the company.[34] In industries such as construction, which still operated in a limited product
market, expansion of the labor market provided the impetus for
centralization. Not only did nonunion workers invade the job territory of unionists and undermine their standards, but the advance
of technology reduced the skill requirements needed for a job and
allowed employers to hire common laborers to perform tasks previously done by craftsmen (a reason why apprenticeship control
was a constant issue of conflict in the building industry). Technological developments also encouraged jurisdictional disputes. As
new materials were introduced to an industry, outside unions claim-
ing authority over the item would compete for work with established
organizations in the trade. These struggles were a prime reason for
centralization within the United Brotherhood of Carpenters. In their
effort to retain control over all things once made of wood, the Carpenters granted their national officers extensive powers including
the right to intervene in local union-management relations.[35]

Augmenting these developments were changes in the field of industrial relations. The years surrounding the turn of the century
witnessed the most important advances in this area until the New
Deal. Increasingly, organized labor confronted organized employers
at the national level. Although employers' associations dated back
to the colonial period, most had been short-lived, local organizations created to achieve a specific goal. Not until the late 1880s did
national employers' associations emerge. In response to several
railroad strikes, the General Managers' Association, composed of
twenty-four roads centering on or terminating in Chicago, was
formed in 1886. The same year the Stove Founders' National Defense
Association was established to combat the Iron Molders' Union.
The following year, the United Typothetae of Ameria organized to
resist the demands of the International Typographical Union for a
nine-hour day. Over the ensuing decade and a half, manufacturers
in a variety of trades banded together to protect their interests in
labor affairs.[36] At Coeur d'Alene in 1892 the workers confronted
the Mine Owners' Protective Association; at Pullman in 1894 the
American Railway Union met defeat at the hands of the General
Managers' Association.[37] In 1897, sixteen strikes occurred in Indiana alone. All were against organized groups of employers.[38] In

countless other instances, organized labor faced national or regional associations in its drive for better wages and hours.

These struggles against organized employers taxed the resources of labor and escalated local conflicts into strikes of national dimensions. With both sides throwing their weight behind the contending parties, the stakes became greater than the immediate success of the local involved, for the future of unionism within the industry was often at issue. Labor mustered its full resources in the struggles and the cost of conflict mounted. The Machinists' national office spent over two million dollars from 1891 to 1910 in strike benefits. This amount was meager compared to the strike expenditures of the United Mine Workers. From 1900 to 1910 the union paid benefits totaling $8,089,986.16; the conflict of 1902 alone cost $1,834,506.53.[39]

The high stakes of combat abetted the drive for centralized authority. Huge war chests had to be maintained to ward off challenges from employers, and locals became far more aware of the need for properly administered strike benefits. "The funds of the International Union," one labor journal pointed out, "are the life blood and backbone of the organization; they constitute strength, stability, and permanency."[40] In 1903, the United Mine Workers alone maintained a defense fund of one million dollars.[41] To promote efficiency, control of strikes passed into the hands of the national executives. For the period 1850 to 1879, nine unions required consent of their national officers or general executive boards before a local could initiate a strike. The figure jumped to fifty unions for the period 1880 to 1900.[42] Moreover, the discretionary authority of the national officers was expanded. Unions required the national presidents, either in person or by deputy, to visit the locals involved, investigate the causes of contention, evaluate the chances for a successful strike, and attempt to negotiate a peaceful settlement. When conflict occurred, they remained on the scene and guided the struggle to a conclusion. The transformation of national officers into professional strike managers added to the more structured nature of labor-management disputes after 1900.

The increased prominence of national officers in labor disputes ironically contributed to their public image as irresponsible agitators. Typical of such feelings, the St. Louis *Globe Democrat* commented in 1894 that "the coal miners strike could be settled in an hour if men like McBride [president of the UMW] were not interested in prolonging it for the purpose of personal notoriety and pecuniary advantages. . . . The worst enemies of the laboring men," the paper continued, "are the vain-glorious and irresponsible leaders who persuade them to strike where their intelligence tells them they have no reason for doing so."[43]

Such views grossly distorted reality, for most labor leaders acted as conservative influences. "The statement that strikes are caused by walking delegates," John Mitchell wrote, "is as naive as the child-ish belief that it is the gong which makes the train move. . . . In nearly all unions, the officials, from the local business agent or walking delegate to the international president, are elements for peace, not for war, and in actual practice the aggressive element is represented by the members of the union, and the steadying and conservative element, by the officers." To the simplistic argument that labor leaders encouraged strikes for personal pecuniary gains, the Mine Workers' president replied:

As a matter of fact, the shoe is entirely upon the other foot. The work of the union official doubles and trebles as soon as a strike is declared, and, likely as not, his salary is lessened. The remu-neration of the union official is not unlike that of the Chinese physician, who, it is said, receives pay only while his patient is well. During the Coal Strike of 1902, the officials of the United Mine Workers contributed 35% of their monthly salary of $70 or $75 a month, ran into debt while working for the union from twelve to fifteen and more hours per day. Unless, therefore, the union official stands for the principle of more work and less pay, he will not call strikes for his own selfish purposes. . . .[44]

The source of labor leaders' conservatism went beyond the detri-mental effects of strikes on their income. Men like Mitchell were sensitive to the human suffering involved.

The sobering sense of responsibility which under these circum-stances comes to the union official, is radically different from the reckless spirit in which it is claimed, the leaders of labor in this country evoke strikes. . . . On the one hand, the leader feels the growing discontent, the increasing recklessness, the sullen irritation of idle men, the hatred between the men who strike and the men who work; he fears the clash between the more reckless on both sides; he fears blows and violence, perhaps even murder; he dreads the hardships, the suffering, the privation, the anguish of men whose wives and children are famished and freezing, the despair that comes at the end and destroys the slow patient work of long years. On the other hand, he sees unfold before him, the whole history of labor; the upward striving through effort and courage and sacrifice; the temporary losses through cowardice or shrinking from the fear of evils, a movement ever upward and onward, but ever beset with difficulties, with danger, with suffering, and, it may be with loss of life.[45]

In more personal terms, labor leaders recognized that their own positions were often at stake in the outcome of a strike. The legacy of Martin Irons, the rejected leader of the 1886 Southwestern Railroad strike, hung heavily above the heads of later leaders.[46] "It is an unwritten law of the labor movement," observed John Brophy, "that lost strikes produce an aftermath of recrimination."[47] "Feeling against our officers who signed the compromise runs high, with no sign of abatement," one correspondent wrote pertaining to the unsuccessful 1894 coal strike, "nothing short of their resignation and its acceptance will satisfy us."[48] In 1904, Michael Donnelly, president of the Butcher Workmen, was blamed for the failure of the packing house strike and forced to resign. Branded a traitor, sentiment against him was so inflamed that he was brutally assaulted and left for dead on the streets of Chicago.[49] To avoid personal odium, President T. J. Shaffer of the Amalgamated Association of Iron, Steel, and Tin Workers attempted to place the blame for defeat in the 1901 steel strike on John Mitchell and Samuel Gompers.[50] The more judicious practice for leaders to follow, however, was to enter upon strikes reluctantly and only when the chance of success seemed good.

The concern of leaders over their own fates paralleled their desire to preserve their institutions. As unions developed strength, their officers became victims of the iron law of oligarchy: championship of the cause became secondary to the preservation of the institution. The expanded authority of the national leaders resulted from the desire by all concerned to protect the union from destruction. The duty of national leaders during labor conflicts, Adolph Strasser maintained, "is to represent the interests of the International Union, regardless of the local instructions of the strike committee. It is also their duty to bring about an amicable and honorable adjustment of the trouble as speedily as possible, thus saving the funds of the International Union, which would be otherwise wasted; and to maintain the honor and reputation of the International Union for fair dealing with union manufacturers."[51] Like Strasser, John Mitchell revealed the emerging institutional outlook when he argued against a strike and for the acceptance of a wage cut in 1904. "This was a different leader than the young man who assumed the presidency of a loose union of 40,000 in 1898," his most recent biographer relates:

> He had constructed a solid organization which now embraced 300,000 men, by far the largest union in the country. But along with this tremendous organizational growth came an unwillingness on Mitchell's part to take chances for fear of something happening to damage this union over which he presided. As he said to the delegates: "I believe that, rather than see this joint movement disrupted, rather than hazard all we have gained during six or seven years, by one great strike, it would pay us to accept this reduction."[52]

Only on the issue of union recognition, which directly bore upon the survival of the institution, were union leaders more adamant than the rank and file. "The members, if left to themselves, would be satisfied simply with better pay and treatment," observed Henry White, the rejected leader of the Garment Workers.

> These granted, they were ready to make peace with the boss. It was my experience that employers were usually willing to make concessions of this kind to avoid trouble. The leaders, however, regarded concessions made direct to the employees as a blow at the union's authority and at their own prestige, and any such arrangement was strenuously resisted. It meant to the leaders buying off the workers for a "mess of pottage" to forestall the union.
>
> Recognition of its authority by both workers and employers is thus the first object sought in every dispute by the union leaders.

Wage conditions are a secondary matter and are even of trifling consequence. That authority recognized, the desired pay, it is held, will follow. . . . This matter of union control as an issue is always pressed, and is, as I have maintained, the vital element in the union situation.[53]

As national leaders extended their authority, the number of strikes for union recognition increased from a low of six percent in 1881 to thirty-one percent by 1905. Meanwhile, the number of strikes over wages decreased from seventy-three percent in 1881 to thirty-three percent in 1905; the number of strikes over hours remained relatively constant at five percent.[54]

The conservatism of the national leaders both encouraged and reflected the development of more amicable relations with certain employers. While the period 1890 to 1905 was marred by extensive industrial strife, a number of companies experimented with peaceful coexistence. The movement by businessmen toward more friendly relations with organized labor was an aspect of the general trend to rationalize the economic system. The same period which witnessed the highest development of negotiatory employers' associations coincided with the great increase of trusts and other business combinations. In forming such groups, businessmen utilized labor unions. "Negotiatory associations made trade agreements with certain unions," relates Clarence Bonnett, an historian of employers' organizations, "and by means of these generally forced the independents to come into the combination or conform to the prices set by the combination if their businesses were not ruined."[55] Organized labor was also interested in rationalizing the economic system, and often encouraged and even aided the formation of management bodies. President Martin Fox of the Iron Molders' Union was instrumental in establishing the National Founders' Association in 1898 in order that trade agreements in the industry might be better drawn up and enforced.[56] John Mitchell also recognized the need for management to unite. "Harmony in the industrial world," he wrote, "will be best obtained by the creation and strengthening of labor unions and employers' associations, and by the inculcation of a permanently friendly feeling between organized labor and organized capital."[57] The UMW leader continued:

. . . in a general way the trade union, in matters of friendliness to employers' associations, set an example to the employers which the latter could advantageously follow. There are many employers who refuse to deal with trade unions because they render labor more formidable and, possibly, more exacting, even though they realize that the effect of trade unionism is also to make the men more reasonable and more conservative. Trade unions recognize that an association of employers is better able to combat them than a number of individual competing employers; but they also recognize that the association is, as a rule, more responsible, more conservative and better disposed than the individual employers of whom it is composed. The incentive to oppose labor is less strong and less direct. . . . In many cases, organizations of employers, by the very fact of their association, make concessions to their workmen which none of the individual employers could separately have made.[58]

Mitchell's optimistic attitude toward employers' associations derived from recent developments in union-management relations. "The clarification of the conception of the trade agreement," Professor Selig Perlman wrote, "was perhaps the main achievement of the nineties."[59] Although sustained collective bargaining existed in a number of industries in the 1870s and 1880s—most notably railroading, glass, and the building trades—the national contract entered into by the Stove Founders' Defense Association and the Iron Molders' Union in 1891 has frequently been described as the first modern national trade agreement.[60] In 1892 national contracts were signed in the glass container industry and in stonecutting, and numerous local and regional arrangements were negotiated in other sectors of the economy. The depression of the 1890s temporarily halted the spread of collective bargaining, but with the return of prosperity the trend moved onward. After a strike in 1897, the bituminous coal industry established the Interstate Joint Conference for collective bargaining.[61] The International Typographical Union wrought an agreement with the United Typothetae in 1898. In 1900 the Operative Potters attained a national contract, and in December of the same year the Bricklayers and Masons entered into agreements with contractors in various parts of the country providing that all differences that arose were to be sent to the national union's head-quarters for adjustment. The International Typographical Union, Printing Pressmen, and Stereotypers and Electrotypers all formed national agreements with the American Newspaper Publishers' Association in 1901.[62] The following year seamen in the coastwise trade of the Pacific, particularly out of San Francisco, entered into formal collective bargaining which was to last nineteen years with various employers' associations.[63] Other agreements in these years occurred in iron molding, stove mounting, brass polishing, machine shop work, overall manufacturing, and Great Lakes shipping.[64] "Though stoutly resisted in certain sectors, collective bargaining was widely regarded and publicized as a method of industrial peace," relates Philip Taft. "It and unionism probably never were more favorably received by the American public than during the five or six years around 1900. Those were the honeymoon years of collective bargaining."[65]

Initiation of collective bargaining lay primarily in the hands of business, for organized labor had always favored negotiation over belligerency. Management's willingness to negotiate was encouraged by a favorable economic environment. Collective bargaining reached its high point in the five years from 1898 to 1902, a period which embraced both the Spanish-American and Boer wars. The increased commerce resulting from these conflicts stimulated prosperity and a demand for skilled workers. To guarantee continuous production, employers were willing to make agreements which in less prosperous times they would resist.[66]

Complementing the economic boom was a desire on the part of both labor and management for stability and order. In the late 1890s many sophisticated industrialists came to realize that the reckless tactics of the Robber Barons were detrimental to business and created adverse public opinion which might stimulate unfavorable legislation. A number of such men joined the National Civic Federation to "help shape the right kind of regulation" rather than to have "the wrong kind" forced upon them.[67] Moreover, they recognized—often after a prolonged strike—that organized labor was here to stay and that some accommodation was necessary in order to prevent the rise of more disruptive radicalism. "Experience shows," the National Civic Federation's organ declared in 1903, that the more full the recognition given to a trade union the more business-like and responsible it becomes. Through dealing with business men in business matters its more intelligent, conservative and responsible members come to the front and gain general control and direction of its affairs. If the energy of the employer is directed to discouragement and repression of the union he need not be surprised if the more radically inclined members are the ones most frequently heard.[68]

Labor's reasons for desiring accommodation paralleled those of management. Industrial strife not only had disastrous effects on the union as an institution, but brought upon labor the wrath of the American people. "The permanency of our movement, the success of our cause," Gompers realized, "depends largely upon not only the confidence and respect of our fellow members, but of the public in general."[69] To allay public fears, Gompers and other conservative labor leaders emphasized the union's role as a middle-class institution. Participation in collective bargaining, membership in conciliatory organizations like the Civic Federation, and unwavering opposition to radicalism, they felt, were the best tactics for surviving within the American environment.

The rise of collective bargaining contributed to the expansion of the national executives' authority. Local labor leaders, who generally worked full time at their trade, were ill suited to deal with the complex issues negotiated or the expanded area of coverage. Increasingly locals demanded specialists from the national office to handle union-management affairs. "There will not be any lasting social progress," wrote one correspondent in the *Typographical Journal* in 1899, "until organized labor understands that it must create a first-class civil service, and by good pay and tenure of office, hold men in its employ who know how to conclude good union bargains with the employers."[70] On each side of the bargaining table there was a feeling that the other side had the more capable negotiators; this sense of unease led to an escalation of industrial relations expertise. During the period of localized union-management affairs, as mentioned earlier, the employees felt at a disadvantage in dealing with their bosses and eventually either established local business agents or called upon the national executives to give aid.

Appearance of these leaders produced a sense of weakness among management. "In bargaining ability," Clarence Bonnett observed,

> the unions have specialists long trained in meeting every type of employer. In knowledge of wages, labor supply and demand, the union officials again have the greater advantage. . . . In strikes, the average or ordinary employer is a novice, the union officials are experts with long and varied experiences, since they spend all their time at such matters while the employer must generally devote more of his time to problems other than labor matters.[71]

The desire to offset this disadvantage, Bonnett argues, was a prime reason for creation of employers' associations retaining their own labor specialists.

In negotiating contracts as well as in enforcing agreements, the leader required effective control over the constituent bodies. The extent of centralization is suggested by the changing authority of the Bricklayers' national executives. The primarily clerical duties of the national staff in the 1860s and 1870s have previously been observed with regard to the limited duties of early officers. By 1897 their role had changed. The new constitution of that year granted them:

> . . . the *entire* control of *all* executive business of this Union, when not in session, *viz.,* all grievances relating to and all strikes and lockouts, the settlement of all disputes between bosses or exchanges and members of this or Subordinate Unions, and the concurrence in the appointment of *all* special deputies or committees. They shall have full and complete control over all strikes. . . .[72]

The increased authority of the national officers as well as the introduction of more businesslike methods in collective bargaining were also seen in the adoption of the concerted wage movement by the Brotherhood of Locomotive Engineers in 1902. Before then, writes George James Stevenson, "the employees' interest in bargaining lay in the hands of the local or general committee of adjustment, and the role of the Grand Chief Engineer was to represent the sustaining power of the whole union for the employees directly concerned, and to act as a mediator between the contending parties." After 1902, with negotiations occurring on a larger regional basis, his activities expanded: "the initiative was taken by the Grand Chief Engineer, not by the members, although they gave him their endorsement."[73]

Under collective bargaining, it was to management's advantage to encourage "conservative" union leadership. Businessmen have always been ambivalent on the question of union government. While publicly they have favored democratic control, as a practical matter they have preferred well-disciplined, "responsible" unions with strong leaders. There is much truth in William Z. Foster's contention that "the employers seek to develop the trade union bureaucracy as a buffer, a shock-absorber, between them and the masses of workers, to break up and demoralize the latter's aggressive attacks against the employers and capitalism."[74] The research of James Weinstein and others support the original allegation of Duncan McDonald— a prominent Illinois Socialist and leader in the UMW and the AFL of the fight against the National Civic Federation—that such groups as the Federation had been conceived to "chloroform the labor movement into a more submissive mood."[75] Businessmen realized they could make deals with leadership-dominated unions without fear of shifts in rank-and-file sentiment. In the pressed and blown glassware industry, for instance, employers complained that although their conferees had complete authority in negotiations, labor's representatives had to submit all important matters to the membership for approval. The resulting inconvenience and uncertainty annoyed management, although few decisions were actually reversed. Finally in March, 1904, the National Association of Manufacturers of Pressed and Blown Glassware notified the American Flint Glass Workers' Union that it would not negotiate unless the labor conferees had full authority. The threat was not carried out, but thereafter the union's executives were given more independence in their dealings with management.[76]

The employers' desire for conservative labor leadership was also a factor in the breakdown of collective bargaining between the Iron Molders' Union and the National Founders' Association. Union President Martin Fox had been instrumental in creating the employers' association, and his cooperative attitude had encouraged management to negotiate from 1899 to 1904. In the later year, friendly relations broke down. In explaining their new belligerent posture, the founders cited two causes related to "irresponsible" union leadership: first, the inability of the officers to prevent workers from breaking the contract and striking illegally; and second, the succession of Joseph Valentine to the union's presidency. Whereas leaders of the association had held Martin Fox in high esteem, they regarded the new president as socialistic and irresponsible.[77]

IV

From 1905 to World War I, collective bargaining continued in numerous industries—including shoemaking, newspapers, coal mining, railroads, coastwise shipping on the Pacific, glassmaking, and pottery—although not without occasional strife.[78] In 1913, the secretary of the AFL reported that forty-five international unions had made 3,190 contracts without resorting to strikes. The actual number of agreements existing that year was far greater, for unexpired contracts made earlier were not included in the figure and several unions simply reported "a great number" of settlements.[79] The National Window Glass Workers alone had contracts with fifty-six firms during the blast of 1916-17.[80]

The complexity of contract details made negotiations a long and specialized task. In 1917 a committee of the Molders' Union and the Stove Founders' National Defense Association spent nineteen days hammering out an agreement. The union had thirty-one trained conferees at the session, "men skilled in all technicalities of the work—who specialized in handling of so-called grievances and demands for their union." The association was represented by "practical employers who knew precisely the conditions of the trade and how its interests should be conserved."[81] Not all negotiations were carried on with so extensive a staff. Within the United Garment Workers, Secretary Henry White dominated the scene. "In dealing with employers," he related, "I was as undisputed as I was in the control of the union. At my discretion firms were selected for a strike or boycott. The privilege of the union label was mine to grant."[82] In 1910, President Tom Lewis of the UMW chose to deal by himself with the operators of western Pennsylvania, Ohio, and Indiana. "Thus Lewis," the union's journal pointed out, "assumed full responsibility for the success or failure of the effort of the miners to obtain the increase in wages they demand. Lewis has kept his own counsel, just as he said he would, and the result is that no one knows five minutes ahead what his next move will be. This is earning for him the title, which one of the operators accorded him, of 'the best politician in the whole outfit.'"[83]

Stable collective bargaining contributed to the conservatism of many union leaders. Through years of dealing with each other, union and management conferees developed mutal respect. According to economist Milton Derber, the domination of a handful of participants in the glass container industry's negotiations since 1896 "meant experience and mutual understanding on both sides of the bargaining table, a restraining hand on new and impetuous representatives, trust in the word and intent of the other party, an understanding of the rules of the game and a willingness to abide by them."[84] In a few industries, union and management collaborated on various projects. The manufacturers of boots and shoes employed trade union agents to advertise their label and also to lobby in Washington for favorable tariff legislation.[85] Unions in the glass industry also joined management in lobbying at the state and national level, particularly in regard to tariffs and prohibition.[86] The National Window Glass Workers went further and conducted advertising campaigns for their employers' products.[87] The outstanding collaborative effort prior to World War I was the creation of the American Railway Employees and Investors Association in 1907. Based on the philosophy of an identity of interests between employer and employee and supported by the railroad companies and the leaders of 1,660,000 workers, the association lobbied in various legislatures for the railroad industry. The head of the organization was P. H. Morrisey, who had resigned from the presidency of the Railway Trainmen to assume the post, which reportedly paid $15,000 a year.[88]

Such cordiality occasionally resulted in the labor leader moving to the other side of the bargaining table. John Alpine, president of the United Association of Plumbers and a vice-president of the AFL, got along so well with the employers in the sprinkler industry that in 1919 he resigned his union post to become an assistant to the president for labor relations of the Grinnell Company.[89] Alpine was not alone in his willingness to change colors. Even labor's hero, John Mitchell, had aspirations. Writing to the president of the longshoremen, Daniel Keefe, a man of equal ambition, the UMW leader related:

> And bye [sic] the way, Dan, the employing side of our committee on Arbitration and Conciliation [of the National Civic Federation] proposes to employ two Commissioners, and Easley seems to favor myself and Justi. His proposition, if it is accepted, will be to give a three year contract, with a salary of five thousand dollars per year. Now I think that would suit me all right; and while I don't want you to say a word about it to a living soul, when the time comes I would like to have matters fixed up all O.K.[90]

Where collective bargaining prevailed, the leaders' role was no longer that of the adamant champion of labor's rights. "It is our intention," President J. M. Neenan of the Window Glass Workers informed his constituents, "to be conservative and ask for nothing but what manufacturers can afford to pay for our labor. . . ."[91] According to the Teamsters' journal, the "Ideal Labor Leader" "has often to act as a mediator between employer and employee, and he must necessarily know the business of both and must keep faith with both, which is at times difficult."[92] Mediation turned into bartering at the conference table, and while labor leaders might preach of the humanity of labor, they dealt with the worker as a commodity. "The function of your power is bargaining. Buying and selling," lectured J. B. S. Hardman's imaginary labor leader. "You sell labor to employers. I will assume you sell on the best of all possible terms. But you sell. Labor is the commodity you sell. Like hot dogs."[93]

Once a contract was consummated, the union leader assumed the role of policeman, endeavoring to make the rank and file abide by the rules. Time and again, leaders of the Shoe Workers lectured that "nothing can justify any union or member thereof for violating its contract or allowing it to be violated."[94] Officers of the Window Glass Workers concurred: "A contract, openly negotiated and freely entered into, must be faithfully carried out, else the whole doctrine of collective bargaining falls into disrepute and the trade union defeats the one great purpose for which it is instituted."[95] At the UMW's 1902 convention, John Mitchell warned that "when the contract is made and signed, if we expect the operators to carry out those provisions that are advantageous to us, we, in turn, must carry out just as explicitly those provisions which are unfavorable to us."[96] When such exhortations failed to produce obedience, more drastic measures were taken. To cite one of many examples, in 1904 when two locals failed to return to work as ordered by the Mine Workers' officials, not only were their charters annulled, but the names of the members were placed on a UMW blacklist and sent to every operator and local in the district.[97]

The leaders' insistence that contracts be upheld stemmed from their belief that organized labor could exist only as a working-class institution which functioned in ways acceptable to middle-class society. Failure to live up to agreements would alienate public support. After 1902 anti-unionism was on the increase, with a number of employers who had previously negotiated with labor becoming belligerent. In explaining their new posture, U.S. Steel, the National Founders' Association, and other employers argued that they had tried to get along with organized labor but that unions were irresponsible and would not abide by their contracts.[98]

While there was some validity in this argument, other factors were equally important in the open shop movement of 1902–16. The economic boom which initiated the collective bargaining honeymoon was declining by 1902 and employers whose earlier cooperation with labor was a marriage of convenience were now willing to resist union demands. Moreover, many employers feared the strength of labor as union membership rose from 447,000 in 1897 to 2,022,000 in 1904.[99] The rise of trusts, as in the steel industry, allowed management to direct a concerted attack on labor where unionism had previously survived through divide-and-rule tactics.[100] Finally, organizations composed of relatively small manufacturers whose plants were highly vulnerable to unionization emerged to challenge labor. The open shop drive generally dates from 1902 when the National Association of Manufacturers, founded in 1895 to promote foreign trade and dominated by leaders of large corporations, was captured by David M. Parry, John Kirby, James Van Cleave and other small producers and transformed into an anti-union organization.[101]

The activities of the National Association of Manufacturers as well as the League for Industrial Rights, the Citizens' Industrial Association of America, and other open shop groups retarded and limited unionism but did not destroy it. From its high of 2,022,000 in 1904, total union membership declined to a low in 1906 of 1,907,300. The most important effect of the open shop movement was to remove labor's weak foothold in the mass-production industries. Labor remained strong in industries which were technologically static or lacked unity and financial strength to push labor out. Unionism abided in a few industries such as coal, partly because management found it to be a stabilizing force in a highly competitive market. On the railroads, labor's own strength plus government intervention insured the survival of the unions.[102]

The impact of the open shop movement on internal union government was to increase the authority of the national executive and foster the leadership orientation of the rank and file. As Kenneth Boulding argues in *The Organizational Revolution,* institutions which exist in an atmosphere of struggle become agencies of conflict. As such, more power is frequently delegated to officials, with more secrecy and fewer controls than in organizations living in a less tense environment.[103] Attacks on labor leaders, moreover, mobilized the rank and file behind them. William D. Haywood and Charles Moyer were union functionaires before the Steunenburg case. Afterwards they were working-class heroes.[104] John J. McNamara, brought to trial for the Los Angeles *Times* bombing, was unanimously reelected secretary-treasurer of the Bridge and Structural Iron Workers.[105] And with the threat of going to jail hanging over the heads of Gompers, Mitchell, and Frank Morrison as a result of the Buck's Stove case, the AFL convention of 1909 voted that if they were imprisoned, all three would receive a salary of $5,000.[106]

In many ways the Buck's Stove and Range case capsulated labor relations in the decade before World War I. The business antagonist in the case was James Van Cleave, president of Buck's Stove and Range Company and a leading figure in the open shop movement. The labor participants—Gompers, Mitchell, and Morrison—were three of the most prominent and conservative national union leaders of the day. To their assistance came some of the more sophisticated representatives of capital, who although by no means prolabor zealots nonetheless shunned blatant anti-unionism. Alton B. Parker, a Wall Street lawyer, presidential candidate, and later head of the National Civic Federation, defended Gompers, while the AFL's side of the case was in part secretly financed by Andrew Carnegie.[107] The case never reached a conclusion; after several years it was dismissed by the Supreme Court on a technicality. Although many capitalists would never have been taken to court for a similar alleged offense, the case ended symbolically, for the most prominent and respectable leaders of labor received "justice" similar to that which many of their business counterparts had long enjoyed.

With the outbreak of World War I, the open shop movement lost momentum. Preparedness at home and war orders from abroad again led some employers to take a more conciliatory stand toward labor in order to more fully participate in the profit making. The few that held out begrudgingly succumbed once the United States began to mobilize and the government increased its intervention in the economy. Organized workers, led by Samuel Gompers, promised their services "in the war for freedom and humanity," but insisted "that their own rights and welfare shall not be filched from them" and that "they shall participate equally with other citizens in determining the mobilization of the nation for effective service."[108] Labor's participation was not fully "equal" with other groups, being denied representation on a few key boards and committees, yet it was incorporated into the power structure in an unprecedented manner. Moreover, in establishing the National War Labor Board, the principle of "the right of employees to organize in associations or groups and to bargain collectively, through chosen representatives" was recognized. "Although this statement of principles was not legally enforceable," economist C. Wilson Randle points out, "it is highly significant as a first step in the government's recognition of the right to organize and bargain collectively."[109]

In terms of union-management relations, labor's participation in the war effort strengthened the already dominant trend toward union centralization. Inclusion of national labor leaders on various war boards and committees served as public recognition of their role as spokesmen for their organizations. Bureaucrats of government and business fostered bureaucratization on labor through the policy of having decisions reached by the national leaders in Washington passed down to the rank and file. Furthermore, the gap between the leaders and the led was widened due to the increased complexity of the issues involved. In 1917 the *United Mine Workers' Journal* correctly interpreted the effects of a proposal to establish commissions to regulate wages, prices, traffic rates, and other subjects: "If such a law is adopted and the provisions thereof put into practice, the miners will need, as never before, a solid organization headed by able men who can present convincingly the miners' side of any controversy that may arise on prices or working conditions."[110]

V

By the end of World War I, the national labor leader's role in union-management affairs had changed significantly from what it had been in the post–Civil War years. His functions in the 1860s and 1870s were largely peripheral and informal, reflecting the decentralized nature of unions. By 1920 the structure of many unions had become highly centralized and the national executive emerged as a key figure in industrial relations. The ideal labor leader was now a general commanding his troops in time of conflict, a diplomat negotiating industrial peace, and a policeman enforcing the trade agreement. Each of these roles raised the leader above the rank and file and increased his insistence on obedience and solidarity within the union. Not all unions had made the transition by 1920, but the pattern of evolution was outlined. "As in biology, life forms repeat or recapitulate in a brief time the previous slow stages of development," philosophized economist George Milton Janes in 1916, "so now unions by direct imitation of older unions, or by stern necessity, approach in many respects a common type of policy."[111]

4.

Leaders and the Led

I

Among the adages which political pundits resurrect at election time is the one about people getting the type of leaders they deserve. While trite and at times condescending, the saying contains more than a grain of truth for private as well as public governments. In the labor movement from 1870 to 1920, the rank and file played a major role in shaping union leadership. They were the ultimate source of authority, and any leader desiring to retain his position had to be sensitive to their wishes.

Rigorous analysis of rank-and-file attitudes presents numerous difficulties. Most obvious is a lack of nonimpressionistic documentation. Manuscript collections of "average unionists" are nonexistent. Letters to the editors of labor journals are only partly helpful, for only a special group among the rank and file engaged in such correspondence. The accessibility of labor papers to all varieties of opinion is also questionable. The historian must therefore rely on less direct sources such as comments from those interpreting rank-and-file behavior, voting returns, and biographical data of individuals who rose out of the ranks to places of prominence. A second difficulty is the complexity of group attitudes. The aggregate of thousands of individual responses, group attitudes constitute an abstract construct. Moreover, the distinctiveness of particular unions' memberships become yet more diluted when blended into a larger conglomerate.

The present chapter does not present a comprehensive portrait of the rank and file. Rather it focuses on those features of union membership which influenced the development of labor leadership. Sometimes these traits were real; at other times they were largely figments of the leaders' imaginations. Despite the subordination of individual unions' characteristics, the attitudes and responses described were common to most organizations.

II

A leader of a national union, observed the *American Federationists,* "finds himself surrounded by a large body of men who have a faith in his integrity, a persistent group who assail that integrity, and a small circle of associates who understand his nature and know its honesty."[1] In the more typical parlance of labor, the three classes of followers were simply "the rank and file," the kickers and knockers," and "the boosters." Each group played a distinct role within the union and had particular influence on the development of labor leadership.

Of the three groups, the boosters, of course, were the most pro-administration in outlook. Known in sociological terms as "the activity," they were the backbone of their organizations' everyday operations. They usually comprised the majority at the sparsely attended local meetings, and from their ranks came many of the minor union functionaries—local officers, check-weight men, business agents, and convention delegates. At election time, less active members often followed their advice, and when the turnout was particularly small, the boosters virtually chose national officers and determined union policy. In 1898, for instance, the International Typographical Union held a referendum on whether it should withdraw from the AFL. One hundred fifty-eight locals submitted returns, while 233 others failed to do so. Of those that did report, five locals had five or less members voting, forty had six to ten members voting, and forty-two had from eleven to twenty members exercising their rights. In short, fifty-five percent of the fraction of locals participating had less than twenty-one members voting yet wielded tremendous weight. Labor leaders could not ignore these few activists.[2]

Realizing the boosters' importance, those in power referred to them in the most favorable terms. To the leaders of the freight handlers, they were "more in touch with the labor movement than the average member. . . ."[3] Mine Worker officials praised them as "calm, sober, thoughtful, conservative men" who possessed "reason and intelligence" and represented "an array of wise cautious conservative, diplomatic talent."[4] The repetition of conservative values clearly reveals the traits which established leaders preferred in their most active followers.

Boosters possessed two basic characteristics: commitment and ambition. "During the early years of the union," observed Henry White of the United Garment Workers, "the uncongenial and trying nature of the organizing and directing work attracted only men of earnest and self-sacrificing purpose."[5] Typical of such enthusiasts was Abraham Bisno, who gave up a lucrative business to become a wage-earner when his fledgling union declared contractors ineligible for membership. Revealing extraordinary altruism, Bisno related in his autobiography: "I knew I could not be both in the labor movement and earn a decent income, and my loyalty to the labor movement was much stronger than my desire to have untorn shoes or a decent place to live in, or fine clothes, or even expensive food."[6]

Although idealism continued to motivate many of the boosters, a number of individuals became activists out of personal ambition. As unions matured, Henry White wrote,

strange men with eyes intent upon the offices began to appear.
The labor union offered opportunities for quick advancement to
people that otherwise might have remained bound to their trade.
In that respect the unions were not unlike the political ward clubs,
excepting that a somewhat different order of ability was needed.
A little fluency of tongue, a capacity to express the wants of
their shop mates, some knowledge of men combined with personal aggressiveness were the requisites for promotion to local
places of influence. Once there, the need of earning their bread
in the shops by the sweat of their brows had passed; for the demands of the cause required their presence here and there at so
much *per diem,* traveling and incidental expenses added. From

the local positions these aspirants found their way as delegates to the National Union conventions, and the foundations for careers in the larger field were laid.[7]

White was far more critical of his contemporaries than was justified, in part owing to his own recent ouster from office. Idealism was not necessarily incompatible with opportunism. As William Sylvis responded: "To the charge of ambition we plead guilty, and if to be ambitious to do good is a crime then we have sinned. We aspired to the honorable position that we now occupy, thinking that we could better serve the cause in this capacity than in any other. . . ."[8]

However, White was correct in recognizing that in its institutionalized form, the labor movement became a vehicle for social mobility. In his autobiography, which reads like an Horatio Alger novel, Robert Watchorn of the UMW revealed the success ethic common to many workers.

Since there was no place to go [as a door-boy in the mines], the stern necessity of sticking to the task was too obvious for contemplation, but the lamp of hope shone none the less brightly in my perplexed and baffled soul, and self-emancipation became a ruling passion, resulting in a determination never for a moment to relax the purpose to be free at the first opportunity from an occupation so terrible depressing, so fraught with perils, and so lamentably unrenumerative.[9]

One day Watchorn's opportunity came. Receiving a telegram offering him a paid union post, he conferred with his family.

My mother was obviously torn between her desire for my advancement and her duty to the younger children, whom she loved no less. My withdrawal from them would, she feared, perhaps imperil their lives. . . . But she rose to the occasion and, drying her tears, she said, "Bob, my boy, you have earned your deliverance from your perilous calling, and I can't bear to see you throw the chance away."[10]

Watchorn proved more successful than most aspirants to wealth and power, eventually becoming vice-president of the Union Oil

Company. But even those who advanced more modestly reaped the reward of greater social prestige. In her biography of John Mitchell, Elsie Gluck observed that union office "was one of the few means open to the miners to secure some distinction for themselves in the community."[11] Edward Flore of the Hotel and Restaurant Employees, in one of the more blatant cases of ambition, originally became a local union activist to gain power and a following for a possible career in Buffalo politics.[12] While ambition led Watchorn, Mitchell, and Flore to positions of prominence, most local activists simply received the benefit of increased status within their own community peer group.

Cooperation between local boosters and the national leadership centered on mutual respect and self-interest. On many issues, the boosters sided with higher authorities out of commitment to common principles and goals. At other times, the ties were more pragmatic. Occasionally the local elite saw itself facing the same opposition which challenged its national counterpart and hence forged an alliance of convenience. More importantly, the national leaders could bestow upon local activists honors which would promote their reputations in return for support at elections and on various issues. A friendly sign of recognition from a high official could improve a booster's standing within his local. At convention time, the leader could promote a supporter's career by placing him in a prominent position. Frank Farrington, beginning his rise in the United Mine Workers, requested President Mitchell to assign him to the constitution committee. "You are aware," he wrote candidly, "that I am going to be a candidate for vice president of District 12 and I want to get before the convention all I can. . . . " Mitchell had to turn down this particular request, but suggested a post on the committee on the officers' reports, "preferably secretary, it would give you a splendid opportunity to get before the convention."[13] National leaders also appointed organizers, some on full salaries, others receiving commissions, and still others purely voluntary but prestigious. Occasionally the leaders could provide government jobs for the faithful. In 1894, for instance, the executive board of the Knights of Labor rewarded one convention delegate for voting along certain lines with a deputy factory inspectorship.[14] John Mitchell was particularly successful in securing public posts for his followers.[15] Such activities, and others to be discussed later, provided strong bonds between national leaders and local activists when idealism was not enough. The significance of the boosters in forging union leadership lay in shaping the office in the mold of a political boss, with back-scratching, under-the-table dealings, and trading patronage for support part of the regular routine.

III

While the small group of proadministration boosters attended to the everyday business of the union with commitment and ambition, the majority of the rank and file seemed completely passive toward such matters. "The most discouraging feature of our work . . . ," complained the *Journal of United Labor,* "lies in the apathy and indifference of the class we would help. People do not care."[16] "When there was neither strike nor political campaign to arouse the workingmen," concurred Joseph Buchanan of the Knights of Labor, "they became careless and indifferent. . . ."[17] Typical of most labor papers, the *United Mine Workers' Journal* carried constant reports of apathy. A local in Wellston, Ohio wrote: "The organization is in fairly good condition. The members, however, do not take the interest they should."[18] Another group from Marissa, Illinois reported: "In regard to our local, we have about 125 members, but we have very poor working material, because the most of them are young men and don't take the interest as they should. . . ."[19] Summarizing such accounts, president Tom L. Lewis informed his colleagues "that there is a feeling of indifference existing among our members."[20] The miners, however, were not the only union plagued by the lack of involvement by the rank and file. In 1898, president William B. Prescott of the printers warned:

> it is imperative that we do something to stimulate interest among
> our members. There is not an earnest worker in our ranks who
> has not been pained and grieved at the slight interest taken in
> union meetings, as testified by the attendance, and I am con-

strained to admit that from the best possible information obtainable this lethargy is becoming more deep seated and widespread, which does not augur well for our future. And, sad to relate, the blight is not peculiar to our organization, but has been responsible for the steady decrease in membership of every considerable American union except ours. . . .[21]

The extent to which rank-and-file unconcern increased between 1870 and 1920 is difficult to determine. To many observers the rise was quite marked. "In the old days when men fought for their unions," Daniel Tobin argued in the mid-1920s, "there was a certain militant spirit pervading the air, and you heard of the union around the freight house, wharves, and other places, you found men at meetings, you heard them out amongst their friends discussing the work of the union. Today you seldom hear members discuss anything of serious importance about the union."[22]

Several facts, however, suggest that the interest of early members was not as strong as Tobin and others imagined. In 1884 signs of impassivity appeared in the Knights of Labor when a survey of more than one thousand locals on the cooperative issue elicited only 212 responses.[23] The casualty rates of unions in the 1870s, 1880s, and 1890s was also extremely high, and those organizations which did survive experienced extreme fluctuations in membership. The International Typographical Union, for example, lost forty percent of its following during the lean years of 1873–78. As time progressed, noticeable improvements occurred; in the depression of 1893–97 the ITU lost only ten percent of its membership including the withdrawal of pressmen and bookbinders into separate organizations.[24] In response to these early signs of indifference, Gompers became an advocate of sickness, death, and out-of-work benefits. "I saw clearly," he related in his autobiography, "that we had to do something to make it worth while to maintain continuous membership, for a union that could hold members only during a strike period could not be a permanent constructive and conserving force in industrial life."[25]

If Gompers's program of benefits indeed kept workers on the union rolls, it did not convert them to activists. Apathy generally characterized trade union life after the turn of the century. Typical of many labor conventions, only 124 locals out of 536 sent delegates to the International Typographical Union's meeting in 1902.[26] Western Federation of Miners' officials, assuming an eagerness on the part of the rank and file to read "the memorable and immortal orations of a number of brilliant Ciceros," published 3,000 copies of the proceedings of their 1910 convention at a cost of $4,000, only to sell a scant 600.[27] More revealing still were statistics on the proportion of members participating in referendums. At its 1912 convention, the AFL presented the results of a survey on the use of the referendum by national and international unions. Thirty-four organizations using the system reported to the federation information concerning their size, the type of questions on which referendums were used, the percentage of members voting, and whether voting was compulsory. The results, while inexact, were indicative.[28]

The proportion of members participating ranged from a high of ninety-six percent for the Tobacco Workers to a low of five to thirteen percent for the Boot and Shoe Workers. The average turnout was between fifty and sixty percent. Those unions which required voting had above average participation, but it was not overwhelming. Compulsion generally produced fifty percent of the Granite Cutters, fifty to seventy-five percent of the Boiler Makers, seventy-five percent of the Brewers, and a high of eighty-five percent of the Tailors.

The proportion of members voting was inversely related to the size of the organization. The ten smallest unions using the referendum had an average of sixty-three percent of their membership participating, while the ten largest organizations averaged forty-three percent. The comparison holds true when considering only those unions which used the referendum for both selecting officers and approving policy. The five smallest unions in this category averaged seventy-one percent; the five largest sixty-one percent. Thus, size played a significant role in determining rank-and-file willingness to take an active role in union affairs.

The questions on which referendums were held also influenced participation. The eighteen unions using the referendum for both electing officers and enactment of laws averaged sixty-seven percent of their members voting. The seven organizations which used the system only for electing officers averaged fifty-eight percent, while the nine unions utilizing the referendum simply to enact laws had only thirty-three percent participation. Such evidence suggests that the rank and file considered electing officers to be the more important function. In short, members tended to be personality rather than policy oriented.[29]

Human frailty also contributed to the indifferent attitude of the rank and file. Young, unmarried workers felt they had better or more exciting things to do than attend union functions. Urban laborers often preferred spending their free time enjoying what recreation the city offered, while rural workers frequently could not motivate themselves to make the long trek to a remote meeting hall. Criticized for not appearing at a local gathering, one miner considered himself a fool "to go after a hard day's work, in the middle of the week, and walk six miles [sic] after dark, and in such weather to attend every meeting of said local union."[30] Many craftsmen no doubt reacted as James Maurer did when first approached by a union activist. "He talked to me about justice and labor's rights, of the need for workers to organize, of their solidarity at the ballot box, and other ideas new to me. They were subjects that I knew nothing about and cared less; he might have well talked about trigonometry or the nebular hypothesis for all the impression he made on me at first." The soft-hearted Maurer, who became Pennsylvania's leading socialist, started going to union meetings with the activist "so as not to hurt his feelings, for outside of what I thought were his foolish notions, he was a good fellow always ready to help me in my work."[31]

Once in the union hall, workers frequently found the experience tedious. The details of everyday business were not stimulating, and the meetings dragged on interminably. Moreover, as the *United Mine Workers' Journal* observed, "the endless brawl of the talkative man who seems to think that he and he alone has been endowed with a gift of speech and an understanding of business methods, destroys the interest of many an otherwise entertaining meeting and causes conservative, thinking men to leave the session in utter disgust and thereafter remain away entirely."[32] With business often consisting of trivial matters, many members responded like young John Brophy. "Perhaps because the union was successful and no burning issue arose calling for active support," he admitted, "I often found something else to do on meeting night. Like Most people, I took the union for granted because it was doing well."[33]

Such circumstances produce indifference in most groups. Yet one particular union policy vastly increased the extent of apathy among the membership. After 1890, a number of organizations turned to closed and union shops to attain security in their dealings with management. At times they achieved this objective only after vicious and costly strikes. At other times the union gained it in exchange for granting the business the right to place a union label on its products. This approach was particularly fruitful in those industries which produced or handled goods for a working-class market, where a prounion label was seen as a means of attracting patrons. Whether attained by strikes or "label contracts", closed and union shops forced workers to join without first convincing them of the value of unionism. Labor leaders and management agreed between themselves that jobs would depend on union membership. In defending this policy, the *Garment Worker* argued:

> The ordinary workingman respects an organization with power enough to force him into it, and he justly reasons that only such an organization can be of benefit to himself and the trade; hence it is why such people eventually as a rule become good members.
>
> A little training and education in the union soon convinces the previously unwilling member that to force him into the union is like compelling people to take a bath against their own will or taking a load from the shoulder of a man foolishly bent into carrying it to the top floor of a building and placing it upon the elevator for him.[34]

The reality of the situation was far different. Establishment of closed and union shops brought into the labor movement a sizable group of workers indifferent to unionism, and many of them remained indifferent after the union card was forced into their hands. A study of female locals in the United Garment Workers revealed, for instance, that those locals most likely to collapse were established by such outside arrangements.[35] Moreover, many workers looked upon the situation "as a sort of conspiracy between the boss and the union agent to levy upon them a tribute for the privilege of working."[36] Powderly was aware of these facts and opposed such methods:

> No person should be forced to become a member of our order
> by the manufacturer, or by the man or firm he may be working
> for. Only those who join of their own free will ought to be ad-
> mitted to membership. The man or woman who cannot cheer-
> fully subscribe to the declaration of principles of the order of
> the Knights of Labor cannot make a good member and must not
> be forced to join.[37]

Failure to attend union meetings or to vote in referendums was the extreme of indifference and apathy. The attitudes of the rank and file most often took more subtle forms. Many of those who did participate in some union affairs displayed what the *Garment Worker* labeled "the lack of independence of character."[38] By and large, union members would submit to the wishes of the leaders without giving the issue under review critical examination. Intending to make a different point, Samuel Gompers suggested the extent of such deference. "In every contingency or circumstance in which I have had to deal with men," he related, "I have found that when a course was presented to them, giving reasons for that position and I appealed to their better judgment to accept that which I advocated, they have voluntarily and gladly accepted my position."[39]

Such deference was in part rooted in the rank and file's feeling of inferiority to the leaders. As sociologist Victor Thompson observed, "people impute superior abilities to persons of higher status, and this imputed superior ability is generalized into a halo of superiority."[40] Letters to the editors of labor journals occasionally contained such revealing comments as "I don't know much, not as highly educated as the honored [executive] board. . . ."[41] Another correspondent was reluctant "to stand face to face with men of experience and great knowledge with figures and all necessary aid to sustain their assertions."[42] One dissenter among the miners recognized this complex and lambasted his fellow unionists: "We have too much fear of our officers! I say let no man who has a mind of his own be afraid of any officer. . . ."[43] "Do not let your officers do all the thinking for you," pleaded another unionist. "Remember, we base all our hopes of bettering our condition upon the intelligent action of the rank and file of the order, and not upon blind obedience to the mandates of executive officers, without reason why."[44]

Far more important than a feeling of inferiority, however, was a genuine appreciation among the rank and file for the work the leaders were doing. "Though it grumbles occasionally," Robert Michels observed of the working class, "the majority is really delighted to find persons who will take the trouble to look after its affairs."[45] Beyond supporting their leaders at election time, the rank and file manifested its gratitude in more personal ways. In 1901, for example, the anthracite miners took a collection to finance a home for Mitchell.[46] The Knights of Labor had earlier raised a similar collection for Richard Trevellick.[47] The Brotherhood of Locomotive Engineers treated P. M. Arthur to a six-month vacation in Scotland, while the International Typographical Union awarded James Lynch a $10,000 testimonial fund upon his retirement as president in 1914.[48] And when William J. Bowen retired from the Bricklayers, he was made president emeritus at a salary of $10,000 a year which he collected for the next two decades.[49]

A tentative case can be made that the rank and file's appreciation of their leaders was related to basic status anxieties. American workers were deeply concerned with their place in the emerging industrial society. In 1899, for instance, coal miners responded vigorously to criticism that they were "abject, immoral and ignorant individuals hardly worthy of citizenship or being entitled to the right of suffrage."[50] In another case, the miner's *Journal* went out of its way to note "that among the names thought worthy of honorable mention by this average daily newspaper is found a goodly quota of miners as usual, and from this last reminder we are persuaded that nothing but perversity or despair on the part of our craft can prevent us as miners from again taking our place among the respected and requited laborers of the country."[51] Such reaction suggests strong status anxieties. The esteem given labor leaders by the larger society reflected on and gave hope to their followers. Contemplating the meaning to the workers of John Mitchell's newly gained prestige, his biographer Elsie Gluck wrote:

> Now men knew his name, knew that he had brought success
> with him, had put back food in houses where there had been

none. They knew, in a vague way, of his childhood, not unlike
their own. They knew of his sudden rise to a position where
newspapers quoted him and political figures associated with
him. He was walking proof that their own hopes might come true.
He had given them a dignity and importance in the country which
they had never had.[52]

Martin B. "Skinny" Madden, an early twentieth-century labor tsar
of the Chicago building industry, was very aware of these sublimated
anxieties and strove to fulfill rank-and-file expectations. Living in
an ostentatious manner, Madden responded to criticism candidly.
"Sure I have an auto," he admitted.

What of it? Don't the hod-carriers, plasterers, and bricklayers
know it? They think a lot more of me because I sport it. They
say, "Well, there's some class to our boss, ain't they?" I spend
money. Sure I do. But most of it is for the good of the service,
as the police department calls it. Nobody can tell me about the
best way to put up a front to the whole class of working men. The
more front you expose the more they will think of you.[53]

Rank-and-file gratitude at times became a cult of veneration.
labor leaders were often referred to in the most eloquent of terms.
"When I listened to John Siney I could see Christ in his face and
hear a new Sermon on the Mount," recalled Powderly.[54] Labor
editor John Swinton viewed the presocialist Debs "as the embodi-
ment and exponent of the genius of the Union of which he is President. The spirit of the Union is in him, and his spirit is in the Union."[55]
The workers who frequented the saloon where Ed Flore worked
mentioned Gompers's name "with hope in their voice. He seemed to
be their towering leader to free them from the grip in which the big
industrialists had them. They talked of him as if he were a knight in
shining armor who would lead them in battle against menancing
ogres."[56] And for Agnes Nestor of the Glove Workers, John Mitchell
was the "great idol in the labor movement."[57]

Several leaders had monuments erected in their memories, a few
were immortalized in song, and some had holidays declared in their
honor. In 1884, the Knights of Labor celebrated the birth of their
late founder and leader, Uriah Stephens.[58] John Mitchell led the

Siney in 1900.[59] The residents of Arnot, Pennsylvania set aside June 13, 1904 to honor their local hero, UMW Secretary-Treasurer William B. Wilson.[60] The greatest event among union miners, however, was October 29th of each year, when they would lay off work and celebrate Mitchell Day.[61]

Such adulation led to commercializing the leader's image. "Every Loyal Workingman," declared one advertisement, "should carry a Moyer-Haywood Souvenir Knife."[62] "Union Men, Smoke the Moyer-WFM & ICC Cigar," encouraged a second.[63] A third pushed "The John Mitchell $2.50 Shoe."[64] Deluged with requests to endorse various items, Powderly became very perturbed at "having my picture used on every notion that men feel like putting it on." The particular object of his scorn was his likeness on flour sacks.[65]

While individual leaders were eulogized, the position of leadership was elevated to sanctified heights. Articles in union papers placed labor leaders in the tradition of "the men of '76 who signed the Declaration of Independence." They were also latter-day abolitionists fighting to end wage slavery just as "Brown, Phillips, and Garrison" had brought the demise of Negro servitude.[66] Even more prominent was the attempt to link the labor leaders with the saints and martyrs of Christianity. One article of this nature was headlined:

HISTORIC STRIKES

The Great Straw Strike With
Moses as the "Ring
Leader."

He Indulged in "Plain Talk" to the
Lord,

And Finally the "Chief Manager," Pharaoh,
Succumbed.[67]

Other articles developed the theme of Christ as "the Greatest Agitator." It was Jesus, the *United Mine Workers' Journal* maintained, "who first espoused the cause of the poor and preached and gave hope and encouragement to the downtrodden."[68] "Christ was an *agitator*," the *Miners' Magazine* sermonized, "and because the doctrines which He preached were at variance with the ethics of the money changers whom He castigated in the temple, he was branded as a criminal, crowned with thorns and finally condemned to die upon the cross on Calvary."[69] Even the radical Industrial Workers of the World employed this imagery. Ben Williams, editor of the IWW's official organ, praised "the Hobo Carpenter from Nazareth," whose call, "stripped of the mystical and mythical veil of Constantine and his successors, and clothed in the original garb of communism and brotherhood, continues to sound intermittently across the ages."[70]

Completing the religious allusions, the leaders' agents were given the status of disciples. "Not more righteous was either Peter or Paul in their sacred work nor more free from sinful affections than is the 'walking delegate,' " preached one correspondent. "Labor is not only noble, but holy, and the person commissioned, under instruction, as an adherent of its purposes and ends for the common weal is as holy in his office as were the apostles as followers of the lowly Nazarene."[71]

Deference and adulation constituted only one trait of a complex rank and file. The same miners who set a day aside to honor Mitchell, publicly insulted him in 1911 by demanding his resignation from either the National Civic Federation or the union.[72] Other leaders met similar fates. John Siney died a rejected and lonely man.[73] Both Powderly and Gompers were thrown out of office in the early 1890s, although the latter was able to return to power. P. J. McGuire, who almost single-handedly guided the carpenters' union from birth to maturity, was ejected from office in 1901. Adding insult to injury, he was paraded through the courts on questionable charges of embezzlement.[74] Even "Big Bill" Haywood, whose name has become synonymous with the IWW, was condemned by many Wobblies when he chose to live out his life in Bolshevik Russia rather than die in a "capitalist" prison.[75]

Such events led labor leaders to view the rank and file as fickle and ungrateful. "In all the train of vice there's not a monster, more foul, more ugly than ingratitude," the *United Mine Workers' Journal* scorned.[76] "The strange part of it all," bemoaned the *American Federationist,* "is that the general body of workers seems to view with unconcern the unusual difficulties that confront their struggling officers. . . ."[77] The ingratitude of the workers was constantly on the leaders' mind. In his last public statement before his death, John Siney lamented: "I care nothing for the abuse of our enemies—it never troubled me for a moment—but the ingratitude of the working-men cut deep into my heart."[78] Over the desk on which Powderly conducted much of the Noble and Holy Order's business, hung a picture of Christ, "the world's greatest, most sublime agitator." At the foot of the cross he tacked a special message:

> Work for self and humanity honors you,
> Work for humanity and it crucifies you.[79]

Powderly met his fate in 1893 when he was ousted from the leadership of the Knights of Labor, his supposed friend John W. Hayes playing Judas by pointing the finger of corruption at him. Even Gompers, the most famous of Powderly haters, was saddened by the episode. "I'll be frank with you," he wrote a friend, "I much regret, not so much the fact of Mr. Powderly leaving the office of the Chief Executive of the Knights of Labor, but rather the manner in which he was forced to do so. . . . It is a repetition of the old cry of Hosannah, followed by that of 'crucify him.' "[80]

At times the leaders' charge of fickleness was fair. Often the loss of a strike, particularly during a union's formative years, resulted in the rejection of the officers from power, whether they were responsible or not. John Mitchell was conscious of this fact. After informing a friend that "the attempt to inaugurate a National suspension [in 1902] is not of my choosing," he continued "but now that we are in it I am going to stay with the boys until they either succeed or fail; and if they fail I shall join the ancient order of has-beens and used-to-be's and become one of its most revered members."[81] Periods of depression also took their toll of leaders. During the lean years of 1893 to 1897, major changes in officers occurred in the Knights of Labor, the AFL, the United Mine Workers, the Machinists, the Railroad Trainmen, and several other organizations. While factors other than the depression were involved, no doubt many of the rank and file were simply reacting to the downturn in business. As ex-president John McBride told the delegates to the 1895 convention of the Mine Workers: "It is at such times that men forget the causes which are responsible for their condition, and without giving a thought to surroundings or taking into consideration their dependence upon craftsmen in competing fields, give vent to their desires, and with their judgment warped by suffering and prejudice and blinded by passion they enter into a wholesale denunciation of persons and things; and officials, no matter how honest, sincere or able they may be are made the victims of their craftsmen's wrath and folly."[82] "It may be a great pity," concurred Gompers, "but it is a fact, that when conditions of life and labor are keenly felt, those in responsible positions, whether in government or in organized labor, are blamed and criticized because they have not either averted such a condition or have not remedied it."[83]

At other times, however, leaders saw ingratitude when other factors were foremost. Frequently union officials held narrow views of loyalty, interpreting independent action as at best ungratefulness and at worst treason. "It is somewhat discouraging how forgetful men can be of the services rendered them during the time in which they are in trouble," Daniel Tobin complained of a group of Teamsters. "After what local No. 710 done for these people and what local No. 753 did, it seems as though you would imagine they would always be, without hesitation, loyal to the International organization, but there is nothing that surpasses the ingratitude of some men who claim to be union men today in the labor movement."[84] Moreover, what leaders mistook for fickleness was often simply another sign of apathy. The ousting of Powderly and McGuire and the embarrassment of Mitchell were engineered by an elite group, and while they needed some popular following they lacked full membership support. Indeed, many workingmen simply were too apathetic and indifferent to union politics to rise up and defend the men whom they once hailed as heroes.

Though leaders perceived their followers as indifferent, submissive, yet potentially disloyal during the normal operations of the union, they held a somewhat different view in times of labor unrest. On the one hand, they suspected the rank and file of being too quick to strike. On the other, they considered them unpredictable once on the picket line.

Leaders particularly attributed impetuous strikes to new unionists. "The truth is," Gompers observed, "that when workers are unorganized they underestimate their own power and influence and overestimate that of the employing class, and newly organized workingmen flushed with enthusiasm really overestimate their power and underestimate that of their opponents."[85] Jacob Magidow, an early activist in the United Hebrew Trades, noted that newly organized Jews "saw no difference between a union and a strike—these were one and the same things to their minds."[86] Like many organizers, William J. Duffy of the Knights complained to his superiors:

> I find, no matter how careful I may be in organizing an assembly, there will get into it an element that is radical, and full of strike, and though the laws in reference to strikes and lockouts have been fully explained to them, the Organizer finds them out on strike or lock-out, the minute he has turned his back, and when I have been asked to come and see said Assy', I have asked them what did they strike for? they were not able to answer.[87]

Such impetuosity distressed established leaders. "I do not know and never did know a labor officer who did not view the strike with gravest apprehension," reflected Powderly. "Nothing can injure the conscientious officer of a labor organization more than to lose a strike unless it be to win one. If he loses he is sure to be charged with selling out, if he wins he'll be expected to keep on striking—and winning right along."[88]

When strikes commenced, leaders were never confident of their followers. Would they stand together in solidarity until victorious, or would they break rank when the going got rough and slowly wander back to work? Would they accept the agreement negotiated by their officers, or would they demand more and possibly bring down upon the union the full wrath of the employers? Or still, would they demand too little, settling for better pay and treatment instead of holding out for union recognition so that their organization could continuously influence the firm's labor policies? Such questions were constantly in the back of a strike leader's mind.

Rank-and-file attitudes exerted strong influence on the development of leadership. Apathy and deference allowed officers to perform the everyday operations of the unions free from accountability to a large, critically concerned following. These traits, combined with the membership's inclination to be personality rather than policy oriented, fostered governments of men as opposed to governments of laws. In the 1860s, William Sylvis established "an unfortunate precedent in labor history" when he used his personal prestige as well as the excuse of emergency to expand his powers far beyond the limits of the Iron Molders' constitution.[89] In ensuing years, numerous organizations followed this lead and accepted the principle that their top officers were free from the restraints of union law.[90] This cult of personality influenced the nature of union elections. In closely contested campaigns, labor politicos resorted to name calling, accusations, and "red baiting" to mobilize an apathetic electorate generally disinterested in policies. With dry humor, one printer noted: "The International Typographical Union is to be congratulated upon an election taking place without the vicious slander and disgraceful charges usually the accompaniment of these biennial affairs. It is true the prime cause for this unusual condition was due to the fact that there was only one ticket in the field headed by a candidate for president. . . ."[91]

Confronted by a complex and often contradictory rank and file, union officials sought to manipulate their behavior. "The leaders' policy was governed by their distrust of the worker," former Garment Workers' Official Henry White maintained. "The voluntary element in the union being small, many strange expedients were resorted to to keep the mass of members in control."[92] In hopes of securing their positions, leaders developed two basic courses of action. The first was to encourage those rank-and-file traits which they saw as helpful to their cause. The second was to institute means of checking seemingly harmful characteristics. To accomplish these ends, they resorted to legalism on the one hand and image building on the other.

The legalistic means by which the leaders sought to check undesirable actions by the led ranged from the rules of the national conventions to procedures to be followed before strikes could be declared. Such policies had other purposes beside simply preventing rank-and-file impulses. Moreover, the majority of the leaders did not really want to thwart the will of their constituents if they could help it. Rather, the legalities and procedures were intended to stop rash and impulsive actions. Whether correct or not, most labor leaders sincerely felt they represented the best interests of their followers. By forcing the rank and file to consider a situation carefully before acting, they reasoned, irrationality would be overcome and the views of leaders and followers would be harmonious.

Image building also relates to the mechanism of power since ultimately the leader's authority rested upon the active, or at least passive, consent of the governed. To attain this support, they mobilized the institutionalized tools of communication in a campaign which some modern observers might label "The Selling of the Labor Leader." Utilizing every forum from organizing rallies to the convention floor, administration supporters warmly proclaimed the virtues of their officers. "All we have to do is keep a boosting and everything will come out all right," asserted one leader who went to the very heart of the image-building philosophy.[93]

The most important medium in this campaign was the union journal. Recognizing the influence of the official organs, such leaders as Gompers, Tobin, Jere L. Sullivan of the Hotel and Restaurant Employees, and J. N. Neenan of the Glass Workers continued to edit the papers of their organizations despite the pressing demands of other work.[94] In other unions, like the United Mine Workers, the editorship became a plum of the president, frequently changing hands each time a new top officer was elected.[95]

The *United Mine Workers' Journal* illustrated the approach of union papers in selling the labor leaders. From its founding in 1891, the miners' press was proadministration and quickly assumed the task of rationalizing and legitimizing official actions. The *Journal* unequivocally approved the cancelation of the eight-hour strike of 1891, and after the loss of the 1894 strike it shielded the officers against charges of selling out.[96] The policy of defending the actions of leaders against criticism became a positive function of promoting the administration's will. Under the editorship of S. M. Sexton, beginning in 1903, the *Journal* was firmly established as an organ of the hierarchy. In March 1904, when the membership was given an opportunity to vote on the practice of making interstate agreements, the paper fully supported President Mitchell's stand and clearly implied that a vote to the contrary was tantamount to treason.[97] Opposing arguments were seldom presented, and then usually to serve as targets for the editor to knock down. In 1908 and 1910 the *Journal* endorsed Tom L. Lewis for the union's presidency and again implied that to oppose him was to do injury to the union.[98]

Besides openly defending and promoting the leaders' actions, policies, and candidacies, the *United Mine Workers' Journal* engaged in more subtle forms of image building. Letters praising the administration frequently received front page exposure, while those critical were buried in the back. Each issue carried accounts of the activities of the officials, and when opportunity permitted dramatized episodes of their lives. Such stories served to remind the rank and file that the leaders were working for their welfare at great personal cost. Moreover, they kept the officials' names before the constituency, and at election time the followers tended to vote for candidates who were best known. Daniel Tobin of the Teamsters advised one aspiring politico: "it would be to your advantage to keep acquainted with the membership through the columns of the Journal, and it is also a means of communication, which at this time, is necessary."[99]

A more indirect method of image building was through articles extolling leadership in general rather than particular individuals. At times this took the form of Max Weber's "routinization of charisma."[100] Labor journals encouraged the cult of veneration mentioned earlier. Consciously and subconsciously, the numerous references to heroes of Christianity, the Founding Fathers, great abolitionists, and pioneers of unionism transferred to the leaders some of the charisma of these historic figures and thereby legitimized their right to obedience. More often, the *Journal* simply published articles which developed the themes of the leaders' virtuous character and the hardships and sacrifices which confronted one chosen to lead.[101]

For those unconvinced by the laudatory portrait of labor leaders, there awaited a special fate. On the one hand, innumerable columns of the *Journal* painted such individuals in an unfavorable light. On the other, the attempts of dissenters to express their views were partly checked. Signs of censorship appeared early in the *United Mine Workers' Journal*. Beginning in 1891, letters to the editors contained statements suggesting that some members were having difficulty airing their views. "Should these few lines escape the bottomless pit of oblivion, *viz.* the waste basket," wrote one correspondent.[102] Another began his letter: "Believing the blue pencil was discriminately used on my last correspondence. . . ."[103] "Now,

Mr. Editor," insisted a third, "I believe The Journal is the property of the miners, and that it is to be used by the miners for the advancement of our craft, and any miner or mine worker who has anything to offer for the advancement of his craftsmen or the laboring people in general should have space for same, which I was not allowed."[104]

Editors admitted censorship, but defended their actions by referring to a principle upheld by most of the labor press. "No letter containing personalities shall be published in this *Journal*," the first editor established.[105] His successors reiterated this policy. In 1898 readers were reminded that it was the editor's job "to obliterate all personal allusions hereafter from any and every communication that may reach us. . . ."[106] Again in 1916, subscribers were informed that the paper "does not invite our members to air their differences with officials, District or International, or with other members of the organization."[107] In reality, this principle only protected the national elite. Some local leaders, and particularly known critics of the administration, were freely attacked in the press, their character assailed, their sincerity questioned.[108] Moreover, the principle became a means of preventing open discussion on candidates for office. In 1898, the *Journal* informed its audience that "all references to the merits or demerits, if any there be, of candidates for office, at our coming annual convention at Pittsburgh, will be excluded from the columns of the Journal." The rationale for this action was that "the Journal is the official organ of the miners, their property, and it would not be proper to make a campaign medium of it for the glorification of some miners and the possible detraction or opposition of others."[109] In reality, the incumbent, in this case Mitchell, was able to propagate his message in the pages of the *Journal* under the rubric of important union business. Only the opposition was eliminated.

While proclaiming the *Journal* would not deal in personalities, the first editor continued: "This does not prevent our members from criticising the policy of the officers of the organization or to suggest remedies."[110] Again, his successors repeated this corollary, but in practice it too was abused. Upon leaving the editorship in 1899 to assume a vice-presidency, Thomas W. Davis nonchalantly confessed "we have tried to exclude all extraneous matter from its columns, especially have we done this when it was of such a character as to seem to us likely to open up an endless, irritating, unjustifiable unity destroying sentiment and action. . . ."[111] In response to criticism concerning the absence of articles by dissenters, another editor retorted in 1908: "The 'Knocker' never has any argument. He deals exclusively with prejudice and a presumption that everything is going wrong unless he is directing its course."[112] Several years later John Brophy met similar opposition when he sent his study on nationalizing the mines to editor Ellis Searles. When it was not published, he inquired as to the reasons. "Searles's reply was evasive," Brophy recorded,

> saying he felt it was unwise to publish the program because it appeared to be "to some extent a denunciation of the policies of the union." This referred to my argument that collective bargaining, as we had been practicing it for so many years, was inadequate to deal with the basic problems in the industry. I sought to allay his fears, but without success; he thought the program was "too controversial," even though I pointed out that it followed the principles laid down in the resolution of the 1919 convention. I knew that he would not take this stand without consulting the national officers, so I concluded that they were opposed to the idea and concentrated on educational work within my district.[113]

Censorship, such as practiced by the *United Mine Workers' Journal* and other papers, had unfortunate consequences for the labor movement. Instead of providing a two-way corridor for ideas to move between the leaders and the led, communications increasingly followed a one-way path from the top down. Rank-and-file sentiment had difficulty filtering up to those in power, thereby contributing to a gap of understanding between officers and followers. Alternative policies which labor might pursue were at times denied a hearing in its marketplace of ideas. The debates on important union questions were frequently channeled into nonunion presses and other media. Most important, the inability of every member to receive a fair hearing undermined a fundamental foundation on which viable trade union democracy could be built.

Other aspects of image building were more defensible. In the realities of union politics, the leader charged with initiating policy had to defend and explain his actions. More explicitly, he had the responsibility to convince the rank and file to follow, and persuasion was preferable to force. Like Edmund Morgan's John Winthrop of Puritan America, the labor leader was confronted with the insoluble dilemma of determining how much divergence a society could allow and still remain a society. Also like Winthrop, he faced the impossible task of living righteously in an impure world.[114]

IV

Much of the propaganda in labor journals attacked the third element among the led, the administrations' critics. Pejoratively labeled "grumblers," "union wreckers," "calamity howlers," "snarlers," and "whiners," they were best known as "the kickers and the knockers."[115] They comprised "the fire in the rear" of which labor leaders unendingly complained. "In all society," William Sylvis wrote in the late 1860s, "we find a class of men possessed of a superabundance of self-esteem, some brains, much cheek, and a little learning." Within the Iron Molders, he continued, these men banded together in a "clique" seeking to capture the union and divide "the profits and honors among them." "Endeavoring to poison the minds of the union men" they conducted their activities "below the surface; but, growing bolder as they hardened in sin, they have lately openly proclaimed in favor of secession."[116] Such men were a "two faced, snarling crew, who act the part of puerile wiffets, . . . fault finding by habit, and treacherous by instinct. . . ."[117]

Sylvis's invectives contributed to his historic prominence as a "Union Pioneer." In ensuing years, other leaders would view the opposition in similar light. "The detective agency," charged the *Miners' Magazine,* "has discovered that the tongue of slander is an effective weapon to shatter a labor organization, and the man whose character is tainted with such traits of degeneracy can always find employment as a Judas and receive the reward of the 'thirty pieces of silver.' "[118] "Disruption, if it comes, must come from within," insisted the *United Mine Workers' Journal.* "Disappointed office seekers; revolutionists in a hurry—men who can not wait for the slow but necessary processes of evolution; plain crooks masquerading as advanced union advocates, these are the disruptive forces that may bring about the dissolution of any or all of the great organizations of the toilers."[119]

The nature of union dissent is difficult to determine. As suggested above, labor papers were often hostile to opponents' views. Consequently, when their arguments were published, it is questionable whether these reflected their true feelings or were simply propaganda to win supporters. More important, the dissidents' camp was comprised of a variety of men whose ideals and purposes were diverse and confusing. In perspective, "the kickers and knockers" resembled the administration boosters. They too were motivated by idealism and ambition. Some sincerely desired labor to adopt an alternative focus; others were promoting their own personal careers. And like the boosters, their motives were often intertwined. Also paralleling their counterparts, the dissenters were active in union affairs. Much to the chagrin of established forces, they attended meetings and at times gained positions of influence.

The character of the disenchanted unionists and the righteousness of their causes was less important in shaping labor leadership than the consequences of their actions and the response of those in power. The presence of a group challenging the leaders created strong tensions within unions. In its most extreme form, the tension splintered organizations and encouraged dual unionism. Sometimes, as with the glass workers, dual unionism weakened the workers' ability to cope with their employer, for one organization would undermine the other in seeking favors from the boss. On other occasions, such splintering improved the workers' position with his employer. The disruption of the lethargic United Garment Workers and the establishment of the Amalgamated Clothing Workers resulted in a far more viable union looking after the interests of the needle workers.

More traditionally, dissenters remained within their organizations where they strove to gain power and remodel the union's program. To some extent, this struggle was healthy for it served as a foundation for democracy. More often, it had detrimental effects. It kept the union in a constant uproar, promoted insecurity, and created backlash. Many good officers, for instance, resigned rather than face a barrage of criticism. In 1891, Edward T. Plank refused to run again for the presidency of the International Typographical Union. "At that time," the printers' journal later explained, "some alleged writers were beginning to exude vile billingsgates and attack the officers by innuendo, which was most offensive to a gentlemen printer like Mr. Plank and he positively declined to be made the target for the mud batteries of self-seeking politicians."[120] Likewise, the infighting in the Mine Workers during 1894 and 1895 was so bitter that Secretary-Treasurer Patrick McBryde resigned.[121] With sensitive men abandoning the field, union offices went to those more fit to survive in the jungle of union politics.

The dissidents also contributed to unions becoming governments of men rather than laws. Even when dissent rested on policy, rebels freely resorted to name calling and accusations. They too realized that the rank and file were basically indifferent to issues and therefore hoped to arouse support by attacking individuals. "We are called upon at all our meetings," complained one unionist, "to listen, hour after hour, to long circulars and charges and counter-charges, and call special meetings of our local assemblies and local unions and stay up till 10 or 11 o'clock, for what? To discuss the honesty and integrity of the McBride's, Penna's, Adams's, Hayes, Sovereign and company, instead of discussing trade matters and political economy and educating ourselves."[122] Such occurrences placed attention on personalities, and drove many of the rank and file from the meeting halls in boredom and frustration. Moreover, these antics could lead to backlash. The majority of the delegates to the 1895 convention of the Mine Workers, a reporter noted, were neutral in the controversy then raging. While they would have liked to abandon the old officers, they were reluctant to do so because the accusations of the antiadministration group were ridiculous. Voting out the established leaders would have been interpreted as approving the opposition.[123]

Infighting also weakened the unions in their dealings with employers. On the one hand, the bickering revealed to a union's enemies the weakness of the organization. "Every time one of our active and leading Members appears in the public Press harshly criticizing Officers, Members, and Methods," pointed out A. A. Carlton of the

Knights, "the real effect is to aid those who are exultingly calling upon the public to witness our dissension and our humiliation."[124] On the other hand, dissension diverted union energies from confrontation with employers. "We have a common enemy to fight and we cannot afford to squabble among ourselves," Powderly observed, "but it seems as if we must assail each other more bitterly than we assail the enemy if the least difference arises between us."[125] William Crawford of the Mine Workers agreed and lectured his bickering comrades: "We can console ourselves with the assurance that we are doing just what the masters, our employers, want us to do. While we are quarreling among ourselves we are not troubling them. . . ."[126]

Adverse consequences of dissension would not have been so severe had those in power answered responsibly to criticism, but in the desire to protect their unions as well as their own positions many labor leaders reacted unscrupulously. The use of the labor journal has already been mentioned and other practices will be suggested in the next chapter. The important point is that long before Lewis, Hoffa, Ryan, or Boyle appeared on the labor scene, their predecessors utilized some of the dubious practices exposed by the McClellan Committee in the 1950s and supposedly outlawed by the 1959 Labor Management Reporting and Disclosure Act. When the opposition captured the largest local in the Cigar Makers' International Union in 1881, for instance, President Adolph Strasser nullified the election and placed a loyal partisan in control.[127] In 1887, Powderly had the Order expel his most vocal critics, Burnette G. Haskell, Joseph Buchanan, and Thomas Berry.[128] He also pioneered in disbanding locals and then rechartering them without the dissident element.[129] Daniel Tobin approved of this tactic. In 1909 he wrote to a friend: "I am in hope that some day we will have peace but the next time we have peace it will be when those who are wrong will be cut out of the general membership."[130] The teamster leader also appreciated the strategy of building a power base on the "sleepy locals" throughout the country. "The little towns and villages," he informed an organizer, "help keep this organization going and are very little trouble to this office, and my object is to try and get to the little places in the woods and remote districts with our organization."[131] In 1909, the Mine Workers adopted an amendment common to many union constitutions:

> Any member guilty of slandering or circulating, or causing to
> be circulated, false statements against any member of the United
> Mine Workers, upon being proven guilty, shall be suspended
> from membership in the International, District or sub-district or
> local union for a period of six months, and not eligible to hold
> office in the organization for a period of two years.[132]

The means by which men were found guilty was the administratively controlled judiciary system. The miners also established an anti-insurgent fund, which in 1921 amounted to $27,000.[133]

The actions which labor leaders at times took against the opposition constitute one of the most unpleasant aspects of trade union history. Yet, without justifying these deeds, they must be placed in perspective. There were elements among the discontented who would, if given their way, follow courses detrimental and perhaps even ruinous to the unions. Leaders felt duty bound to prevent such developments by whatever means necessary. That they overreacted was unfortunate but entirely human. Indeed, the degree of suppression and manipulation by labor leaders was probably no greater than that of politicians and far less than that of the Robber Barons, whose concern for democracy was academic.

5.

Mechanisms of Power

It is necessary to stress at this point that the tendency toward the upward shift and concentration of power is inherent in the very nature of the organization as it grows, its functions multiply, and its responsibilities increase. Thirst for power, where it does exist (and it naturally exists almost everywhere), is essentially a secondary factor, aggravating, accelerating, but certainly not originating the tendency.

Will Herberg[1]

I

While a leader's right to rule originated in the consent of the rank and file, his immediate authority derived from his control and influence over the mechanisms of union government. The evolution of labor leadership was closely tied to the institutional development of the trade unions. Over the years from the Civil War to the end of World War I, union structure evolved in a manner which placed the national leaders in pivotal positions of power.

Several themes weave their way through an analysis of the mechanisms of power. One is the progressive expansion of the labor movement in both size and functions from 1870 to 1920. In 1869 there were twenty-nine national trade unions. Despite the high mortality rate among them, the number rose to 79 in 1889, 120 in 1899, 171 in 1909, and 163 in 1919 (the slight decline resulting primarily from the merger of existing bodies).[2] The number of trade union members correspondingly increased from roughly 300,000 in 1870 to 865,000 in 1900, to over five million in 1920.[3] Membership in the International Typographical Union grew from 25,165 in 1891 to 62,661 in 1918, while the increase was even more marked for the Teamsters, whose rolls lengthened from 32,000 in 1903 to 112,453 by 1920.[4] Union functions expanded concomitantly. The increased involvement of the national office in the field of union-management relations has already been mentioned in chapter three. Unions also initiated for their members such activities and services as training institutes, hospitals, clinics, retirement homes, and health and life insurance. By 1913, 72 out of 134 organizations provided benevolent relief, and the funds disbursed that year totaled $11,500,000.[5] To support such programs along with strike relief funds, unions increased their treasuries to respectable proportions.

Closely associated with these developments was the continual conflict between the forces of local autonomy and decentralization and the advocates of centralization and national union dominance. This theme was also discussed in chapter three with reference to the evolution of union-management relations, and many of the points developed there are equally applicable to an understanding of trade union government. In the loosely structured bodies of the 1860s and 1870s the national office "secured little obedience from the constituent local societies" which were bound to it "by such slender ties that threat of suspension had little effect in compelling obedience to international rules." By 1920 trade unions had evolved into relatively centralized institutions in which a majority of locals were "a product of the international or national, chartered by it, largely directed by it, bound to obey it in matters of policy and method or suffer revocation of charter, loss of counsel and financial support in time of trouble—all of which ordinarily means speedy dissolution."[6] Absorption of power by the national union did not proceed unchallenged, and a number of the institutions of trade union government including executive boards and referenda were originally designed as means of preventing concentration of power in the hands of a few top leaders. Plans for decentralization, however, were not always intended to foster trade union democracy. In numerous instances, advocates of decentralization were local power elites attempting to forestall encroachment on their domain by the national office. Proponents of centralization, in contrast, generally adhered to the images of the union as an army and a business and explained their tactics in terms of the need for order and efficiency.

An equally important theme underlying the development of union government was the labor movement's rather weak adherence to constitutionalism. While all unions possessed a declaration of their laws, policies, and structure, they did not hold these documents sacrosanct. "To a certain extent . . . ," John Mitchell observed, "the formal written constitution of a trade union is rather a statement of principles and a formulation of present policy of the union than a hard and fast determination of its future laws." Contributing to this situation was the ease with which the documents could be changed. "The constitution of the United Mine Workers," Mitchell continued, "may be altered by a majority vote in convention, and in a large number of other organizations the fundamental law of the organization may be changed by a majority vote either of the delegates in convention or of the members voting by referendum, although in some unions a two-thirds vote is necessary."[7] The relative facility by which constitutions could be, and were, amended undermined the sanctity of the documents, for what was accepted policy today could very well be rejected tomorrow.

Lack of an independent judiciary responsible for interpreting the document also contributed to the weakness of constitutionalism in the labor movement. Within most organizations the national president or secretary possessed power to pass upon the the meaning of the constitution, generally subject to review by the executive board or convention, both of which increasingly came under his dominance. The leaders who exercised this function were not unusually devious, but they were men of action directing organizations designed for accomplishments. When officers felt the constitution inhibited effective action, they did not hesitate to stretch or abridge its provisions. "I am prepared," the president of the Iron Molders declared in 1867, "to lay the constitution on the shelf and to do what seems best to save the organization, believing that it is better to have an organization without a constitution than to have a constitution without an organization."[8] Beginning in the 1860s, when William Sylvis extended his authority beyond its defined limits, the concept emerged that top union officials possessed extraconstitutional powers.[9] The Teamsters' General Secretary-Treasurer Thomas L. Hughes revealed this attitude in a letter to a unionist requesting special privileges. "President Tobin is still President of the organization," he wrote, "and I must receive any orders that are contrary to the constitution from him before I will take any action whatsoever." Again he repeated, "I do not intend to deviate from the constitution, *at least not without his instructions.*"[10]

The general attitude toward constitutionalism, among the top leaders at least, is perhaps best revealed in a letter from Samuel Gompers to an associate who complained that the document restrained him in his work. "Dear Sir and Brother," Gompers replied,

> At a railroad station a young man was about to enter a car on the train. Seeing the conductor, he asked him whether he could smoke his cigar in that car. The conductor peremptorily said, "No," when the young man retorted:
>
> "Why, I saw a man coming out of that car smoking a dirty old pipe." The conductor replied: "Well, he did not ask me."
>
> Your letter of the 7th to hand, and I make this private reply.
>
> Fraternally Yours,
> Samuel Gompers[11]

II

In a newly formed union, the governing authority generally resided with the convention. Here delegates from constituent bodies gathered to determine the organization's priorities and supervise the national officers. The delegates were the citizens of the national body, and they chose the leaders from their ranks. By 1920, however, the sovereignty of the convention had been severely undermined. The servants had become the master as union officials assumed responsibility for policy decisions and guided the work of the delegates. Maneuvering by the leaders only partially accounted for the weakening of the conventions. More importantly, the system itself had serious shortcomings.

Trade union conventions have never been purely democratic. The early gatherings were designed to protect the interests of the locals and only indirectly to express the sentiment of the members. Rigid instructions frequently circumscribed the authority of the delegates, yet such pledges were primarily designed "to safeguard the power originally held by the local unions" rather than "to retain governing authority in the 'voice' of the membership."[12] Local unions were the actual constituencies of the delegates, since the rank and file were not citizens of the national organization.[13] Representation at conventions was initially based on the senatorial principle in which each local received an equal number of votes regardless of size, and while most organizations eventually moved to proportional representation, few, if any, unions achieved a stage where every delegate represented an equal number of members.[14]

The inability of locals to send delegates to the national convention further hindered fair representation. "Nearly one-half of our total membership of over 18,000," reported the secretary of the International Typographical Union in 1885, "are practically disfranchised in the way of representation in the international body, owing to the poverty of small local unions and the great expense necessarily incurred in sending representatives long distances. . . . As an illustration of this disfranchisement, it may be mentioned that at the last annual session of this body less than one-third of the enrolled unions were represented at all."[15] Nor did the situation improve over time: seventeen years later the union's journal published an already familiar report of convention attendance. Of 536 locals enrolled on the books, 124 sent delegates while 412 were unrepresented.[16] Other unions experienced the same problem since the cause was common to all: "The small unions simply can not afford to send representatives."[17]

Various unions instituted a number of reforms to rectify the situation, but these measures in turn created difficulties of their own. One proposal suggested that the convention meet in a different region of the country each session so that small locals might send delegates whenever the gathering was held in their vicinity. This was no solution at all for the problem of incomplete representation at each convention remained.

A proposal that small locals be represented by proxy, when adopted, also failed to make conventions more democratic for it concentrated power in the hands of the national executives or leaders of a few large locals who controlled the absentee votes. W. C. Pomeroy, for instance, gained dominance over the Hotel and Restaurant Employees in the 1890s because from his Chicago stronghold he was able to wield the proxies of many outlying locals. Once in power, Pomeroy chartered ghost locals with false memberships, and since he controlled the books, he could avoid detection. If challenged at a convention to reveal the state of the union, he could defeat the move by using his proxies.[18]

Payment of delegate expenses by the national administration constituted a more constructive reform. The Iron Molders' Union had always paid the mileage costs of the delegates and beginning in 1882 provided them with three dollars a day "to defray expenses." As a result, attendance at their gatherings was far better than at such conventions as the Typographers', where there was no provision for aid. The drawback to the plan, however, was the financial burden on the union's treasury. From 1876 to 1902, the length of the Iron Molders' conventions doubled, the number of delegates rose almost five-fold, while mileage and per diem costs increased thirteen times, from $3,844.60 to $50,670.72.[19] Likewise the plumbers' 1913 convention cost over $72,000, the 1917 session over $96,000, and the 1921 gathering a record $154,000.[20] One of the more common reasons given by national unions for resorting to referenda was the prohibitively high cost of conventions.[21]

A more popular solution to the problem of poor attendance was to hold conventions less frequently. Whether the expenses of sending a delegation rested on the local or was assumed by the national organization, this proposal reduced costs. Moreover, as unions matured and no longer existed in an openly hostile environment, many labor leaders felt that frequent gatherings were uncalled for. The sense of mission and solidarity which early conventions stimulated was no longer necessary. Nor was there need for frequent policy directives from the delegates, as the administrative bureaucracy had developed a momentum of its own. Indeed, many unionists perceived fewer conventions as a means of stabilizing their organizations, for delegates to annual gatherings seemed unable to resist the temptation of tinkering with the union's structure and policies. Accepting such views, the Journeymen Plumbers called off their 1903 convention to avoid the excessive cost and because "to make any change in our constitution . . . would upset our system."[22]

Several unions allowed considerable time to pass between conventions. The Cigar Makers' convention of 1912 was the first in sixteen years. The Granite Cutters held a session in 1880 and then did not convene again until 1912. In the meantime, business was conducted in both organizations by referendum and specially elected committees.[23] In 1939, the rank and file of the Tobacco Workers had to get a court order to force the organization's officers to call a convention, the last one having been held in 1900.[24] Most unions, however, met at reasonable intervals. The Iron Molders held conventions annually from 1859 to 1868, biennially from 1868 to 1878, quadrennially from 1879 to 1886, biennially from 1886 to 1890, and quinquennially from 1890 to 1899.[25] The Journeymen Plumbers, founded in 1889, held annual sessions until 1913, when the constitution was changed to require only triennial meetings.[26] The International Association of Machinists held annual conventions from 1889 to 1893 and biennial meetings from 1895 to 1911; it had no provision for a specific meeting date from 1912 to 1916 but met quadrennially thereafter.[27] Fewer gatherings naturally resulted in less direct control over the leaders. In many cases the term of office was lengthened to correspond with the meetings, providing officers greater freedom and flexibility in their actions.

When conventions met less frequently, the duration of each session was often inadequate for the amount of work to be done. In 1913, economist Theodore Glocker clearly perceived the problem this development posed:

> The governmental efficiency of the trade-union convention is limited because it can be convoked so infrequently and can remain in session such a very short time. None of the unions hold conventions oftener than once a year, and many of them less frequently. The length of each session has been more and more protracted as organizations have grown in size and number of their activities. For example, the convention of Iron, Steel and

Tin Workers lasted for three days in 1876 and for seventeen days in 1902; that of the Cigar Makers lasted for five days in 1866 and for eighteen days in 1896. Nevertheless, in fifty-six associations from which information was obtained the average length of the convention was seven days; in only twelve of these was the convention in session for more than ten days. The most protracted sessions are those of the Iron Molders, whose delegates continued to meet together in 1902 for twenty days. Certainly a week or even two weeks seems a very short time in which to adopt needed legislation, clear the docket of judicial cases, elect officers, audit accounts, levy dues, appropriate funds, declare strikes, and transact the numerous other items of business which have been accumulating during the year or more since the last convention.[28]

Added to these shortcomings was the increasingly large size of convention delegations. Gatherings of the Cigar Makers, for example, expanded in size from seven delegates in 1877, to 85 in 1883, to 245 in 1896.[29] Likewise the number of delegates attending the conventions of the plumbers started at 40 at the first session in 1889, dropped to 22 in 1897 as a result of the depression, rose to 240 in 1906 after the national office started to pay expenses, and reached 460 in 1917.[30]

Enlarged attendance further contributed to inefficiency and inability to supervise the executives properly. The early conventions of a union, generally small in size, were arenas for conflicting views; the delegates were earnestly devoted to the serious business of building an organization and cared little for social functions.[31] A representative to an early Hotel and Restaurant Employees' convention reported "I was under the impression that the principal business of the delegates was to have a good time; but I was speedily made aware of my mistake."[32] But as time passed, the delegate's original impression became more accurate. "In too many organizations," complained a printer in 1915, "the trip to the convention is regarded as a junket, and only a junket. In too many organizations the practice prevails of passing the 'honor' around, first to this and then to that personal favorite, to good mixers and to those whom we would like to give an occasional vacation because we like the man."[33]

"Anyone who has attended our international conventions," argued a mine worker in 1912,

> must realize that they have reached a size where delegates can no longer take intelligent action on the questions that come before them. . . . This convention is so large that at least one-half of the delegates are paying no attention . . . because it is impossible for them to hear the debates that are going on. And if the mining industry is ever thoroughly organized in this country, imagine the conventions we will have! They will be mobs and nothing else . . . mob rule would prevail more than intelligence.[34]

The delegate's fear that large conventions would become mobs contained considerable truth. As sociologist Robert Michels observed:

> It is easier to dominate a large crowd than a small audience. The adhesion of the crowd is tumultuous, summary, and unconditional. Once the suggestions have taken effect, the crowd does not readily tolerate contradictions from a small minority, and still less from isolated individuals. A great multitude assembled within a small area is unquestionably more accessible than is a small meeting whose members can quietly discuss matters among themselves.[35]

Small, early conventions were described in the union press as parliaments for debate and exchange of views, while later and larger sessions were defined as serving an educational function and promoting harmony.[36] An approving editorial in the *United Mine Workers' Journal* suggests the emerging mob-like harmony of union gatherings:

> Former conventions of miners have been more or less marked by individual spleen and rancor, but these with which we are now dealing were marked by a determination on the part of each and every delegate to squelch any notoriety hunter or common disturber who might have the hardihood to show his head at a time when the calamitous and perilous position of our craft demand unity and harmony in as full a measure as possible.[37]

Reformers continued their efforts to correct the shortcomings of conventions. The most popular alternative in the years around the turn of the century was the referendum, to be discussed shortly. Another standard proposal called for reduction of the number of delegates attending the sessions. This plan was proposed in the Typographical Union as well as the United Mine Workers, where it was defeated three times, the last in spite of the disorder that prevailed at the 1916 convention when 1,511 delegates tried to negotiate business. The reluctance of delegates to accept the measure sometimes revealed a desire to protect their own positions, yet it also reflected a yearning to keep the union representative. Several plans were formulated, including one advocated by the Mine Workers' leaders, which would transfer the unit of representation from the local to the district level and thus dilute the convention's ties with the average unionist.[38]

A third reform would transform the meetings into "business conventions." Most vigorously advocated within the Typographical Union, this proposal reflected the emerging image of the union as a business. "Instead of leaving ourselves to decide on a new man or men every year," argued an advocate of the plan, "instead of keeping ourselves in doubt as to whether we will be represented at all or not, we ought to so change our constitution as to make the delegate an officeholder with a term of three or five years, send him off on business principles, pay him his regular union scale just as if he were at work in his shop at his branch of the trade, and meet his legitimate railroad fare and hotel expenses in addition, and no more."[39] This plan to create a corps of professional delegates had a number of variations. Among the more popular was the designation of local leaders as representatives, creating "a convention of subordinate union officials." While appealing to the more bureaucratic-minded, the idea was distasteful to rank and file unionists and not officially accepted. Ironically, however, delegates to the national conventions came increasingly from the local power elites who developed an almost sacred right to the position. "At all the conventions, excepting the early ones," recalled Henry White of the Garment Workers, "the sameness of representation from year to year was a marked feature. The faces at one convention could be counted on to appear at the next. In the personnel of the national officers there was also this peculiarity. It seemed as if a settled class of place-holders had grown up, a condition best adopted to the development of a governing trust."[40]

The weaknesses of conventions made them susceptible to domination by the national executives. In preconvention planning and during the sessions, the officers wielded the extensive influence of their positions and personal prestige. As national unions centralized and local leaders, increasingly reliant upon the blessings of headquarters, became delegates, the national executive's powers of persuasion grew. In addition to the informal pressures which the leaders could bring to bear, they were granted certain explicit powers which enabled them to manipulate, for good or evil, the nature and conduct of the gathering.

Control over membership records and charters proved one of the leaders' most useful tools. In 1914 the officers of the United Garment Workers successfully prevented the seating of delegates from locals, particularly in New York City, on grounds that they were in debt to the union and consequently ineligible for a voice in the convention.[41] On the other hand, if a leader wanted the representation of a friendly local which was in bad standing, he could conveniently arrange to cancel its debt. Secretary John Hayes of the Knights of Labor, for example, wrote to an amenable local leader:

> If you will write me a letter dated back thirty or forty days, say about the middle of June, asking that I exonerate them from back taxes and request that I right their standing, that upon your recommendation I have granted your request for their exoneration, I am of the opinion I can add them to the list of good paying locals in the future. Besides, if this is done as I direct, it may be the means of seating you as the 3rd delegate in the G[eneral] A[ssembly]. I have said enough.[42]

Similar tactics included withholding charters to potentially independent-minded locals until after the convention, as Powderly did in 1887; or, as Mitchell did in 1905, in requesting cooperative leaders of large locals or districts to buy several thousand fake membership cards in order to send a larger delegation to the forthcoming convention and thereby weaken a growing opposition.[43] In each case the leader's power to appoint the credential committee chairman, and in some instances the entire committee, enabled him to carry off the coup.

Other methods by which leaders manipulated conventions ranged from holding them in a community favorable to their interests, to determining who should get paid, and how much, for services rendered at the meetings. Examples can be found in numerous biographies and union studies.[44] Yet the cry of manipulation was most frequently raised over the election of officers.

The practice of selecting officers at the convention posed basic philosophical and practical questions as to the nature of representative government. Was it the delegate's duty to represent accurately the views of those who sent him by voting for the man they desired? Or should he use his own judgment, independent of the rank-and-file's will, and support the man he felt most fit for the job? In the main, the later concept received the greater support from union leaders. "I do not believe in the practice of pledging representatives to vote for any man at the G[eneral] A[ssembly]," wrote Powderly in 1886. "After they arrive on the ground they may see a better man, or a man better fitted to perform the duties than the man they are pledged to vote for and if the interests of the order require it I believe they should pay no attention to such pledges."[45] The officers of the Garment Workers held similar views. "The best fitted to make laws and elect officers for any international organization are the men who act as delegates to convention," they reported to the AFL. "They are usually the workers and know what is best for the organization."[46]

Underlying this position was a basic and not entirely unreasonable distrust of the rank-and-file's discretion. "The rank and file is too far removed to have the requisite knowledge of the personality of the officers to be as well equipped as a delegate who has attended one or more conventions in estimating the fitness of the man for office," insisted the leaders of the Plate Printers.[47] Likewise, Gompers counselled the International Association of Machinists in 1903 to reject the referendum because its members labored at their trade too many hours to have time to understand complex issues and to evaluate candidates. Such feelings also led the AFL leader to disapprove of direct democracy in his own organization.[48]

In those unions in which the delegates chose the national leaders, politics dominated the conventions. The high point of the meetings was the balloting, and many delegates left for home soon after the choice was made, regardless of what business might still be pending.[49] Frequently politics resulted in the actual work of the convention being conducted outside the hall. Praising the adoption of a more democratic way of choosing leaders, one mine worker pointed out that previously

> our officers were always elected in the hotel corridor or on the street corner or, in other words, the button holing process. Under the old plan the rank and file didn't know who would be nominated for offices in the convention and consequently instructed their delegates to vote for the best man, but instead in a great many instances they voted contrary to their own opinions and why? Mr. A would have a man that he would like to see elected to a certain office; Mr. B has a man that he wants for the same office the consequence is that they will begin to hold caucuses and the one will say this and that about the other to defeat him, when in fact both of them might perhaps be the grandest rascals in the whole business. . . .[50]

Along with politics and caucuses, the power of the incumbent created suspicion against electing officers through conventions. The maneuvering both before and during the 1899 UMW convention and John Mitchell's rise to the presidency suggests the uses of the incumbent's power. In late September 1898, UMW President Mike Ratchford, after emphatically vowing to the rank and file during his reelection campaign that he would not accept a government appointment, succumbed to the temptation and assumed a seat on the newly formed United States Industrial Commission.[51] He then proceeded to prepare the way for his first vice-president, John Mitchell, to rise to the presidency. While remaining official head of the union, Ratchford persuaded the executive board to install Mitchell as acting president, a post not provided for in the union's constitution. With this advantage Mitchell was able to build up a following by freely distributing strike aid to win support and by using his organizers to undermine the prestige of the opposition.[52] At the January 1899 convention, Mitchell was immune to

direct criticism, for Ratchford was official president and as such presided. He appointed men favorable to Mitchell to all the important
committees, including the one on credentials which admitted delegates and determined voting strength. One of Mitchell's opponents,
Pat Dolan, complained of these tactics and charged National Secretary-Treasurer W. C. Pearce with making false entries into the cash
book to pad the roll of delegates in Mitchell's favor. A move to call
for the official union books was defeated and Mitchell won the coveted office.[53]

III

The shortcomings of the convention—its inherent unwieldiness,
inefficiency, and susceptibility to manipulation—led many unionists in the decades around the turn of the century to champion the
referendum as a substitute for, or at least a supplement to, the official meeting. Labor's interest in the referendum, as well as initiative
and recall, manifested Populist and Progressive influences. In the
1890s and early 1900s men from all walks of life—farmers, lawyers,
educators, doctors, as well as workers—promoted a variety of reforms with the intent of shaping government more closely to the
ideal of participatory democracy. Under this influence a number of
unions and the American Federation of Labor went on record supporting referenda in civic affairs, and it was to be expected, given
the democratic impulse of the labor movement and the inadequacies
of the convention system, that these reforms would be advocated
for the trade union polity.

While a few champions of the referendum in union government
saw it as a means of manipulating their way to power, most workers
supported it on grounds of democratic principle—"namely, that each
individual member should be given a chance to express his opinion
on the questions submitted."[54] Believing in the wisdom of the
masses, they felt that giving everyone a voice in determining policy
and electing officers would prevent the rise of an oligarchy. To this
extent, the referendum was a decentralizing reform, transferring
authority from the few to the many.[55]

Advocates of the referendum also viewed it as a means of creating greater support for the union. "The success of any law," a printer pointed out, "depends very largely on the extent in which it is backed up by the sentiment of those to whom it is applicable. . . . It is better that the members should retain the right to pass upon all laws than that they should be restricted to complaining about them for a year [between conventions], without any opportunity to secure their amendment or repeal."[56]

Finally, advocates of referendum saw it as a means of supplementing conventions and making them more efficient. Fewer sessions would be necessary when much of the business was conducted by referendum. Within many organizations a direct correlation existed between the use of the referendum and the frequency of gatherings. During the sixteen-year interval, 1896 to 1912, between conventions of the Cigar Makers, and the thirty-two-year span between the Granite Cutter meetings of 1880 and 1912, both unions conducted most of their business by referendum.[57] The Furniture Workers' Union held its sessions biennially, the Machine Wood Workers' Union annually, but after they amalgamated, the conventions were held triennially and the referendum was introduced.[58] The quality of conventions also improved with the direct election of officers. "It was remarked on more than one occasion by those at Syracuse who had also attended previous sessions," observed a printer,

> that there was a marked improvement in the tone of the gathering, and that it was more business-like in every way, just because of the elimination of all the wire-pulling and caucusing incident to an election. It has been the experience at other conventions that the delegates seldom really got down to work until after the officers had been chosen, and as the practice was to have this on the fourth day—a proper idea, too, because it gave the delegates a chance to size up the merits of the candidates—a great deal of time was wasted. From the point of view of the transaction of convention business alone the present system of electing officers ought to be retained.[59]

Influenced by such arguments, several unions introduced some form of referenda. In response to a questionnaire sent out by the AFL in 1912, thirty-two unions reported that some form of referendum was used to elect officers, although seventy-nine reported that their conventions made the choice. At the same time fifty-two of the unions stated that the convention was the sole law-making body, while another fifty-two also made use of the referendum in determining policy. While not a clear majority, the number of unions utilizing the system was impressive.[60]

The gap between the number of unions using the referendum to enact laws and the number using the system to elect officers leads to an interesting observation. Using the same 1912 AFL study, it was pointed out in chapter four that while an average of fifty-eight percent of the membership voted in unions using the referendum to elect officers, only thirty-three percent voted in those organizations using the system only to enact laws. From this discrepancy it was concluded that the selection of leaders seemed to be the important force in turning out voters and that the rank and file were not policy oriented.[61] Yet the figures above show that significantly more unions were willing to allow the rank and file to vote on laws than were willing to have them elect officers. In short, the members were frequently given the right to vote on subjects that did not interest them and denied a voice on the business which they felt were important.

This discrepancy no doubt contributed to the failure of the referendum to live up to expectations. Even the system's most avid champions were forced to admit after time "that the referendum as we have had it has not been all it was intended to be."[62] In referendum after referendum, membership participation fell short of even minimal expectations. In 1901 the *Typographical Journal* lamented, "Of a membership of 32,105 in the typographical union and allied crafts, 11,741 succeeded in developing sufficient energy to cast a vote and have it counted."[63] In 1912 the Stationary Engineers held a referendum on providing death benefits in which only 3,000 out of 18,000 members participated.[64] In a referendum on the constitutional amendments proposed by the 1895 convention, only thirty-seven of ninety-three eligible unions sent in returns, leading the *Garment Worker* to bemoan: "This is not an encouraging showing, and indicates much apathy on the part of the members in the important changes made in the fundamental laws of the Union."[65] "Our experience with what we call referendum voting," summarized the Hotel and Restaurant

Employees' officers, "has been rotten. We have used every known device except penalizing our members to secure a fair measure of action and votes, but we have failed miserably."[66]

Nor did the results of the referendum substantiate the belief in the wisdom of the rank and file. There was, indeed, a flaw in the logic of the system's proponents. "The referendum was introduced because faith was lacking in the good, disinterested judgment of the convention delegates," observed economist Mark Perlman. "It is hard to see, however, how venality or stupidity among them can be prevented by referring all questions to the electorate who selected them."[67] Time and time again convention delegates would hammer out in debate resolutions which when submitted for approval to the membership would be defeated by the relatively few locals which bothered to vote. Any resolution which threatened to increase the financial burden on the members was almost predestined to defeat regardless of its worth.[68] A number of unions noted that the referendum resulted in excessive and inconsistent legislation and made the introduction of minor reforms a cumbersome process.[69] The Stationary Engineers, who beginning in 1904 required rank and file approval of all changes in their constitution, sought to clean up the document without making substantial alterations in its content. To do so they had to submit 102 different items to referendum votes and in the end the entire process created more confusion than it clarified.[70]

The judiciousness of the rank and file was most suspect in electing officers. While the direct election of officers provided a more democratic means of choosing leaders, it hardly improved the quality of men gaining office nor did it hinder the development of a power elite. Indeed, economist Theodore Glocker intimated in 1913 that popular elections in unions tended to prolong the tenure of existing administrations for "an outsider has greater difficulty in unseating the officer in power under the system of popular elections than under the system of election by conventions."[71] A number of unionists supported this view. "The difficulty of changing officers is very great," reported the ILGWU, "since the new men are unknown outside of their locality, while the old officers can retain their position through their influence. It is absurd for people to vote for officers whom they have never seen and know absolutely very little about."[72] "The failure or shortcomings of the initiative and referendum in the election of officers," concurred the Granite Cutters, "is that popular men are supported for election irrespective of their ability to perform their duty."[73] "I believe our organization in its entirety should have a vote on anything in regard to the organization," maintained a member of the Stationary Engineers, "but when it comes to the election of officers I want to know how you are going to educate the members of your different unions in regard to the men you nominate for office. . . . If you cannot trust the delegates who come here to the convention to elect proper officers you cannot trust your local organizations . . . I can go back to Syracuse and say, 'Murphy is a good fellow, Commerford is a good fellow, vote for them.' I cannot say that in the convention. The delegates see for themselves."[74]

On top of these shortcomings, the referendum proved as vulnerable as the convention to manipulation and corruption. Resolutions could be worded in such a manner as to circumscribe the real choice available to the electorate.[75] Another way to induce the rank and file to vote according to administration's wishes was, as Samuel Gompers advised the secretary of the National Union of Textile Workers, to delay the referendum until a period when "your trade will be most brisk" and discontent from unemployment reduced. Gompers also agreed to send out a circular on the proposal to the union's members in order to lend his prestige to that of the officers.[76] Desiring to circumvent the "unfounded prejudice" of the "self-governing masses" against increased levies, the delegates to one convention of the United Garment Workers' Union went into secret, executive session. As Secretary Henry White recalled:

> there each delegate was pledged to a plan to carry a referendum vote in favor of the question by causing a small attendance at the meeting at which the proposition was to be voted on, and by counting the absentees as voting in the affirmative. The national executive board being the court of last resort on all points of law, the success of the plan was never in doubt. Before the motion was carried, every aspiring delegate had to be assured privately where he "came in" on the jobs. In the discussion of the

proposition of imposing a tax in this way, the argument was made and generally assented to that the "benighted masses" had to be helped against their will, even by strategy and force. Since the members were unwilling to pay for the self-sacrificing work done for them, a way had to be found.[77]

Within the Typographical Union, reported one disgruntled member, many locals "took no steps to enable any but those present at the meetings to vote, while in some cases the secretary was instructed to cast the votes of the entire membership in favor of or against the proposition without consulting them."[78] Abuse of the system was particularly marked in the United Brotherhood of Carpenters after the turn of the century. According to Robert Christie, historian of the union:

One referendum vote compilation committee reported that "the present method of election of General Officers seems . . . to be a clumsy and costly one, and if continued will ultimately wreck the organization." The report went on to complain that the referendum system placed a "premium on illegal voting" and that the recording secretary of a local union could disfranchise the whole union by making some minor mistake in filing the returns "either through carelessness or intent."

Nor were such practices uncommon. Referring to the 1912 election, Thomas Ryan of New York, one of the tabulators, said "You could stretch out fifty or one hundred ballots on the table and even to a little curve on the cross all were alike." In the counting of the votes, "ballots were thrown out because they were folded and some were thrown out because they were not folded." Almost every election from 1904 to 1912 was disputed. The administration won each of them. President William L. Hutcheson subsequently admitted that the election in which he first assumed office (1913) was rigged.[79]

After several years of actual application, enthusiasm for the referendum began to wane among top union leaders and significant elements of the rank and file. As early as 1898, members of the Typographical Union began considering modifying or abandoning the system, and members of other unions soon followed suit.[80] By 1912, the comments of union leaders reporting to the AFL on their organizations' use of the referendum were for the most part pessimistic and unfavorable. Only twelve of the thirty-four unions were enthusiastic enough to recommend that the federation adopt it.[81] In the emerging arguments against the system, the opponents projected the values of efficiency, order, and centralization, basic to the image of the union as a business. In their eyes, the advocates of referendum were "radical students of social and political rights." "The theoretical dreamer," declared one opponent, "who can study the returns from the recent typographical union vote and not awaken to the futility of his plans, and the absurdity of their performance, holds to a nonsense which will, sooner or later, result in stoicism or idiocy." He continued, "To my mind the future usefulness of the International Typographical Union is gravely threatened by the recent vote. Centralization, the bugbear with which our agitators are want to conjure, is the goal that means our salvation."[82] Thomas Kidd, Secretary of the Amalgamated Wood Workers concurred, and in his parting remarks upon leaving office after fourteen years came down hard on referendum while at the same time promoting the virtues of bureaucracy:

> No fault can be found with the principles of the referendum, because all men should have a right to a voice and vote in the conduct and management of their organization. They ought to have a voice in the election of their officers. They ought, in fact, to have as much to say about the affairs in which they are interested, as any one else in the organization.
>
> But, after all, democracy in unionism is a hideous failure, and this applies with considerable force to at least 50 percent of the advanced unions, including the Amalgamated Wood Workers.
>
> We send our delegates to conventions to frame laws for us. These delegates adopt proposed amendments by unanimous vote, but if these amendments are likely to take a solitary cent from the pockets of the members, the members defeat them. The same is true in connection with the election of officers. Members will abuse the officials to their heart's content, and at the same time manifest absolute indifference in electing competent successors.
>
> Democracy in unionism is a failure. This was never demon-

strated to us more clearly than it is demonstrated in the Amalgamated Wood Workers' Union to-day. Certain propositions were approved by our second convention that would have meant much to our organization. Yet returns at present indicate that these much needed reforms will be defeated.

As we are retiring from the executive office of the Amalgamated organization, we can say without fear of being charged either with mercenary motives or a desire to acquire additional powers, that from our experience the only organization that can succeed effectively is one where power and responsibility are centralized. Never before have we been so firm in the belief that the so-called one-man power is the best power after all. The organization, however, should never surrender its right to recall an official who fails in the performance of his duty. If power and responsibility are centralized on men who are honest, able, and conscientious, then the power and responsibility will be used for the common good of all.[83]

IV

The conflict between the desire to prevent the aggrandizement of power in the hands of a few and the desire for harmony, unity, and efficiency also characterized the development of the executive board as an instrument of trade union polity. Prior to 1873, executive boards as such were nonexistent among major unions. The executive committees of such bodies as the Cigar Makers and the Bricklayers consisted of the national officers exercising judicial power; they did not represent distinct institutions. As unions matured and the powers of the national office expanded, however, delegates to union conventions—still champions of local autonomy—saw the creation of executive boards as means of preventing the concentration of authority in the national leaders' hands. "After 1875," Theodore Glocker observed, "a tendency to form general executive boards became manifest, and by 1880 such boards were being mantained by practically all existing national unions."[84] To curtail excessive authority, powers formerly exercised by the president and secretary were transferred to the newly formed boards. In many unions they became a court of appeal in judicial cases; they were also given authority to levy assessments, appoint temporary officers, and have a voice in declaring strikes.[85]

The composition of the emerging boards also revealed an attempt to counterbalance the power of the national officers. Unlike the earlier executive committees, the new bodies contained significant proportions of nonadministrative personnel. The Iron Molders' revised constitution of 1879 explicitly stated that board members must be "other than officers," and in many other organizations the executives were limited to a voice but not a vote in their board's deliberations. In a few unions including the early Carpenters', board members were chosen from the locals in the headquarter city so that they could easily be called together. Far more popular among unions was the practice of choosing the members on a district basis so that various regional interests would be represented.[86] A third method was for the board to be elected at large by the convention or the membership. In practice this often evolved into informal geographical representation. In 1892, for example, the seats on the United Mine Workers' board were filled without Illinois or Iowa having secured representation. As a result the convention simply increased the size of the body from four to six and chose Mr. Crawford of Illinois and Mr. Scott of Iowa as the new members.[87] Whether formal or informal, regional representation was a manifestation of decentralizing influences.

In the main, national officers strongly resisted the rise of executive boards, and conflict between the two parties abounded as long as the principle of checks and balances was upheld. Many leaders, including Terence Powderly, felt hurt that their authority and good intentions were questioned. To one correspondent the grand master workman revealingly wrote:

> If the matter of which you speak concerns the G.M.W. and he alone can attend to it, come up, if it requires action of an Executive Board nature, it must go to Philadelphia, for I will never again assume any responsibilities or take upon myself to do anything not strictly in line with my duties as laid down in the law, then if a wrong is done to any one it must be blamed upon

the law and not me. At any rate I will never again be called a dictator by men who profited most by the dictatorship. There was a time when this Order could not afford to employ an Executive Board, the G.M.W. then did all the work and paid for the privilege of doing it; the Order did not die under his management and if the day ever comes when a like service is necessary, the present G.M.W. is willing to undertake the work, but under present laws, present conditions, and under the present torrent of abuse that is being poured down upon me without a cause, I shall not stir hand or foot except in accordance with the strict letter of the law.[88]

A large part of the officials' resentment derived from the fact that the new boards attacked them personally. Thus, when the Iron Molders created a board which immediately charged President William Sylvis with misappropriating funds, he responded by dismissing most of its members.[89] Adolph Strasser fought a bitter battle with the Cigar Makers' executive board in 1883 as it sought to investigate charges that he had overstepped his authority.[90] Within the United Brotherhood of Carpenters the executive board became an instrument of the opposition in their efforts to overthrow the administration, first used in the 1890s against P. J. McGuire, and then in the 1900s against the William Huber–Frank Duffy machine.[91] Upon assuming the presidency of the Teamsters in 1908, Daniel Tobin was confronted with a cleavage in his executive board with half of its members openly hostile to him. In one instance the dissidents attempted to remove him from office on grounds that his election was illegal; at the same time they were encouraging a secession movement and organizing independent unions.[92]

Such disunity between officers and board members hindered the effectiveness of the respective organizations. "I think that it has been a detriment to our organization," observed one teamster, "to have members on the Board that did not work in harmony and it has handicapped us in lots of the fights that has [sic] come up."[93] Eventually, it became clear to unionists that some accomodation was needed for the sake of unity and efficiency.[94] Within some organizations, officers were given a vote in the board and were thus able to influence decisions. The Knights of Labor went even further in

1888 by choosing board members from a list of nominees drawn up by the general master workman.[95] As part of an administrative reorganization around 1903, the Electrical Workers curtailed the duties of their executive board and transferred many of their functions to the president.[96] The Typographical Union simply reduced the size of its board in 1900 to include only the union's president, secretary-treasurer, and three vice-presidents. "Many of us were afraid at the time we were making the Executive Council too small," a convention delegate later explained. "But we took the risk and the fruits of that action are apparent in the history of the Typographical Union. It has made the greatest progress since the [1900] convention . . . and it has been due absolutely I think to the centralization of authority and responsibility in the hands of a few men."[97]

Along with structural changes, more informal forces undermined the independence of the boards. Most unions failed to compensate board members adequately, forcing them to seek posts as organizers from the officers and thus fall under their purview. Moreover, the leaders' influence over conventions and referenda meant that aspiring board members desirous of advancing in the union hierarchy generally could not afford a direct confrontation with the leaders.[98]

Such developments, some consciously planned and others the result of circumstance, transformed the executive boards in much the same way as conventions had changed. The board's independence and its role as critic and conscience of the national union were sacrificed for the sake of harmony. Rejecting a plan for regional representation on the board, one printer expressed the emerging ethos in 1908 when he wrote that his union "is, and should be, one complete, harmonious, single body, in which sectionalism has had, and should have no place."[99] "To permit the members to properly place responsibility for the ails of the executive officers," explained another printer, "there should be no divided responsibility."[100] Even the AFL desired harmony among its officers; the 1908 convention went on record that it was the duty of officers who disagreed with various policies to resign their posts. "Such action would be honorable to themselves and advantageous to the movement."[101]

The diminished status of executive boards had its most unfortu-

nate consequence on unions' judicial processes. Unionists frequently expressed discontent with the vesting of judicial power in the
hands of the national executives. "To clothe any man or set of men
with judicial as well as administrative power," one printer raged,
"is undemocratic and un-American, is a violation of the rules of
common sense and the laws of logic, and ignores absolutely the
lessons of history and the teaching of universal human experience."[102] In response to such complaints, early executive boards
were empowered to serve as a court of appeal independent of the
officers. Yet their authority in this area was at times more fancied
than real. During the twelve-year period 1883 to 1895, for example,
the Cigar Makers' executive board received 264 appeals from the
decision of the president, but only overruled his judgment four
times. To be sure, the concurrence of the Cigar Makers' board in
the president's decisions reflect in part his basic judiciousness, yet
it also suggests that the board members were not as independently
minded as may have been wished.[103]

V

While the institutions designed to supervise and check the activities
of the executives—conventions, referenda, and executive boards—
proved inadequate for the task, the position of the national leaders
was strengthened by the creation of large administrative staffs. In
the sixty years prior to 1920, the executive branch of trade unions
passed through three general stages of development. Among the
early national organizations, when local autonomy prevailed, the
rather limited powers and duties of headquarters were divided
among several officers. The first constitution of the Typographical
Union in 1851 established a president, vice-president, recording
secretary, corresponding secretary, and treasurer, while the Iron
Molders' constitution of 1859 created the posts of president, recording secretary, corresponding secretary, treasurer, and door-
keeper. In general, the president acted as chairman of the conventions, the vice-president took his place when he was absent, and the

recording secretary kept the minutes of the sessions. Between gatherings, the corresponding secretary handled communications with the locals, the financial secretary collected the dues, and the treasurer managed the funds. Their work was seldom taxing. In 1863, the Iron Molders' financial secretary reported that he had neither corresponded with any of the local officers nor performed any work for the organization during his term. The union's corresponding secretary also complained of having too little to do, while the president pointed out that in order to feel useful each officer had tried to do the work of all the rest.[104]

As the responsibilities of the national headquarters increased and a desire for some efficiency emerged, union administration entered the second stage, in which a single paid officer performed all duties between conventions. Within the Iron Molders' Union after 1864, for example, all power—executive, judicial, and even legislative—was vested in the president when the convention was not in session. Similar authority was granted the head of the Sons of Vulcan. Within both organizations the leader acted as financial and corresponding secretary, organizer, editor of the journal, as well as judge in cases over the constitution and work rules. The only sphere where their powers were limited was over control of strikes. In this area, as pointed out in chapter three, local autonomy still prevailed.[105]

The third stage of development and the actual beginnings of administrative bureaucracy occurred when the business of the national office exceeded what one man could handle. Generally after considerable agitation by the overburdened leader, the offices of vice-president, treasurer, corresponding secretary, editor, and others were reinvested with power, given full-time salaried status, and made supervisory over a number of assistants.[106] From the days in 1886, for example, when the office of the newly formed AFL consisted of Samuel Gompers and his son Henry, who served as errand boy, the staff of the federation grew until by 1920 its payroll included 125 paid organizers alone.[107] That same year, the United Mine Workers employed 202 persons and paid $408,324 in salaries and another $368,223 in expense money. Beginning in 1916 there were enough traveling auditors on the union's staff for them to hold their own annual conventions.[108]

Centralization of power and an increase in staff did not in themselves create an administrative bureaucracy. Equally important was the emergence of a bureaucratic mentality among the participants, as the working-stiff was transformed into an organizational man. "Students of trade union development," economist Theodore Glocker cautioned, "must not forget that the early unionist was ordinarily without parliamentary or executive experience."[109] What little administrative background they had generally derived from dabbling in politics, membership in fraternal societies, or in the case of some of the foreign-born leaders through participation in unionism in their home country. New unions generally failed to establish any special criteria for office holding. Hopefully, a secretary could write and a treasurer could add, but on occasion their abilities were obviously limited. Men were often chosen for reasons other than administrative skill. In the United Mine Workers' union of the 1890s, for example, both Patrick McBryde and Michael Ratchford were placed in office partly because they had been injured in mining accidents and were unable to work in the coal fields.[110] Nor were most early labor leaders able to gain much experience on the job. Usually serving without pay, they labored at their trade by day and performed their union work during their free time at night. The responsibilities of leadership were so burdensome and the compensation so poor that men would only serve for a brief time; a number of offices consequently remained vacant. Moreover, some newly formed unions including the Journeymen Plumbers, in order to protect local autonomy and prevent the rise of a ruling clique, prohibited reelection of officers after a certain number of terms, thus limiting their ability to gain competence through experience.[111] Finally, the task confronting these ill-prepared men was enormous. "The General Secretary," the first issue of the Teamsters' magazine reported, "on taking hold of his office found himself in a position few men have been in. Fancy a man starting a new business venture without the customary preliminary of building up to the high standard gradually, and you have the situation which confronted the General Secretary on October first."[112] "Hell is paved with good intentions," Powderly had earlier explained to a disgruntled unionist, "so is the office of G[eneral] S[ecretary] T[reasurer], and the work rolls in so rapidly that the good intentions are sometimes forgotten."[113]

The problem of creating efficient administration, however, went beyond enlisting the services of skilled men for national posts. One of the major difficulties of the early labor movement was the fostering of a bureaucractic ethos in which each participant from the highest to the lowest would understand his responsibilities. The work of the national leaders was doomed to frustration unless their subordinates, particularly local and district officers, cooperated and conducted business through proper procedures.

Absence of bureaucratic values among early unions is reflected in the fate of Terence Powderly as he attempted to direct the Knights of Labor. Powderly has been continually faulted by historians for his shortcomings as an administrator. According to Norman Ware, he was "a talker, writer, agitator, but lacked executive ability and inclination;" he was "a windbag whose place was on the street corner rousing the rabble to a concert pitch and providing emotional compensation for dull lives. They should have thrown him out, but they did not."[114] To support their case, Ware and others have pointed to Powderly's extensive complaining about being overworked. Yet an examination of his correspondence reveals that these critics were insensitive to the problem and unresponsive to the evidence.

Powderly may not have been the best of all possible administrators. Yet his conduct as mayor of Scranton, Pennsylvania (a city of 45,000), from 1878 to 1884, commissioner-general of immigration from 1897 to 1902, and chief of the Division of Information of the Bureau of Immigration from 1907 to 1921 suggests that he must have had some talent along these lines. He accepted the position of grand master workman of the Knights in 1879 on a part-time basis, receiving $200 a year plus expenses while the grand secretary, who was to do most of the work, received $800.[115] Thus he felt justified in dividing his energies between the Order and his duties as mayor, his tea and coffee business, and the Irish Land League. Yet such an arrangement could not last long; the rank and file, ignoring his part-time status and the constitutional divisions of power, demanded his attention on every issue that arose. "One thing I do not like and that is the manner in which I must perform my duty," he wrote in 1883. "I sit here day after day as busy as a man can be for some eight or ten hours and answer questions that should be answered elsewhere. . . ."[116] Under such pressure, he abandoned his other activities and became a full-time servant of the Order. Yet the burden did not let up. "From behind the piles of letters ever before me," he wrote in 1884, "I can see but little of what is going on in the world except such matters as come directly before the order of the Knights of Labor. . . ."[117]

Powderly clearly perceived the lack of obedience and under-standing of proper administrative procedures on the part of sub-ordinates as a major cause of the Order's administrative difficulties. "I find as many letters ahead of me as you have at your office all from new Assemblies," he wrote to a fellow officer at the height of the great upheaval of 1886:

the organizers are woefully ignorant and I must add very unrea-sonable as well. Nearly every one of them ask for dispensation. There are over two hundred requests for dispensation to orga-nize, we must send out another circular and tell these men that our order was issued to be obeyed and if they do not feel dis-posed to comply with it then send back the Commission. If the men who teach will not obey their superior officers, then it can-not be expected that those whom they teach will do so.[118]

In another instance he wrote:

A man having in charge the welfare of hundreds of thousands must necessarily have matters of great importance thrust upon him at all times. The great, weighty questions of labor reform, demand that his attention should not be taken up with mere matters of detail: time and again have I notified the Order, through the Journal, to send such business as related to the Gen. Ex. Bd. to the Secretary of the same, yet in the face of that, thousands of letters that should go to brother Hayes are poured in upon me, this you will see can have but one effect, and that, to take up my time in matters of detail when I should be allowed to watch over the field at large.[119]

Typical of the "matters of detail" of which he complained was the following:

Dear sir and brother;—

The new charter was especially designed so that it could be suspended from the walls of the sanctuary. You do not require my permission to so suspend it.

With kind wishes I remain

Fraternally yours,
T. V. Powderly
G.M.W.[120]

In a sense, the Knights and their sister organizations served as schools for future union bureaucrats. A large number of later labor leaders at both the national and local levels gained their initial union experience in the Noble and Holy Order. Here they learnt the rudiments of administration, often to the detriment of the Order, by trial and error. The result of such experience became evident in more mature unions by the turn of the century. While not models of administrative efficiency, their press, convention proceedings, and files reveal a certain bureaucratic outlook. In selecting men for office, skills in administrating a union became more important than rhetorical talent. Local leaders knew their responsibilities and conducted business through proper channels. Neither Tobin nor Mitchell were flooded with the picayune correspondence which earlier had made its way across Powderly's desk. Moreover, the national labor leaders could delegate authority to trained, competent subordinates. Backing up Daniel Tobin in the Teamsters were Michael Casey, George W. Griggs, Michael Cashal, John M. Gillespie, as well as Secretary-Treasurer Thomas Hughes, all men with experience in running a large organization. A similarly competent crew including William B. Wilson, Tom L. Lewis, Chris Evans, Pat Dolan, and others supported John Mitchell. Indeed, when Mitchell stepped down in 1908, an excess of experienced men were eager to replace him.

VI

One of the most important developments in forging strong, national administrative staffs was the transformation of their positions from part-time offices receiving little or no remuneration to full-time, adequately compensated posts. During the formative years of the labor movement, the desire to protect local autonomy, a belief that the functions of the national office were not extensive enough to warrant a professional staff, and the simple lack of funds contributed to the unwillingness of newly created unions to provide for the financial needs of their national executives. As a result, early labor leaders were severely limited in advancing unionism. For example, Henry Miller, who was elected the first grand president of the National Brotherhood of Electrical Workers in 1891, was not compensated for his work. In attempting to extend the membership of the new organization, he was obliged to seek temporary employment in each city he visited. Not surprisingly, the results were unimpressive.[121] Likewise, both President White of the Bricklayers and President Tom Phillips of the Boot and Shoe Workers were among the many labor pioneers unable to fulfill their constitutional responsibilities because their respective conventions failed to provide funds, either in salaries or for traveling expenses.[122]

Even those early labor leaders fortunate enough to receive salaries often found them grossly inadequate. As head of the National Labor Union, Richard Trevellick was allotted $1,500 a year; John Siney was to receive $1,200 as president of the Miners' National Association; and the salary of Iron Molders' President William Sylvis was raised to $1,600 in 1867, "making him probably the highest paid labor leader in the United States. . . ."[123] The incomes stipulated in constitutional clauses or convention resolutions, however, bordered on fantasy, for the actual compensation given these men was generally far less. Of the $1,500 promised Trevellick, he received only $700.[124] Nor did Siney get his proposed $1,200. The Miners' National Association owed him a large sum in back pay when he left office in 1876, and his last official act was stoically to deny his secretary permission to raise the money.[125] The deflated incomes of these men were used to run the national administrations as well as to provide for their personal and family needs. Lacking an expense account, John Siney was obliged to pay out of his own pocket the cost of traveling and organizing.[126] Sylvis likewise was destined to remain on the edge of poverty, for as his biographer points out, "if something had to be done and there were no union funds with which to do it, he paid expenses out of his own pocket. He paid for the furniture in the International Union office; he paid large amounts on 'loans' to needy molders; he paid for his secret service to spy on employers, and when the union demanded an accounting, he chose rather to bear the expense personally than to reveal activities that publicity would render useless."[127]

Despite the heavy burdens created by their meager incomes, Sylvis, Siney, and Trevellick were nonetheless better able to contribute to the development of trade unionism than most of their fellow labor leaders. Working at trades during the day and for the union at night taxed the energies of many potentially valuable men, and this situation combined with inadequate remuneration led them to shun union office. In general, a correlation existed between compensation and the willingness of an incumbent to seek reelection. During the International Union of Stationary Engineers' first eight years, nine men held the sparingly paid, part-time post of general president.[128] Within the Iron Molders' Union, founded in 1859, the period of long presidential incumbencies dates from 1863, one year before the office was given a stipulated salary. From 1886 to 1900 the unremunerative office of president of the Carpenters was occupied by eight men, each serving one two-year term. Meanwhile, P. J. McGuire retained the post of secretary-treasurer which carried with it a salary amounting to $2,000 a year by the turn of the century.[129] Likewise, from 1892 to 1897, M. J. Counahan held the full-time, $1,200 a year position of secretary-treasurer of the plumbers' union. During his tenure, five men held the unpaid office of president and the eight non-salaried vice-presidencies had all changed hands.[130]

The initial drive to compensate national officers derived from the gradual realization by the rank and file that unions needed qualified men to handle their affairs. The fact that the officer performing clerical duties was frequently the first, or at least the highest paid functionary, reflected this awareness. The secretary-treasurer was the first full-time salaried post among the Carpenters, Journeymen

Plumbers, Hotel and Restaurant Employees, Sons of Vulcan, Brotherhood of Locomotive Engineers, Steam Engineers, as well as the Knights of Labor. In other organizations such as the Iron Molders, the Workingmen's Benevolent Association, the National Labor Union, and the AFL, the president was the first paid officer, but he performed many clerical tasks. There is some indication that centralized unions were more willing to give their leaders salaries than decentralized bodies which lacked the need for strong national officers, but the evidence, however, is by no means conclusive.[131]

Once unions decided to retain full-time, paid leaders, the issue of proper compensation emerged. Involved were not only financial considerations, but basic questions of union ideology. Should all leaders be paid equally or according to the task; or further, should their pay be commensurate with their skill and ability? Should they be paid the going wage offered by the capitalists to the working class or on the basis of what the workers ought to receive? Or perhaps should they be given salaries equal to their business counterparts?

These questions were posed in almost every union. "To the present and future officers," argued a typographer, "we should pay a salary more in keeping with the work that is to be done, the reputation of our organization, and the quality of brains that we require—and, last but not least, more nearly approximating what we ask our employers to pay us. . . ."[132] An old miner suggested that the salaries of UMW officials be based on a sliding scale adjusted to the prevailing price of three tons of coal, an arrangement which "would stimulate them to work for the advancement of the miners as it would also be an advancement to themselves."[133] The organ of the Window Glass Blowers reminded its readers that "you are the employer in this instance and should give your employees the same fair consideration you expect for your services. . . ."[134] The *Typographical Journal* agreed: "The Union should be a model employer."[135] "In order to get first-class leaders," the *Pattern Makers' Journal* maintained, "the union must pay first-class salaries. That is the only way the corporations can enlist capable men in their service, and trade unions can accomplish the same results only by doing likewise."[136] Some unionists were skeptical of business parallels. "Fair wages for all our members and good salaries for our officers should be the slogan," insisted one printer, "but we had better not follow the example of the corporations too far along these lines."[137] One Wobbly took a more adamant stand. After pointing out the meager earnings of the average working-stiff, he concluded: "I do not believe our officers should be paid a bourgeois salary of $1,500 a year."[138]

Despite rigorous debates, the issues discussed generally had little impact on the original salaries paid the officers. The realities of the situation limited the sum to whatever the union's treasury could afford, one which was frequently below the wages of the membership. Advances in salary came slowly at first, and occasionally the leaders lost ground. The salary of the secretary of the Brick-layers is a case in point:

> The international union was formed in 1865; in 1867, the secretary was voted a salary of $500, which was eliminated in 1871, restored to half its former amount in 1871, reduced to $150 in 1877, to $100 the following year, and eliminated in 1879. In 1882 it was decided, "That if it be found at the next Convention that more than sufficient money is on hand to defray the expenses of the Union for the past year, Brother Carpenter, National Secretary, shall receive the surplusage, provided the same shall not exceed one hundred dollars." Brother Carpenter received $100 for his labor. In 1883 the salary was raised to $250; the following year to $300; and in 1886, it was doubled so that, for the first time, it exceeded the level at which it stood in 1867. Nor had the heady inflationary process spent itself: the secretary was paid $800 in 1887, $1,000 in 1888, and $1,200 in 1889.[139]

Such experiences lend justification to the lamentations of the *Pattern Makers' Journal* that "it has always been an unfortunate characteristic of workingmen that, while they ask for higher wages, they are unwilling to pay high wages to their own representatives."[140]

After the turn of the century, however, earnings of labor leaders improved considerably. Between 1900 and 1920 the salary of the Typographical Union's president rose from $1,475 to $5,000; that of the head of the Journeymen Plumbers from nothing to $3,000. The income of the president of the Operative Engineeers went from zero to $6,000; the compensation of the Grand Chief of the Locomotive

Engineers from $5,000 to $10,000; and Gompers's remuneration as head of the AFL went from $2,100 to $10,000.[141] A debate may prevail among economists on the ability of unions to improve drastically their members' earnings, but the figures above leave little doubt of the ability of unions to increase their leaders' incomes.

The rationale for wage increases after the turn of the century was connected with the emerging image of the union as a business. After pointing out the contributions of Samuel Gompers and Frank Morrison to "the splendid growth and high standing" of the AFL, a resolution offered at the Federation's 1914 convention continued: "The salaries paid these officials in comparison with salaries paid to officials occupying positions of far less importance and responsibility in our industrial establishments is much too small. . . ."[142] A typographical worker, impressed by the increased workload of the national officers, pointed out that "when a business house or corporation increases the work and responsibility of its officials, an increase in salary usually goes with it, or follows shortly afterwards," and called upon his fellow workers to pursue the same policy.[143] "Many will say that they [labor leaders] are paid enough to meet all the advances in living expenses, and still be able to save a little by the practice of economy," wrote another printer.

> If we would, however, look at the corporations we might learn
> something from them. Although they are generally deemed soul-
> less, it is a fact that they recognize ability, and they have, and do
> from time to time, advance the salaries of the men employed in
> executive positions. I do not believe that there is a corporation
> in the United States doing one-third the business of the Inter-
> national Typographical Union that does not pay larger salaries
> to their executive officers than we do.[144]

By and large, the leaders were pleased with salary increases. To be sure, there were a few stoic figures like Andrew Furuseth, head of the International Seamen's Union, who would accept only such compensation as would cover his minimum needs (Furuseth fortunately being a bachelor).[145] But the protestations against salary increases by most labor leaders were more self-serving than sincere. In 1882 Powderly threatened to resign as grand master workman if the Knights increased his salary; probably he feared the commensurate amount of work he would be called upon to perform.[146] Three years later, however, after his work load had increased anyway, in order to pave the way for a salary raise, he let it be known that he had been offered a $1,500 a year position with the Provident Life and Trust Company. This tactic worked, for the following year he was granted a yearly income of $5,000, making him the highest paid labor leader of the Gilded Age.[147]

Samuel Gompers also struck the posture of opposing large salaries for labor leaders. "It is a mistake," he argued in 1894, "to pay a man so high a salary in the labor movement that he shall be in his method of life so far removed from the wage-workers as probably to ween them from their conditions and interests and possibly from sympathy with his fellow-workers."[148] This statement, one suspects, was made partly for public relations purposes, as it came after six years of subtle agitation by Gompers for a wage increase during which time his salary rose from $1,000 in 1887 to $1,800 by 1892. Nor did he press his case against large salaries hard enough to forestall further advances: in 1899 his salary was made $2,100; 1902, $3,000; 1907, $5,000; 1914, $7,500; 1919, $10,000.[149] Gompers mildly objected to the last two raises, not because he did not think a labor leader should receive such sums—by then he clearly thought they should—but because of the false impression they gave the unorganized. "When I was in Europe as a fraternal delegate five years ago," he asserted in 1914, "one of the biggest things that was hurled against our movement and against me in Paris was the idea of a man in the labor movement getting 25,000 francs a year. We have a great mass of men and women of labor who are yet unorganized and while you who have worked with me so long would understand, to them a salary of such character would be appalling. . . ."[150]

Several leaders in the labor movement were more open about wanting higher salaries. While John Mitchell acted as though pay raises were a secondary consideration for him and maintained that he would not accept one if anyone opposed, his vice-president, Tom L. Lewis, was more candid. "I am one of the people who if I think my services are worth a certain sum are going to ask for it, and if I don't get it I am going on strike," he informed the 1900 UMW convention.[151] Daniel Tobin of the Teamsters took a similar stand, and even Sidney Hillman of the newly formed Amalgamated Clothing Workers revealed anxieties over his income when he complained that it could only be raised by a referendum vote.[152] Perhaps the most revealing attitude on the subject is found in a private letter from Daniel Keefe of the Longshoremen to John Mitchell, dated 1901:

> The Convention held at Toledo turned out just as I wanted it. They gave me an increase in salary of $300.00 for the year, leave of absence of two months and allowed me some $500.00 and some odd dollars which I expended for the Organization in one way and another during the last year, so you can see that things were handled in a practical and business like way.[153]

Initial pay increases were justified on the grounds of the immense amount of work which labor leaders performed as well as to compensate for the past hardships of self-sacrificing men. "In accepting the position of chief officer of the Knights of Labor at a salary of $1,500 a year," Powderly wrote to a carping critic, "I did it knowing that the compensation was not in proportion to the amount of work to be done. I work from sixteen to eighteen hours a day, I have not known a holiday for the last seven years. You will see by that that my actual pay for labor done is about 23 cents an hour. If I were actuated by a desire to accumulate wealth I would not give my services for that figure."[154] To this argument, Gompers added: "It is true that I am receiving a salary to-day and have received a pitiable one for a number of years, but these upstarts may not be aware that hundreds of men have worked for years in the cause without any recompense whatever. They do not know that from 1881 to 1886 there was not one solitary cent paid to any officer of the Federation, and but a very few dollars were expended except for printing, stationery, and postage."[155]

One may believe, however, that increasingly after the turn of the century, salary advances were related in part to status anxieties of both union members and leaders. Advocates of pay raises constantly brought forth comparisons of the salaries given to leaders of other unions. "What do the railway engineers and firemen, who pay their executive officers $5,000 a year think of us? Or the mine workers, who pay their president $3,000 and their secretary $2,400, or the glass bottle blowers, who pay their president $2,400, or the Carpenters who pay $2,000?" asked the *Typographical Journal* in 1907.[156]

By 1920 many labor officials were receiving incomes of $5,000 and above, and a leader's prominence in the movement was roughly correlated to his salary. As Victor Thompson writes in *Modern Organization:*

> Above a certain level it would seem that salaries are to some rather large extent a function of status—the higher the status, the higher the salary. In fact, it would seem that salaries operate chiefly as symbols of status rank. That the perquisites and conveniences of the work situation are distributed according to status rather than organizational need is common knowledge, and it has been argued that they are distributed in inverse ration to need. These perquisites also act as symbols, and along with other symbols . . . help to maintain the status system by increasing its visibility.[157]

Creation of full-time, salaried executives had a tremendous impact on the evolution of labor union leadership. Grants of authority through constitutional provisions or convention resolutions bore little relationship to a leader's actual power as long as he was unable to fulfill his assigned duties for lack of financial backing. The 1891 constitution of the Electrical Workers, for example, created a centralized organization with considerable power granted to the national leader. Yet, prior to 1903, the International officers went without regular salaries and were forced to work at their trade to earn a living. Unable to devote sufficient time to the affairs of the union, they were incapable of making locals comply with constitutional provisions. As a result, members frequently disregarded national obligations and the more powerful locals came to regard themselves as virtually autonomous. They plunged into illegal and poorly planned strikes, while the International was too weak even to exercise its expulsion powers. Finally, at the 1903 convention, the delegates granted the Electrical Workers' president a sufficient salary and instructed him henceforth to devote all his time to the Brotherhood. "The adoption of this policy," commented Michael Mulcaire, a student of the organization's early development, "was an important event in the history of the Union, because it marked the transformation of the International from a decentralized and discredited association to a centralized and respected organization."[158]

Besides enabling leaders to control union affairs better, the establishment of salaries made union posts more attractive to qualified men. Within many unions, the earnings of the national officers compared favorably with those of workers in the trade as well as small businessmen. In 1910, for example, the salaries of the president and secretary of the Journeymen Plumbers were more than twice the estimated yearly income of an average plumber in Chicago, a high wage city.[159] With fattening pay checks, as was noted earlier, leaders were more willing to remain in office for several terms. And as a number of advocates of efficient union administration maintained, longer tenures in office enabled men to develop expertise and also strengthened the organization by promoting a continuity of policy.

Finally, salaries paid to leading union officials by 1920 contributed to the widening gap in life style and outlook between the leaders and the led. *Literary Digest* exaggerated when it declared in 1920 that "Labor Pays Its Leaders Capitalist Wages," yet their remuneration was impressive. As president of the AFL, Gompers received $10,000 a year, the same sum given Warren Stone, head of the Locomotive Engineers. Longshoremen President T. V. O'Connor got $7,500; Marden Scott of the Typographical Union, $5,000; and William Johnson of the Machinists, $4,200, raised to $7,500 the following year. The basic compensation of other national leaders in 1920 fell between $4,500 and $10,000.[160] On top of these figures, the leaders were reimbursed for money spent on union work, a practice not enjoyed by earlier union pioneers. In 1907, for example, James Lynch received a base salary of $2,000 as president of the ITU. Another $400 was added for being an officer in the Union Printers' Home Corporation, and $1,947.19 was paid as "expenses."[161] In 1918, Gompers's reimbursement for expenses exceeded his salary for the year, $8,516.61 to $7,500.[162]

The reporting of such figures should in no way detract from the sacrifice such men made for the labor movement. They worked hard for their money, and many could, and several eventually did, earn more in private business. "I should say, considering the general ability and the powers for organization which Samuel Gompers has," appraised George E. Holmes, general manager of the Industrial Relations Service, "that he would be worth $100,000 a year to large interests which could afford to pay him all that he is worth."[163] Yet their salaries were clearly beyond the income of the average work-man. As of 1917-18, Scott Nearing wrote:

> The American wage—the amount paid by American industry to its workers—may be characterized briefly in these terms. A comparatively small percentage (from 5 to 10 in 100) of the persons gainfully employed in modern industry are on a salary basis. The vast majority of the employees (from 90 to 95 in 100) are paid a wage or its equivalent. Among those who work for wages, the great majority (about nine-tenths of the adult males) receive wage rates of $1,000 per year or less. The wage-rates of two-thirds of the males falls below $750; a third below $500. These statements make no allowance for unemployment, which is a constant, irreducible factor.[164]

VII

The most important addition to the personnel of the national office was a corps of organizers. Although in some early unions organizers were elected by the convention delegates or chosen by the executive board, by the turn of the century they generally were dependent upon the national officers who hired, fired, and paid them and directed their activities. Union constitutions usually provided little guidance as to the work of organizers; they were to be utilized as the national executive saw fit. In performing their assigned tasks, they were of invaluable service to the labor movement—in spreading unionism to unorganized territories, in conducting strikes and aiding in collective bargaining, and in giving general guidance to locals. They were the liaison men of unionism, coordinating the activities of the subordinate bodies with the desires of the national office; they were the eyes and ears of the national executives, increasingly isolated from personal contact with the rank and file by barriers of excessive duties and bureaucracy.

Yet organizers were also the ward heelers in a leader's political machine. Whichever officer commanded the organizers generally commanded the national staff. For this reason, power struggles between the secretary-treasurers and presidents of the Carpenters, Hotel and Restaurant Employees, and other unions and federations frequently focused on control of organizers. The positions were of considerable patronage value for the officer who controlled them. The work was interesting, not excessively demanding, and respectably compensated. Around 1902, agents for the Carpenters were receiving a healthy four dollars a day, while eight years later the salaries of organizers for the Journeymen Plumbers were more than eighty percent higher than the earnings of workers in the craft.[165] Those blessed with the posts carried into the field all the powers of the executive, which they were expected to wield in the officer's favor. In a 1912 report, President William Huber of the Carpenters expressed a familiar hope among labor leaders "that every officer of the Brotherhood, as well as all of our organizers and business agents will . . . see to it that a favorable vote is rendered from their district."[166]

A humorous but revealing incident stemming from the use of organizers for political purposes occurred in the United Mine Workers in 1899. In John Mitchell's campaign for reelection as union president, he faced a forceful challenge from Pat Dolan, head of District 5 in western Pennsylvania. To undermine his opponent's support in his home territory, Mitchell forged an alliance with the district's secretary-treasurer, William Warner. With this aid Mitchell won the coveted post, and a month later received a request from Warner asking him to reciprocate, for Dolan was after the secretary-treasurer's scalp. Against the district president's protest, Mitchell sent two of his most faithful organizers to work for Warner's reelection and also instructed his friend to pick one or two men from the Pittsburgh area to campaign for him and to send the bill to the national office.

Somehow Dolan got possession of the letters and showed them around, thereby creating strong anti-Mitchell sentiment. To offset this turn of events, Mitchell sent the following to Warner:

> I desire to ask you to come on to Indianapolis so that we can fix up letters from you to me which will justify answers such as I sent, so that I shall be in a position to defend myself. If everyone knew Dolan as well as you and I do there is no reasonable miner who could take exception to those letters, but the fact that the

mine workers generally do not know whether Dolan is a good or a bad man makes it necessary that I be placed in a position that will not compromise me in the eyes of the miners, or in our convention.[167]

Warner made the requested trip and the necessary falsification occurred. He then took the "revised" correspondence back home, where he arranged to have it published in the *Lonaconing Review* as a counterattack on Dolan. Ironically, the incompetent Warner, who first blundered by letting Dolan get the original letters, now gave the *Review*'s editor the doctored correspondence *plus* Mitchell's letter cited above explaining that they were fake. Warner caught the mistake before the printed copies were distributed and under orders from Mitchell had them all destroyed at union expense. As an epilogue to the story it should be noted that Warner lost his bid for reelection, but Mitchell took care of him by appointing him a national organizer![168]

Mitchell's use of organizers, while ethically suspect, was condoned by the informal canons of labor leadership. If the tables had been reversed, Dolan undoubtedly would have done likewise. As Robert Christie pointed out for the Carpenters, the men who attacked P. J. McGuire for running a leadership dominated, undemocratic union, turned around after gaining power in 1902 and "filled the void with swarms of professional organizers and hence a political machine. . . ."[169] Jere L. Sullivan, secretary-treasurer of the Hotel and Restaurant Employees, was able to make and break presidents through his control of organizers. Desiring Ed Flore to win the post of president in 1909, he appointed a number of the candidate's friends as organizers and sent them to those parts of the country where Flore needed support. When the incumbent president complained, Secretary Sullivan simply hid behind legalities:

> You forget that International Organizers are *my* jurisdiction. Kovaleski is a competent organizer. What he does in his free time is his own business. As soon as he falls down on the job, I'll take him off the payroll and not before.[170]

The backbone of the Gompers machine in the AFL likewise was a corps of organizers. Numbering about eight in 1888, the ranks grew to seven hundred by the turn of the century, over two thousand by 1919, about one hundred twenty-five of which were receiving regular salaries.[171] "Their chief function was to organize workers into unions," biographer Bernard Mandel points out, "but they also served as Gompers' informants on local conditions and as his agents in helping settle disputes, to advise the local unions, and to carry out his policies. They were responsible to no one but Gompers, and their jobs depended on their performing in a manner satisfactory to him."[172]

VIII

Complementing the mechanisms of power within each organization, particularly after the turn of the century, were associations of unions designed to advance their common interests. Dominated by the leadership of the member unions, associations in the building trade, railroading, and other industries saw as one of their functions the suppression of rebellion and secession movements, and thus by implication the perpetuation of the existing power elites. Five printing trades which joined together in an alliance around 1909 pleged

> that when any union or members or groups of members subordinate to any one of the five International Unions making up the International Allied Printing Trades Association secede from the present organization, the five International Unions will join in a general movement against the seceders and to the end that the supremacy and authority of the International organizations affected may be clearly and permanently established, the five International Unions pledge their moral and financial support. . . .[173]

The most powerful of such alliances in terms of total membership was the American Federation of Labor. The ethos of the Federation had changed markedly from its pioneer days in the 1880s. After the turn of the century, AFL President Samuel Gompers functioned as the servant of business union bureaucrats. "And business unionism," Bernard Mandel points out, "had a different meaning in 1900 than it did in 1875. Gompers had established business unionism in the cigar industry primarily as a means of bringing order and regularity into the union. It was a means of strengthening the union in its battles with the employers; it was a disciplined solidarity. But in the twentieth century, his conception of business unionism was that of unions run by their leaders—machine rule by the 'experienced officers'—engaged in the business of supplying labor to employers at prices fixed by contractual arrangement."[174]

The Federation's labor conventions reflected the domination of the organization by national union leaders. At the 1919 convention of the AFL, Margaret Bonfield, a visiting fraternal delegate from the British Trades Union Congress, implied in a speech that the gatherings of the TUC were far more democratic than the present meeting since delegates to the congress were mostly rank and file while the convention of the AFL was composed of labor leaders. Delegate John P. Frey—who was also vice-president of the Molders' Union, perennial secretary of the Committee on Resolutions at the AFL conventions, a member of the first and second labor missions sent to the Allied countries by the AFL during World War I, and soon to become president of the Ohio State Federation of Labor—felt compelled to reply. With such credentials it was obvious that in his rejoinder he had to admit that the Federation was leadership dominated, so he challenged Miss Bonfield with the argument that the same situation existed in England.[175]

In order to encourage national unions to join the Federation, the AFL established at its founding the principle of noninterference in the internal affairs of affiliates. The organization violated this policy on several occasions, in one instance by preventing W. C. Pomeroy of the Hotel and Restaurant Employees from expelling his opposition from the union.[176] Yet the principle remained the official stand of the organization and increasingly was construed in a manner which perpetuated the existing power structure within unions. Hiding behind the principle, the AFL's executive council allowed corrupt leaders to retain their positions of power. In 1905, for example, the council turned down an appeal from San Francisco Teamsters to remove President Cornelius P. Shea, indicted for extortion in relation to a strike at Montgomery Ward in Chicago. "He is a disgrace to himself, a dishonor to the teamsters of the country and a stain to the labor movement," the plaintiffs pleaded. Yet the executive council, which had breached the principle in other cases, did not feel that these grounds warranted a violation of the union's autonomy.[177]

The policy of noninterference was more blatantly used to perpetuate the existing leadership of a union at the AFL's 1914 convention. Earlier that year the United Garment Workers experienced a major rank-and-file revolt spearheaded by Sidney Hillman against the corrupt and tyranical administration of Thomas A. Rickert. At the following AFL convention both factions sent delegates and demanded representation. The Hillman UGW was never allowed to testify before the gathering, and the Credentials Committee, comprised of established labor leaders, recommended the seating of the Rickert faction over the rebels on the grounds that the former had been known to the AFL as the officers of the Garment Workers and the latter were unknown. "If the labor movement should follow this rule in all cases," the frustrated rebels pointed out, "it would make it impossible for any union ever to change its officers, for the old officers are always the ones that are 'known' and the new are always 'unknown.' Yet, this strange rule, laid down by the Credential Committee, was accepted as sufficient grounds for seating as tailor delegates persons not representing tailors."[178] Continuing with the perverted policy of noninterference, President Gompers and Secretary Morrison sent to the members of the divided union a circular under the AFL letterhead declaring the Rickert faction as the official United Garment Workers.[179] Turned away by the convention, the rebels took the only honorable course left open and formed the Amalgamated Clothing Workers. Now they confronted the problem of being branded a dual union by the Federation.

The AFL's policy toward dual unions added to the importance of the leaders' power to revoke charters of rebellious locals. If the expelled local decided to go it alone as an independent body, it found the whole of the American Federation of Labor against it. According to the AFL's constitution:

> No Central Labor Union, or any other central body of delegates, shall admit to or retain in their councils delegates from any local organization that owes its allegiance to any other body, or that has been suspended or expelled by, or not connected with, a

National or International organization of their trade hereinafter
affiliated. . . .[180]

Thus a local union which displeased the parent organization and had
its charter withdrawn was placed outside the pale of the labor movement. Limited to its own resources, its contracts and strikes were not
recognized by the Federation and the jobs of its members were open
game for any interested union.

Finally, the AFL served as a refuge for labor leaders rejected by
their followings. John A. Moffitt, president of the United Hatters
since 1898, was finally removed from office by reform forces in 1911.
Samuel Gompers quickly came to his aid and made him an AFL
legislative agent.[181] Likewise, after his ouster from the presidency
of the Machinists in 1912, James O'Connell continued to serve as a
vice-president of the AFL and was made president of the Metal
Trades Department with Gompers's aid.[182] Albert Berres of the
Pattern Makers, John B. Lennon of the Journeymen Tailors, and
Hugh Frayne of the Sheet Metal Workers were among the other
union leaders who retained positions in the AFL after they no longer
held offices in their respective unions.[183]

IX

By 1920 the general structure of union government tended toward
leadership domination. On the one hand, the institutions designed to
check and supervise the executives had proved inadequate for the
task. Conventions met too infrequently, were too large, and were too
dependent upon the directions of the national officers to serve as a
meaningful control. Referenda failed to provide a medium for rank-
and-file sentiment, and led to confusion and chaos detrimental to
the efficient operations of the union. Conflict and bickering between
the early executive boards and the national officers was also detrimental and eventually resulted in the boards transformation from
instruments to check the authority of the leaders to an agency to
work harmoniously with them. On the other hand, the executive's

position was directly strengthened through creation of an extensive administrative bureaucracy. Staff positions were a source of patronage by which the officers could build their own political machine. Through their chosen agents the leaders effectively wielded their basic powers of the press, purse, and punishment. Finally, in supporting their authority, the established executives were aided by various craft associations as well as the American Federation of Labor.

The dominance of the national leaders over their unions enabled them to work effectively on labor's behalf. They could make those quick decisions frequently needed to turn the tide of events to the union's favor. Strategy could be developed and negotiations pursued without the constant threat of an uninformed rank and file taking blundering action. Yet domination could also lead to abuse. When an irate rank and file rebelled against its leaders, the national administration controlled the means of suppression. As Sylvia Kopald points out repeatedly in her study *Rebellion in Labor Unions*:

> the officials controlled the union treasury upon which they could draw "to save the union", while the funds of the insurgents were of necessity uncertain and inadequate. They could get out anti-insurgent propaganda through official letters and circulars and spread them over a wide territory. They possessed full membership address books and established publicity machinery. They had the advantage of superior training in propaganda, publicity and procedure. They could place at strategic points experienced "talkers" and organizers. They could promise the full power of the central office to protect the "loyal men" and could distribute awards and punishments. They could wield the last weapon by ejecting the too stubbornly rebellious from the union. They made full use of all this machinery.[184]

6.

The New Men of Power

I

The preceding chapters have explored the forces underlying the evolution of union leadership in the decades prior to 1920. They have focused on the changing images of the union in terms of its internal power structure; the impact of evolving union-management relations on union officers; the role of the rank and file in encouraging leadership domination; and the evolution of the mechanisms of power toward creating strong national executives. Throughout, the men holding national office have been treated as playing a subordinate role in the process. In a sense, they were prisoners of historical forces, unknowingly confined by the perimeters of their situation. Within these limits, however, their activities added to the evolution of union leadership.

The life of a national labor leader was not an easy one. Union work probably taxed least the earliest officers, whose duties were limited in order to protect local autonomy. The burden on the leaders correspondingly increased as the central headquarters assumed greater responsibilities. An unending torrent of mail to answer, records to keep, charters, receipts, and funds to disperse bogged down the poorly paid secretaries. Amidst the frantic routine, they dashed off articles for the journal, sent the edition to press, and then addressed envelopes hoping to have the journal in the mail only a week behind schedule. Meanwhile, presidents and vice-presidents dashed across the country, lecturing here, advising strikers there, organizing a local elsewhere; all the while living in cheap hotels or accepting makeshift accommodations from sympathizers they met along the way. In 1869, President Richard Trevellick of the National Labor Union spent 169 days traveling and holding meetings, a record to be surpassed by a number of later leaders, among them John Mitchell, who recorded on June 1, 1906 that he had not seen his children since Christmas.[1] Weary from travel, the early leaders' spirits were seldom bolstered by the reception they received. The initial volumes of the *United Mine Workers' Journal* as well as other labor publications contained countless stories of men journeying

> from ten to fifteen miles at a time over mountains and rivers and forging the same up to their knees in water in the midst of rain and snow in order to keep their promises and not disappoint their constituents. After surmounting all these obstacles, both footsore and hungry and wet to the skin, they were rewarded with the presence of 20 or 30 men when there should be at least two hundred. Was this not discouraging to men who suffered so much to give us an idea of what our duty is to ourselves and our fellow men. . . .[2]

Larger salaries, expense accounts, and an increased staff reduced some of the basic discomforts for later labor leaders. While on the road at night, they could go to sleep after a good meal in a comfortable hotel or a rolling Pullman car, secure in the knowledge that their families were adequately fed and clothed and that some minor but annoying piece of union business was being handled by a competent subordinate. Yet they needed that good night's sleep, for their job was still extremely taxing. Controlling their own organizations and participating in union-management affairs constituted heavy burdens in themselves. Moreover, the increased influence of unions and the resulting prominence of their officers put greater demands on the leaders' time. They conferred far more frequently than their predecessors with presidents, governors, mayors, Congress, state legislatures, and a host of investigatory commissions; and served as members on numerous governmental committees as well as in private groups from the National Civic Federation to the Federal Council of Churches to the American Legion. Middle-class clubs and universities asked them to lecture, while popular magazines constantly sought their views. And added to the expansion of their duties was the increased pace of work. Improved transportation got leaders more places, faster, and with less time for contemplation. Better communication, likewise, enabled quicker decisions which were often more advantageous to the movement but more tiring to their maker. No wonder when Grand Chief Warren Stone of the Locomotive Engineers was asked in 1911 the secret of his success he attributed it "largely to the fact that I have an iron constitution and can work eighteen hours a day year in and year out; success you know is only another name for hard work."[3]

Illustrative of the demands on union leaders and the pace with which they moved was Samuel Gompers's itinerary during one month in 1902:

> The Federation convention in New Orleans adjourned at three in the morning on November 23, 1902. The same day he held a conference with representatives of various labor organizations and a meeting with the Executive Council. Two days later he was in Birmingham to address a mass meeting. He returned to Washington on the 28th, and four days later went to Hartford, Connecticut, to attempt to adjust a dispute between the Horse Nail Makers Union and the Capewell Horse Nail Company. The following day he was in Boston, where on successive evenings he lectured at Faneuil Hall and debated with Louis D. Brandeis on the incorporation of unions. Stopping at New York to address the National Civic Federation, he returned to the capital to make appearances before a Senate committee considering the eight-hour bill. He went back to New York the next day to lecture on strikes to the League for Political Education, returned to Washington, and stayed only a few hours, when he was called to Scranton to testify before the Anthracite Coal Strike Commission. He returned to his office on December 18. During that month he sent out some 5,000 letters, of which he probably dictated 500 personally.[4]

Even when Gompers stayed at headquarters, his work day was exhausting. "More often then not," he recorded, "it was midnight before I got home—there were meetings, speeches to make, conferences to attend, for the cause of labor is no easy mistress to serve."[5]

Added to the strain of long hours and hard work, leaders were under constant tension from fear of personal danger. Defenders of the status quo in America have always been preoccupied with the role of leadership in social movements. Like the misguided terrorists of the Left and Right, they believed that by separating the leaders from the led they could abate the challenge to their authority. The actions of various anti-union employers, their henchmen and sympathizers should have awed even the more extreme advocates of "propaganda by deed." "Last Thursday morning," reported the *United Mine Workers' Journal* in May 1894, "President McBride received, through the mail, what, to all appearances, was a diabolically constructed infernal machine, composed of death-dealing constituents."[6] The next month the *Journal* disclosed that "a Dastardly attempt has been made to kidnap W. B. Wilson, a member of the national executive board, in the Frostburg, Md. district, by certain coal operators there. 'Billy' escaped the trap, but has evidence that a cowardly conspiracy and scheme existed to spirit him away for an indefinite period."[7] On his way to Pueblo, Colorado in March 1904, sixty-three-year-old Chris Evans, a member of the Mine Workers' executive board and previously secretary of the AFL, was brutally assaulted while on a Chicago and Southern passenger train by three masked men who used the butt end of their revolvers on his head and face, inflicting from fifteen to twenty deep gashes.[8] In Clarksburg, West Virginia in 1910, ten thugs ganged up on two more UMW executive board members, leaving them both badly injured.[9] And in Glassmere, Pennsylvania in October 1916, gunmen presumably hired by nonunion coal companies made an attempt on the life of UMW President John P. White.[10]

Nor were the officers of the Mine Workers the only victims of terrorism. While precise records are unavailable, the pioneers of unionism no doubt lived in greater anxiety than their more established successors. During a strike in Leadville, Colorado in 1880-81 and the Rio Grande Strike of 1884-85, Joseph Buchanan of the Knights of Labor lived in fear of assassination or lynching by a mob. In the second strike he went so far as to hire a detective to investigate menacing rumors, and spent most of the conflict boxed up in his newspaper office under the protective guard of a shooting club composed of about forty radical socialists.[11] The audacity of the terrorists almost equalled the hideousness of their acts. In Chicago on July 17, 1905, "Five men, flourishing bright blue magazine guns, broke in the hall where the election of the Federation of Labor was held, and, after smashing the ballot boxes and tearing up the tickets, attacked Michael Donnelly, international president of the butcher workmen, who was left lying on the floor in a pool of blood, with probably fatal injuries. The assailants, whom no one recognized, escaped."[12] Similar gang-land drama occurred on the night of December 26, 1912 when President Charles Moyer of the Western Federation of Miners and organizer Charles Tanner were brutally attacked in their room at the Scott Hotel in Hancock, Michigan by a mob of Citizen Alliance members and imported gunmen.[13] Acts of violence against leaders and members of the Industrial Workers of the World have become enshrined as part of the unpleasant folklore of the American labor movement along with many other incidences, the details of which are enough to disturb even the most hard-core cynic.

While terrorist acts might cause the victims to become more cautious, their consequences did not always favor the instigators. Rather than rendering workers docile, acts of violence frequently led to greater militancy and allegiance to the leaders. Disclosure of the incident by the press could inflame public opinion against the employer and possibly result in government investigation. Thus terrorism was both ineffective and at times counter-productive, a fact which its perpetuators have recognized belatedly. The more sophisticated anti-unionists perceived a more subtle and respectable means of doing away with unwanted labor leaders—through legal prosecution, and, when possible, imprisonment. With the aid of anti-union judges like John J. Jackson—who in one decision labeled labor leaders "vampires" who "have nothing in common with the workingman"—harassment of union officers under the facade of justice proceeded at a pace.[14]

Throughout the period from the Civil War to 1920, labor leaders faced the constant threat of legal action. Several of the cases are classic examples of justice and misjustice in America—the Clearfield trial of John Siney and Xingo Parks in 1873; the Debs trial of 1894; the Haywood-Moyer-Pettibone case of 1905-6; the Buck's Stove and Range case of 1907-14; the prosecution of the Wobblies during World War I.[15] Along with these more spectacular episodes were hundreds of lesser-known trials of labor leaders for crimes ranging from murder to contempt of court. For two years in the mid-1890s, William B. Wilson had conspiracy charges hanging over his head before they were finally dropped.[16] In 1898, while vice-president of the miners, John Mitchell was indicted by a grand jury in Braidwood, Illinois for intimidating other laborers during a strike. Along with Mitchell, charges were brought against twenty-one state and local leaders.[17] January, 1900 saw John P. Reese of the UMW's executive board imprisoned for violating an injunction.[18] The following month another board member, George Purcell, appeared before the bar in London, Kentucky to answer to an indictment of having induced miners to strike when under contract, and then a few days later was again arrested in another part of the state for violating the Kentucky "disturbance" statute.[19] On January 14, 1918, UMW President Frank Hayes, Vice-President John L. Lewis, Secretary-Treasurer William Green, and seven other leaders were ordered before the United States Supreme Court to show why they should not be adjudged guilty of contempt for violating an injunction restraining them from organizing employees of the Hitchman Coal and Coke Company.[20] •

While the miners were having their troubles, James Hughes, master workman of the clothing cutters' branch of the Knights of Labor, was convicted of extortion in 1891 when he attempted to collect a fine from employers violating the contract.[21] That same year Joseph Barondess of the garment workers was also convicted of extortion. Upon hearing the verdict, this immigrant from the Pale quipped: "Russia has its Siberia and New York its Tombs."[22] Twenty-four years later, Morris Sigman and six other leaders of the ILGWU were tried and acquitted of murder charges.[23] The leaders of the Carpenters were particular targets for lawyers. "From 1910 to 1913 injunction servers constantly harassed various officials of the Brotherhood," recorded Robert Christie. "At one time, twelve different suits were in progress in New York City alone. In total, almost a hundred suits were entered in the largest court assault directed against a trade union to that time."[24]

Attacks by anti-union employers—whether by terrorism, legal prosecution, or other means—added to the strain on the overburdened labor leaders. Yet these challenges they expected and could take in their stride. "We are in this business knowing full well that it is no bed of roses for anyone," observed Thomas Hughes of the Teamsters, "and must expect trouble and lots of work if we will do anything for the movement."[25] Far more unnerving were the attacks against them by their supposed friends and comrades. The "kickers and knockers" continually challenged their authority, while the sleeping mass of the rank and file, potentially fickle and ungrateful, could turn against them at any moment. "It is an awful life to live, this labor movement," bemoaned Teamster Vice-President George Golden, "and all we get is abuse from our members."[26] Gompers, whose strength of character contributed so much to the labor movement, was constantly seeking to reinvigorate the spirit of mission within his dejected cohorts. "It is needless to say to you," he wrote to an organizer, "that if one is to be deterred from active participation in the labor movement because of adverse criticism by some of our well meaning friends, we would have few or no active men. Persistency despite criticism is as much a necessity in the labor movement as in every other field of human existence."[27]

In spite of such words of encouragement, many leaders did bend under the strain of their jobs. Secretary-Treasurer Pat McBryde of the miners and President Edward Plank of the printers both chose to resign rather than face the bickering of their followers.[28] Numerous others sought posts in business and government in hopes of leaving the long hours and insecurity of union work behind. Some who stayed with the movement sought relief from the strain through drink, a vice which got the best of P. J. McGuire of the carpenters and Frank Hayes of the miners, and which also contributed to the serious illness which led Mitchell to resign. Even the stout Sam Gompers felt the only way he could relax was to take a few drinks, and in his later years he occasionally appeared intoxicated in public.[29] However, those who could bear the strain for as long as Gompers did with only this slight indiscretion were truly unusual men.

II

Union officers who withstood the hardships of their job to become prominent labor movement figures reveal in their character certain traits which help explain their success. To be sure, not all labor leaders had the same personality orientation, yet enough of them shared certain anxieties and drives in common to warrant a discussion of these traits in a study on leadership development.

Among these characteristics was a strong desire for social esteem. Union journals devoted extensive space to general articles on labor leadership, many written by the officers themselves. Some were positive in tone, stressing their strength of character and dignity. "The ideal labor leader," the Teamsters' magazine declared, "is an ideal man in every particular, whose ready brain quickly grasps each new situation as it presents itself and whose cool, level head instantly directs the proper course of action. . . ."[30] Far more were negatively oriented, lamenting the hardships of leadership and the lack of respect union officers received from their own following and the larger community. "It is safe to say," both the *Mine Workers' Journal* and the *American Federationist* bemoaned, "that the average labor official is the best abused man on earth."[31] Innumerable essays complained of "the cowardly attacks made upon labor leaders by the hirelings of the daily press. . . ."[32] Others explicitly objected to the fact that "Labor leaders are barred from all high social functions. They are excluded from all fashionable clubs. Even in the average university settlement they receive the curious attention that is given to tame bears."[33] The labor leader's name "is not found in the society columns of the newspaper, he is not invited to afternoon tea at the home of the capitalist, and reception committees do not give him a seat on the platform unless the function is a political one and votes are needed. All this would be of small moment, however," rationalized the *Garment Worker,* "were it not that it retarded the progress of his work; but, this being the case, social recognition and support become important factors in the labor movement and to secure and hold them is the work next in line for the organizers."[34]

Individually, union officers were equally concerned with their status and image, as several trivial incidents revealed. "Why dont you have some style about you," lectured the aspiring Powderly to the Knights of Labor's secretary. "What do you use tea paper for when you write me? it looks as if we were going into bankruptcy."[35] Agnes Nestor of the Glove Workers plowed through the 1916 reports of the Industrial Relations Commission before which she had earlier appeared and was "elated" to learn "that, next to John Fitzpatrick, I had the greatest number of pages of testimony," a fact she felt compelled to record in her autobiography.[36] Executive board member William C. Webb of the miners complained that a politician was "more toothsome to the owners of hotels, halls and churches in West Virginia than a mere labor organizer." During his journeys in the state he felt slighted because "political spouters are given all the comforts and accommodations that the localities in which they are sojourning can afford, while men who are engaged in spreading the gospel of truth as applied to labor, must gather their little congregations around them in open air under the most adverse conditions. . . ."[37] John P. Frey of the Molders constantly whined about his failure to gain respect. In a letter to one friend he envisioned a conspiracy by his union's president to undermine his increasing social prominence, and in another letter to Gompers he expressed the belief that it was debasing for him to be expected to give free lectures on the labor movement when men from other walks of life were compensated for their talks.[38] Many other labor leaders used up reams of paper, filled hundreds of columns in the union press, and consumed hours of convention time to defend their names, reputations, and characters from a variety of insignificant charges and insults.

In his biography of William L. Hutcheson, Maxwell Raddock utilizes David Riesman's archetype of the "other-directed man" as a key to his subject's character.[39] Within limits the concept is applicable to other labor leaders prominent after the turn of the century. Their concern over status and respectability suggests the radar reaction of the other-directed personality. Extensive membership in social clubs and fraternal organizations reveals a strong desire "to belong." As a young man Samuel Gompers joined a variety of groups, including the Arion Baseball Club, the Ancient Order of Foresters, the Independent Order of the Odd Fellows, the Society of Human Progress, and Felix Adler's Ethical Culture Society.[40]

Edward Flore, whose ambition led him to join the Hotel and Restaurant Employees as a base for a potential career in politics, at one time belonged to thirteen social organizations.[41] Memorabilia from the Masons and Shriners comprises over half of the volume of the collection of Joseph Slight, Secretary-Treasurer of the National Window Glass Workers.[42]

Yet, while sharing characteristics of "the other-directed man," labor leaders were not willing to simply blend into "the lonely crowd." They wanted to be in the limelight, as central stars in the drama of life rather than be buried in crowd scenes. As youths Samuel Gompers, Agnes Nestor, James Maurer, John L. Lewis, and other labor leaders were captivated with the theater and had dreams of becoming thespians.[43] This need to capture an audience, to dramatize the pathos and dignity of existence, and to receive the applause after the performance was over stayed with these individuals in their roles as labor leaders. Twentieth-century America surely knows no greater Shakespearean figure than John L. Lewis.

Desiring to be in the center of public affairs, the more prominent labor leaders worked hard to achieve their goal. "[Tom L.] Lewis is a man of ambition," observed the *United Mine Workers' Journal* in 1908 of the union's new president. "Ambition it was that took the boy of seven out of the breakers and made him a coal miner at eleven; that kept him in night school when other boys were playing; that gave him the meager savings of $105, seven months in the National University at Lebanon, O., and that when through the nights of three years, while he was still working in the bowels of the earth during the day, kept him reading."[44] William L. Hutcheson's biographer describes him as a youth "proud of his 'superiority.' . . . It inflamed his desire to convince, to influence, perhaps to command. His instinct for leadership was profound and irresistible. He loved politics, though he never quite regarded his interest in that field as an end in itself. Nothing could quite satisfy him entirely but the feeling that he was leading men by serving their cause in a common objective. His natural traits forced him to want to be a chief. . . ."[45]

Wanting to lead was the first prerequisite of a successful labor leader; the second was to convert ambition to action. This entailed not only developing widespread rank-and-file support, but also a foothold in the union's power structure. There developed within the labor movement an informal protégé system in which young aspirants to power attached themselves to an established union figure who helped advance their career. Uriah S. Stephens's backing of Terence Powderly to assume his post of grand master workman in 1879 was an early manifestation of the process, as was the support Adolph Strasser offered to the ambitious Samuel Gompers.[46] The protégé system did not fully come into its own, however, until the mid-1890s when unions assumed more institutional forms. William D. Ryan, head of the Illinois miners, played the role of Mark Hanna for John Mitchell and maneuvered him into the first vice-presidency of the national body. From this post, Mitchell became the protégé of President Michael Ratchford, who kindly paved the way for the young man to become his successor.[47] Mitchell in turn became the mentor of William B. Wilson, who in his earlier career had received the support of John L. Sexton, publisher of the *Advisor,* and his son Sam Sexton, who became editor of the *United Mine Workers' Journal.* His chief opponent, Tom L. Lewis, marshalled his strong family connections. His father, Thomas J. Lewis, had been active in miners' unions since the days of John Siney. His older brother, William T. Lewis, had been a leading spirit in the Knights of Labor as master workman of the miners' District Assembly 135, labor commissioner of Ohio during the governorship of William McKinley, and then one of "the right-hand lieutenants" of Senator Mark Hanna. Another brother, Stephen L. Lewis, was the vice-president of the iron and steel workers' national organization, while a third, Isaac Lewis, was at age twenty-nine the mayor of the mining community of Martin's Ferry, Ohio.[48] John L. Lewis, who had no kinship with the previous Lewis dynasty, was groomed for power by both Samuel Gompers and UMW President John P. White.[49] Outside the miners' union, the protégé system also prevailed, although probably not as extensively. In the Western Federation of Miners, William D. Haywood received the backing of President Edward Boyce; Jere L. Sullivan of the Hotel and Restaurant Employees helped elevate Edward Flore to the union's presidency; Milton Snelling rode to power in the Operating Engineers on the coattails of Arthur M. Huddell; and Max Zuckerman of the Cap Makers fostered the career of young Max Zaritsky.[50] The protégé system was potentially rewarding to both parties involved. The young understudy received the post to which he aspired, while the benefactor attained the ego satisfaction of making men leaders, and was able to wield behind-the-scene influence on union policy, even after he broke his formal ties with the organization.

Even more revealing of the drive of many labor leaders was the manner in which several attained top union posts without running for election. The classic example of such maneuvering was the rise of John L. Lewis to the presidency of the Mine Workers. The highest office to which Lewis was elected before becoming chief executive of the union was that of president of his Panama, Illinois local from 1908 to 1911. During these years he was also a member of the union's state legislative committee and used this position to court John H. Walker, president of the Illinois miners. Upon Walker's recommendation, Samuel Gompers appointed Lewis an AFL legislative agent in 1911. While performing his duties at this post, Lewis developed contacts with mine union leaders throughout the country which were strengthened when Gompers assigned him to serve as liaison agent between the AFL and the UMW at the outbreak of the war. As a result of the ties he had nursed, Lewis was appointed statistician for the national body in 1917 and also served as manager of the miners' journal from February to July of that year. In October 1917 John P. White, president of the UMW, resigned his office in order to work full time for the Fuel Administration. Vice-president Frank Hayes moved into the presidency and, in accordance with an apparent deal between himself, White, and Lewis, nominated Lewis to the now vacant vice-presidential post. In spite of strong dissent from the Illinois members, the national executive board ratified Hayes's choice. From here fate took its course. Under the pressures of the presidency, Frank Hayes took to heavy drinking and by September, 1918 was unable to perform his job. Lewis became acting president, presided over the union's 1919 convention, and used the resources available to him to prepare his own election to the highest office in 1920.[51]

While dramatic, John L. Lewis's maneuverings were not unique. As related earlier, John Mitchell utilized a modified version of this technique to win the UMW presidency in 1899. In the Hotel and Restaurant Employees, it was established custom for departing executive board members to pick their successors. Thus in 1904 resigning Fred Seames designated Ed Flore to take his place as an International vice-president.[52] At the same time that John L. Lewis was manipulating his way up the Mine Workers' hierarchy, his later enemy William L. Hutcheson was following a roughly parallel, although less scheming, path within the Carpenters' Union. In 1913 he won election as second vice-president of the union in a contest he later admitted was rigged. When the first vice-president resigned later that year, Hutcheson moved into the vacant post and from there into the presidency when its occupant, James Kirby, died of food poisoning in 1915.[53] In the Operating Engineers, Milton Snelling was the last president to be elected to his first term by convention or membership vote. Every president since 1916 has either died in office or resigned between conventions, and his successor has been appointed by the general executive board.[54]

The ambitious drive of labor leaders did not subside with the attainment of union office. Some including Daniel Tobin and George Leonard Berry went on to build up influence within political parties.[55] Others like Warren Stone used their unions as a base for financial empires.[56] For many, the union became a vehicle for social mobility into careers in business and politics. The correspondence of John Mitchell, for instance, reveals a man with ambitions outside the labor movement. On the one hand, he entered into a variety of speculative business ventures, always hoping to "clean up a handsome little stake each year."[57] On the other hand, he teamed up with Daniel Keefe of the Longshoremen, and William B. Wilson and W. D. Ryan of his own organization in search of government patronage positions for themselves and their friends. At the local level they received cooperation from minor politicians solicitous of the coal miners' votes.[58] On the national level, Mitchell had the good fortune of being friendly with Senator Mark Hanna, whom he casually called "the Captain." "While in Washington I called upon the Captain," he wrote to Keefe, "in fact he sent me an invitation—and had a heart to heart talk with him concerning some of the good things. He told me that he had the District Superintendency of a free postal delivery in view for you; that he had told the Postmaster General that you must have it."[59] On another occasion Mitchell wrote Keefe: "If we cannot land the place we want, put in a bid for the Chief of the Bureau [of Immigration], at New York City, which pays almost as much, and there is considerable patronage to be disposed of. One thing sure, we must have a good berth."[60] "Of course," he cautioned, "I think it good policy to preserve our dignity, and not appear to be tumbling over ourselves in getting the good things."[61]

Through this correspondence over patronage, it becomes strikingly clear that the opposition of "business unionists" of the Mitchell-Keefe stripe to Terence Powderly and other traditional labor leaders was based on something other than conflicting ideological views. "I think, John," Keefe wrote to the miners' leader, "that if you would write Ryan and have Ryan see some others and write Senator Hanna opposing the re-appointment of Powderly [as commissioner-general of immigration] without mentioning my name, that it would be a long step in the right direction"—by which he meant his own appointment to the post.[62] "As a matter of fact, Billy," Mitchell explained to the future secretary of labor in 1903, "both Powderly and [Robert] Watchorn are members of that faction that has sought to keep our best friends out of [appointed government] office."[63]

III

By the end of World War I, offices in established unions were well worth striving for. Despite the troubles which still accompanied the posts, the rewards of the job were highly attractive to men of humble birth. In material terms, the labor leaders lived in the style of the middle class. With incomes considerably above the earnings of the average worker, they often owned their own homes, sent their children to college, and belonged to prominent social groups. Gone were the shabby, poorly fitting suits of men from the working class. Earlier labor leaders like P. J. McGuire had been noted for their unkempt looks, with long drooping mustaches and garments wrinkled by night-long travel on bounching freights. The men who replaced them, like Harry Lloyd of the Boston carpenters, "dressed well in dark clothes, wore a heavy gold chain and charm and might have been mistaken for a young lawyer."[64] The rising prestige of the AFL was reflected in Gompers's more natty wardrobe, accented by a diamond pin in the cravat.[65] And radicals like Henry D. Lloyd and

Clarence Darrow delighted in dating John Mitchell's "corruption" by men of business from the day in 1902, when on a trip to New York to attend the National Civic Federation he traded "the black soft felt hat by which he is universally known" for the silk derby of fashionable society.[66]

The biographies and autobiographies of union pioneers—men like William Sylvis, John Siney, Samuel Gompers, Terence Powderly, Joseph Buchanan, Abraham Bisno, and William B. Wilson—relate the economic sacrifices these men made to become active in the labor movement. After World War I, new recruits to the labor movement were largely spared such suffering. David J. McDonald, the future president of the United Steelworkers, was a typist for the Wheeling Steel Company earning $80 a month when, in 1923, he landed his first union job as personal secretary to Philip Murray of the UMW. His starting salary was $200 a month, which, he relates in his autobiography, "sounded to me about one cut below what Andy Carnegie must be making."[67] On his first three days on the job he was whisked to New York City, during which time he enjoyed such previously unknown comforts as his own berth in a Pullman car, a room to himself in the Hotel Pennsylvania, and his "first meal in a big city hotel dinning room."[68] More than the new comforts he enjoyed, young McDonald was impressed by the expanded horizons opened to him—of meeting men he never dreamed of meeting and touring places no common laborer could hope to reach. The workers' "existence is all routine and headaches, and it's apt to contribute very little to personal growth," observed David Dubinsky several years later. "In my job I meet all sorts of people—government officials, labor leaders from every corner of the world, politicians, business men, journalists. That is what opportunity is all about—being able to touch the world at many points."[69]

To domestic radicals as well as many Europeans, the most distinctive feature of American labor leaders after the turn of the century was the extent to which they had adopted the lifestyle of the bourgeoisie. In speech after speech, Socialist Eugene Debs attacked established labor leaders for succumbing to "the blandishment of the plutocrats," while Communist William Z. Foster penned *Misleaders of Labor* to expose trade union officials as "agents of the bourgeoisie in the ranks of the workers," and "often petty capitalists themselves."[70] In Robert Michels's classic study, *Political Parties,* written in 1915, the radical European sociologist's only extensive reference to the American scene concerns the *embourgeoisement* of the labor leaders. Since "the United States of America is the land of the almighty dollar" in which "public life seems to be dominated . . . by the thirst for gold," he writes: "We cannot wonder, then, that North America should be preeminently the country in which the aristocratic tendencies of the labor leader, fostered by an environment often permeated . . . by gross and unrefined materialism, should have developed freely and upon a gigantic scale. The leaders of the American proletariat have merely followed the lead of the capitalism by which the life of their country is dominated."[71]

Michels's equation of *embourgeoisement* with cultural conditioning provides a far more sophisticated explanation than the "chloroform-conspiracy" implications of Debs, Foster, and other American radicals. Labor leaders strove for place and power in order to fulfill the nebulous American Dream; to attain success in a society dominated by middle-class values. Despite the presence of various radical groups which hoped to fundamentally alter the nature of our society, the dominant impulse of the labor movement has been simply to gain for the workers a larger piece of the American pie— Samuel Gompers's famous demand for "more, more, more." Terence Powderly confronted time and again the petty-bourgeois anxieties of his followers, who at rallies and conventions were eager to proclaim that "Property is Robbery," "and yet," he observed, "they are all striving to acquire property, how inconsistent, but I did not intend to moralize."[72] IWW organizers were likewise unable to transform into a revolutionary force individuals from the gutters of society, who "thought only of rising to the sidewalk, and once there entering the house."[73]

Desirous of climbing the social ladder themselves, the rank and file generally looked favorably upon the advancement of their leaders to posts in government and industry from which they could achieve "recognition, fame, and fortune."[74] The rise of the labor leader out of the movement, explained one sympathetc miner, "is to be expected; the natural dread of poverty and deprivation is always, under present conditions, a factor to wheedle away from their allegiance men to whom that poverty is magnified by the glare of prospective ease and comfort. . . ."[75] James Lynch, one printer commented in 1914, "used the prestige gained as president of the International Typographical Union to get a better job, and got one, which was all right. And he resigned, to accept a more lucrative job, which was all right."[76] Such views differed greatly from the early years of unionism, when a rule had prevailed that "when the daily press and the employing class begin to praise a labor 'leader', it is time for workingmen to keep an eye upon him."[77] By the turn of the century, the glare of suspicion was becoming a gaze of admiration. In a 1905 article on Robert Watchorn—one-time secretary-treasurer of the UMW, who left the union to become chief factory inspector of Pennsylvania, then worked his way up the hierarchy of the Bureau of Immigration to the post of commissioner for the Port of New York, and later became a vice-president of the Union Oil Company—the *United Mine Workers' Journal* jubilantly declared:

> Such is the general outline of a successful career which should be an object lesson to every man who reads it. It indicates that by honesty, devotion to his ambition, hard work and determination what a man may accomplish. Contrast the rise in station, earning capacity and power from the little boy in the English coal mine to the present position that Mr. Watchorn holds. There are similar opportunities for every man in the union to advance himself, and Mr. Watchorn's career will doubtless serve as the inspiration for many young men to try to equal his great success.[78]

Only the radical minority sincerely questioned the propriety of such mobility, although occasionally conservative union politicos would treat such advancement by a member of the opposition as a sign of their insincerity in order to undermine their prestige.

An astute young worker, studying the careers of men like Watchorn, soon came to recognize the valuable role union offices played in the drive for upward mobility. "Great prestige," C. Wright Mills observed, "increasingly follows the major institutional units of the social structure." "To be celebrated, to be wealthy, to have power, requires access to major institutions, for the institutional positions men occupy determine in large part their chance to have and to hold these valued experiences."[79] By the second decade of the twentieth century, the AFL and several of its affiliates had become recognized by the power elite as established forces in American society. Office-holding in the Federation, Mine Workers, Carpenters, Teamsters, Typographical Union, or the various railroad brotherhoods brought with it social prominence where earlier occupants had been lam-basted as scalawags, demagogues, blatherskites, and loafers. In the 1880s labor leaders of the stature of Powderly and John Jarrett of the Amalgamated Iron and Steel Workers lobbied hard to win for themselves the post of chief of the Bureau of Labor Statistics, only to lose out to a Massachusetts gentleman, Carroll D. Wright.[80] Yet by 1904, the post was deemed unworthy of John Mitchell. "You are better off, more important and influential," James Duncan wrote, "as President of the United Mine Workers than you would be as successor to C. D. Wright; the Vice Presidency is another proposi-tion."[81] And Mitchell concurred: "I recognize the fact that as Presi-dent of the United Mine Workers I have more prominence, influence and prestige than I could have by holding any position with the Government unless it were one in the Cabinet or the Vice-Presi-dency."[82] Apparently William B. Wilson held a similar estimate of the miners' top post, for having already won a seat in Congress he chose to run for the union's presidency upon the retirement of Mitchell in 1908.[83] Albert E. Hawley gave up a job as inspector for the Interstate Commerce Commission in 1909 to become secretary-treasurer of the Brotherhood of Locomotive Firemen and Enginemen; Emanuel G. Hall relinquished his post as Assistant Commissioner of Labor for Minnesota to become head of the state's Federation of Labor in 1911; and in 1924 James Lynch returned to the presidency of the Typographical Union after holding several important posts in government and business.[84]

Changing attitudes by the nation's keepers of culture reflected the increasing prominence of labor and its leaders. In the 1890s both John R. Commons and Richard Ely faced hostility from uni-versity circles for their championship of the workers' cause.[85] As late as 1915 the University of Pennsylvania forbade Samuel Gompers from speaking on campus. Disgruntled by the decision, more than a thousand undergraduates defied the university authorities and passed a resolution of censure directed at the institution's high-handed methods.[86] Yet signs of change appeared after the turn of the century as a number of schools, most notably the University of Wisconsin, established programs in labor studies. By 1919 the University of Cincinnati went so far as to attempt to hire a real labor leader, John Frey, for a chair in the department of industrial relations.[87]

The religious establishment also demonstrated a more favorable attitude toward unions. Beginning with James Cardinal Gibbons's support of the Knights of Labor, the Catholic church strove to influence the conservative labor movement, an effort which resulted in the founding in 1910 of the Militia of Christ under the direction of Father Peter Deitz.[88] The accommodation of the Protestant churches with organized labor was less extensive, yet through the efforts of the Social Gospelers and men like Charles Stelzle a rapport was established: by 1910 practically every denomination designated one service a year as Labor Sunday; labor leaders served on the governing board of the Federal Council of Churches; and various faiths sent fraternal delegates to labor union conventions.[89] For their part, the business unionists were generally delighted at their increased respectability within the churches, and participated more extensively in church activities than their earlier counterparts. In the America of 1920, to become a respectable leader of society it was helpful to be a pillar of the Church.

Nothing else quite symbolized the growing status of conservative unions and their leaders as the dedication of the new AFL building in Washington, D.C. on July 4, 1916. Like many of the labor leaders in attendance, Sara A. Conboy, secretary-treasurer of the Textile Workers, was overwhelmed with the respect paid to labor by dignitaries of government. "As I looked over the number of people on the reviewing stand," she gloated, "and saw the President of this United States and Mrs. Wilson, Secretary Lansing and Mrs. Lansing, Vice President Marshall with Mrs. Marshall, Secretary Wilson and so many other notables, I could scarcely help exclaiming that Labor has indeed come into its own."[90]

IV

By 1920 the nature of modern labor union leadership was clearly discernible. A number of the leaders whom C. Wright Mills would label "the New Men of Power" had already gained office and were behaving in the manner which Mills would belatedly describe. Within the more established unions, the national executives were the focal point of power, giving the labor movement its oligarchical character which has been both a source of strength and a cause of injustice. In the larger society, the conservative labor leaders had attained a place on the fringe of the power elite to which they have largely been confined. During World War I they served on a variety of commissions to direct the war effort, aided the government in undermining antiwar sentiment through the Alliance for Labor and Democracy, and, as historian Ronald Radosh has shown, began their activities as instruments of American foreign policy.[91] In the election of 1924, both parties considered choosing labor leaders for their vice-presidential candidates. John L. Lewis was pushed for the Republican nomination by the Harriman interests, while George L. Berry of the Pressmen lost the Democratic nomination by only three votes.[92] The fact that they lost symbolizes the less than total acceptance they enjoyed.

The consequences for the labor movement of the rise of strong, national executives were both favorable and detrimental. The emergence of professional leadership was a major step in transforming the unions into stable, permanent forces in the economy. From their secure base in their own organizations, men like John L. Lewis, Sidney Hillman, and David Dubinsky were able to weather the "lean years" of labor and launch their spectacular drive to organize the unorganized in the 1930s. Yet the same base which allowed boldness on the part of the CIO founders encouraged conservatism and lethargy on the part of many of their fellow officers. Whatever visionary plans they had when entering the labor movement dissipated under the immediate pressures of the job. The unions, which were originally to serve as vehicles to a better world, became for these men an end in themselves, to be guarded from adversity regardless of cost. Maintaining that "in the American labor movement order is the first and greatest of laws," they discouraged rank-and-file spontaneity, which led to a number of undemocratic practices and the emergence of the increasingly familiar unionist alienated from his organization.[93] The cautiousness of the labor leaders in the political and economic fields led to their qualified acceptance by respectable society. And with the *embourgeoisement* of its leaders, whatever radical potential had existed in the labor movement was defused.

Notes

Chapter 1
The Traditional Labor
Leader and the New
Business Unionist

1. Terence V. Powderly, *The Path I Trod,* ed. Harry J. Carman, Henry David, and Paul N. Guthrie (New York, 1940), p. 3.
2. For the fullest presentation of this interpretation see Gerald N. Grob, *Workers and Utopia* (Chicago, 1961) and Norman J. Ware, *The Labor Movement in the United States, 1860-1895* (New York, 1929). For briefer treatments see John R. Commons et al., *History of Labour in the United States* (New York, 1918-1936), 2:482-501; Foster Rhea Dulles, *Labor in America,* 3rd ed. (New York, 1966), pp. 150-54; Joseph G. Rayback, *A History of American Labor* (New York, 1966), pp. 168-207; and Samuel P. Hays, *The Response to Industrialism, 1885-1914* (Chicago, 1957), pp. 63-65.
3. Grob, pp. 38-43, 132-37; Selig Perlman and Philip Taft, *History of Labor in the United States, 1896-1932* (New York, 1935), pp. 3-12; Robert H. Wiebe, *The Search for Order, 1877-1920* (New York, 1967), pp. 123-32.
4. Grob, p. 39.
5. Commons et al., 2:308.
6. For various aspects of this stereotype see Grob, pp. 39-43; Perlman and Taft, pp. 3-12; Com-

mons et al., 2:308; Wiebe, pp. 66-69; Hays, pp. 35-37; and Selig Perlman, *A Theory of the Labor Movement* (New York, 1928), pp. 182-99.
7. Ware, pp. 20-21.
8. For various aspects of this stereotype see Perlman, *Theory,* pp. 192-200; Perlman and Taft, pp. 3-12; Commons et al., 2:308-10; Wiebe, pp. 123-32.
9. For the type of documentation see Grobe, pp. 39-43; Perlman and Taft, pp. 3-12; Perlman, *Theory,* pp. 182-200.
10. The use of such terms can be found in most standard discussions of the Knights of Labor and the AFL. They are given fullest play, however, in Grob, pp. 34-137. See also the biographical portraits of Powderly and Gompers in Charles A. Madison, *American Labor Leaders,* 2nd ed. (New York, 1962), pp. 44, 50, 73, 78.
11. Madison, pp. 73-78; Lafayette G. Harter, *John R. Commons* (Corvallis, Oreg., 1962), pp. 190-91.
12. Harter, pp. 17-19, 183-86.
13. Compare the image and concept of good leadership implied in Perlman, *Theory,* pp. 192-200; Perlman and Taft, pp. 3-12; Commons et al., 2:308-10 with Philip S. Foner, *History of the Labor Movement in the United States* (New York, 1947-65), 3:136-73.
14. Samuel Walker, "Terence V. Powderly and the Social Context of the Early American Labor Move-

ment" (Paper read before the Missouri Valley Historical Conference, Omaha, Neb., March 9, 1973). See David Montgomery, *Beyond Equality* (New York, 1967) and Herbert G. Gutman, "The Worker's Search For Power: Labor in the Gilded Age," *The Gilded Age: A Reappraisal,* ed. H. Wane Morgan (Syracuse, N.Y., 1963), pp. 38–68.

15. The information from which these sketches were drawn came from several sources. The most helpful secondary source was Solon DeLeon, ed., *American Labor Who's Who* (New York, 1926), which contains biographical material on a number of labor leaders elected to office during the Progressive era and still at their posts in the mid-1920s. A number of other secondary works also contain useful biographical sketches including George E. McNeill, *The Labor Movement* (Boston, 1887); Lewis Lorwin, *The Women's Garment Workers* (New York, 1924); Clifton K. Yearly, Jr., *Britons in American Labor* (Baltimore, 1957); and David Montgomery, *Beyond Equality* (New York, 1967). Reference sources such as the *Dictionary of American Biography, The Cyclopaedia of American Biography,* and *Who Was Who in America* were of limted value. The largest proportion of biographical material was derived from unorganized information found in biographies, autobiographies, union histories, labor journals, and manuscript collections. Newspaper obituaries proved the least helpful source, except in rare cases.

16. Grob, pp. 119-162; Perlman

and Taft, pp. 9-10; George E. Barnett, "The Dominance of the National Union in American Labor Organization," *The Quarterly Journal of Economics* 27 (May 1913):455-81.

17. Arthur, Mann, *Yankee Reformers in the Urban Age* (Cambridge, Mass., 1954), pp. 188-98.

18. *Journal of United Labor,* June 1883, pp. 485-86; Yearley, pp. 137-39.

19. John Laslett, *Labor and the Left* (New York, 1970), pp. 10-11, 145-48, 298.

20. Eli Ginzberg, *The Labor Leader* (New York, 1948), p. 45.

21. Although a quantitative analsis of labor union leadership between 1870 and 1920 has not previously been attempted, there are several statistical studies which are useful as a means of checking the conclusions of this work. David Montgomery's study of labor leaders prominent during the Reconstruction era is a benchmark for an analysis of the traditional unionist. Montgomery (pp. 197-229) has examined leaders prominent during a period earlier and shorter than that of the present study; he has included local union leadership, labor journalists, and politicians, as well as national labor figures. Moreover, his sample has a decidedly political orientation. Pitirim Sorokin, "Leaders of Labor and Radical Movements in the United States and Foreign Countries," *American Journal of Sociology,* (November 1927), pp. 382-411, and Louis Stanley, "A Cross-Section of American Labor Leadership," *American Labor Dynamics,* ed. J. B. S. Hardman (New

York, 1928), pp. 412-20, provide a partial check on the conclusions regarding the business unionists. These studies relate only to leaders in office in the mid-1920s and suffer from the biases both of the authors and the sources of the sample. *American Labor Who's Who,* from which these scholars took their data, contains sketches of local as well as national and foreign labor leaders, and reflects the preconceptions of its editor, Solon DeLeon, the son of the famed leader of the Socialist Labor party, and hence contains a disproportionate number of sketches of socialists, La Follette Progressives, Jews, and leaders of the needle and textile trades. Eli Ginzberg's study of labor leaders prominent from 1900 to 1940 is also helpful in understanding the business unionists, but it is primarily concerned with leaders in office at the later date.

22. Statistics based on sample of ninety-five.

23. George James Stevenson, "The Brotherhood of Locomotive Engineers and its Leaders, 1863-1920" (Ph.D. diss., Vanderbilt University, 1954), pp. 25-26; Ware, p. 28; Harry C. Bates, *Bricklayers' Century of Craftsmanship* (Washington, 1955), p. 11. A similar conclusion is arrived at by Montgomery, pp. 199-200.

24. Grob, p. 56; Montgomery, p. 466; Eleanor Flexner, *Century of Struggle* (New York, 1959), pp. 134-36, 196-200; George C. Kirstein, *Stores and Unions* (New York, 1950), p. 12.

25. Montgomery, pp. 200-201.

26. Statistics based on 107 leaders whose place of birth are known. Fifty-five of these were native born and fifty-two were foreign born. Montgomery, p. 196, concludes that fifty-eight percent were foreign born.

27. Statistics based on information known on thirty-two foreign-born labor leaders.

28. Thomas Phillip Papers, State Historical Society of Wisconsin, U.S. Mss. 12A, box 1; Yearly, pp. 94-106, 139, 143-45, 271-82; *American Federationist,* January 1901, p. 26; *United Mine Workers' Journal,* May 6, 1909, p. 6; H. M. Gitelman, "Adolph Strasser and the Origins of Pure and Simple Unionism," *Labor History* 6 (Winter 1965):74-77.

29. This emphasis differs sharply from that of most historians who follow the path of Grob, Commons, Perlman, and Ware in treating the pre-AFL labor movement as a continuation of the Jeffersonian-Jacksonian influence. These scholars recognize the role of foreign influence on the AFL, but tend to overlook or treat as exceptional such influence on the earlier movements. Behind this approach are assumptions that America is unique and concomitantly that labor reformism in America is unique. They have also tended to exaggerate the size and influence of the Jacksonian labor movement. If one assumes that the Jacksonian labor movement was as large as they maintain then it would be fair to expect a continuation of values into the Gilded Age, but, as Maurice F. Neufeld has shown, such as assumption is grossly unjustified. Moreover,

both Neufeld and Edward Pessen have demonstrated the great influence which Britons had on the American labor movement in the 1830s and 1840s, just as Montgomery and Yearley have done for the later period. As a result of such studies, it is becoming increasingly apparent that what has been considered a unique Jeffersonian-Jacksonian ethos was to a large extent Chartism transplanted. Maurice F. Neufeld, "Realms of Thought and Organized Labor in the Age of Jackson," *Labor History* 10 (Winter 1969):5-43; Edward Pessen, *Most Uncommon Jacksonians* (New York, 1957), pp. 129-72; John F. C. Harrison, *Quest for the New Moral World: Robert Owens and the Owenites in Britain and America* (New York, 1969).

30. Montgomery, p. 199.

31. Yearley, p. 86.

32. Samuel Gompers, *Seventy Years of Life and Labor*, 2 vols. (New York, 1925), 1:33.

33. John Brophy, *A Miner's Life*, ed. John O. P. Hall (Madison, Wis., 1964), p. 12.

34. Ibid., p. 73.

35. The New England states are Maine, New Hampshire, Vermont, Massachusetts, Rhode Island, Connecticut; the Middle Atlantic states New York, New Jersey, and Pennsylvania; the East-North-Central states Ohio, Indiana, Illinois, Michigan, and Wisconsin; the West-North-Central are Minnesota, Iowa, Missouri, North Dakota, South Dakota, Nebraska, and Kansas; the South Atlantic states Delaware, Maryland, District of Columbia, Virginia, West Virginia, North Carolina, South Carolina, Georgia, and Florida; the East-South-Central states Kentucky, Tennessee, Alabama, and Mississippi; the West-South-Central states Arkansas, Louisiana, Oklahoma, and Texas; the Mountain states Montana, Idaho, Wyoming, Colorado, New Mexico, Arizona, Utah, and Nevada; the Pacific states Washington, Oregon, and California.

36. Population of birthplaces based on U.S., Bureau of the Census, *Seventh Census of the United States, 1850*. Before 1880 an urban area was considered a community with 8,000 inhabitants or more. Beginning with the Tenth Census the base population was lowered to 2,500 inhabitants. For a breakdown of the proportion of the Amrican population living in urban areas as defined by both criteria see U.S., Bureau of the Census, *Thirteenth Census of the United States, 1910*, 1:53-54.

37. Population of residences based on U.S., Bureau of the Census, *Tenth Census of the United States, 1880*. For the definition of regions see note 35.

38. Stevenson, pp. 117-19; Mark Perlman, *The Machinists* (Cambridge, Mass., 1961), pp. 4-9; Edward Pinkowski, *John Siney, the Miners' Martyr* (Philadelphia, 1963), pp. 111-12; *Journal of United Labor*, July 1883, pp. 513-14; Mann, pp. 188-89; Joseph R. Buchanan, *The Story of a Labor Agitator* (New York, 1903), pp. 37-78.

39. *Typographical Journal*, February 1916, pp. 170-73; Montgomery, p. 210; Powderly, p. 178.

40. Ginzberg, p. 53.

41. Jonathan P. Grossman, *William Sylvis* (New York, 1945), p. 38.

42. Howard H. Quint, *The Forging of American Socialism* (New York, 1953), p. 15; Thomas W. Gavett, *Development of the Labor Movement in Milwaukee* (Madison, Wis., 1965), pp. 33-94.

43. Montgomery, p. 214; Ware, pp. 80-91.

44. Robert Watchorn, *The Autobiography of Robert Watchorn,* ed. Herbert F. West (Oklahoma City, 1959), pp. vii-xi; *United Mine Workers' Journal,* June 11, 1891, p. 4; *Journal of the Knights of Labor,* December 21, 1893, p. 1; *United Mine Workers' Journal,* February 18, 1892, p. 4; Gompers, *Seventy Years,* 2:164-5.

45. Montgomery, pp. 214-15.

46. *New York Times,* April 15, 1944; *United Mine Workers' Journal,* July 6, 1905, p. 2.

47. See Ware, p. 21.

48. For the best discussion of the influence of the Catholic church on labor leaders see Marc Karson, *American Labor Unions and Politics* (Carbondale, Ill., 1958), pp. 212-84. Karson's conclusions, however, should be compared with Grob, pp. 165-66, footnote 8; and Laslett, pp. 54-55.

49. Based on U.S., Bureau of the Census, *Ninth Census of the United States, 1870.*

50. Donald B. Robinson, *Spotlight on a Union* (New York, 1948), pp. 122-23.

51. Stevenson, p. 237; DeLeon, p. 247; *Dictionary of American Biography,* 12:544-45.

52. John Llewellyn Lewis Papers, State Historical Society of Wisconsin, Mss. 91, Guide.

53. *Who Was Who,* 1:1032; *National Cyclopaedia,* 25:29-30.

54. *National Cyclopaedia,* 42:14; *New York Times,* March 13, 1949, p. 76.

55. *Who Was Who,* 1:721; Warren R. Van Tine, "Ben H. Williams, Wobbly Editor" (M.A. thesis, Dept. of History, Northern Illinois University, 1967), p. 7.

56. Harold Seidman, *The Labor Czars* (New York, 1938), pp. 9-10.

57. Based on U.S., Bureau of the Census, *Thirteenth Census of the United States, 1910.*

58. Stanley, p. 417; Perlman and Taft, pp. 17-19.

59. Ginzberg, pp. 49-54; Theodore W. Glocker, *The Government of American Trade Unions* (Baltimore, 1913), p. 55; Lloyd Ulman, *The Rise of the National Trade Union* (Cambridge, Mass., 1955), p. 4.

60. *United Mine Workers' Journal,* November 15, 1949, p. 1; *Who Was Who,* 3:934; *National Cyclopaedia,* 42:14.

61. Bernard Mandel, *Samuel Gompers, a Biography* (Yellow Springs, Ohio, 1963), p. 431.

62. DeLeon, p. 55.

63. John Hutchinson, *The Imperfect Union* (New York, 1970), pp. 146-47.

64. John Mitchell to W. D. Ryan, September 14, 1899, Mitchell Papers, file 12, Catholic University of America.

65. William Z. Foster, *Misleaders of Labor* (Chicago, 1927), pp. 128-29.

66. *National Cyclopaedia,* 22: 225-26.

67. DeLeon, pp. 17, 146, 148, 243, 137.

68. *Who Was Who,* 1:1193; *Na-*

tional Cyclopaedia, 42:14.

69. Stanley, p. 420, arrives at a similar conclusion: "Somewhat more than half of the unionists were so little interested in politics or so much concerned about concealing their political affiliation that they omitted stating their politics altogether. In either case they are not politically aggressive and, therefore, do not count for much in the determination of the political action labor takes."

70. See Karson, pp. 42-73.

71. Hutchinson, pp. 94-95; *Who Was Who,* 3:434.

72. Max Danish, *William Green* (New York, 1952), pp. 11-20.

73. *Biographical Directory of American Congress,* pp. 617, 670-71, 1315, 1835.

74. *American Federation of Labor: History, Encyclopedia, Reference Book,* compiled by W. C. Roberts (Washington, 1919), pp. 471-74.

75. *Proceedings of the National Arbitration and Peace Congress,* New York, N.Y., April 14-17, 1907.

76. *Miners' Magazine,* July 29, 1909, p. 3.

77. DeLeon, pp. 133, 143, 43.

78. *Who Was Who,* 2:60.

79. *Literary Digest* 44, no. 3 (January 17, 1920): p. 84.

80. American Federation of Labor, *Report of Proceedings of the Thirty-Fifth Annual Convention,* November 8-22, 1915, p. 66.

81. *Literary Digest* 44, no. 3 (January 17, 1920): p. 84.

82. See Foner, 3:136-73; Philip Taft, "On the Origins of Business Unionism," *Industrial and Labor Relations Review* 17 (October 1963):20-38.

83. The one serious effort to cope with some of these questions is David Brody, "Career Leadership and American Trade Unionism," *The Age of Industrialism in America,* ed. Frederick Caple Jaher (New York, 1968), pp. 288-303.

Chapter 2
Four Images of Unions

1. *American Federationist,* May 1910, pp. 417-18.

2. T. V. Powderly, *Thirty Years of Labor* (Columbus, Ohio, 1890), pp. 133-38.

3. Ibid., p. 134.

4. Ibid., p. 116.

5. Ibid., p. 127.

6. Ibid., pp. 26-27.

7. George James Stevenson, "The Brotherhood of Locomotive Engineers and Its Leaders, 1863-1920" (Ph.D. diss., Vanderbilt University, 1954), pp. 11-12.

8. Ibid., p. 12.

9. *Constitution of the Order of Sovereigns of Industry,* revised 1874, Sovereigns of Industry Papers, U.S. Mss. 4A., State Historical Society of Wisconsin.

10. Stevenson, p. 14.

11. Norman Ware, *The Labor Movement in the United States, 1860-1895* (New York, 1929), pp. 382-83.

12. Stevenson, p. 53.

13. *Secret Circular,* n.d., p. 2.

14. Charles A. Madison, *American Labor Leaders,* 2nd ed. (New York, 1962), p. 46.

15. Powderly, *Thirty Years,* pp. 167-68; for an analysis of labor's use of evangelical rhetoric see

Herbert G. Gutman, "Protestantism and the Labor Movement: The Christian Spirit in the Gilded Age," *American Historical Review* 72 (October 1966): pp. 74-101.

16. *Secret Circular,* p. 2; see also Terence V. Powderly, *The Path I Trod,* ed. Harry J. Carman, Henry David, and Paul N. Guthrie (New York, 1940), p. 51.

17. Samuel Gompers to B. F. Gordon, June 9, 1893, Gompers' Letterbooks, vol. 9, p. 183, Manuscript Division, Library of Congress.

18. Powderly, *Path,* p. 38.

19. *Journal of United Labor,* June 1882, p. 248.

20. *Adelphon Kruptos,* n.d., p. 13.

21. Powderly, *Thirty Years,* p. 172.

22. Ibid., p. 281.

23. Ware, p. 378.

24. Powderly, *Thirty Years,* p. 280.

25. Terence V. Powderly to Charles A. Brannon, January 9, 1888, Powderly Papers, Letter Press Copy Books, vol. 32, p. 65, Catholic University of America; *Journal of United Labor,* January 29, 1887, p. 2265.

26. *United Mine Workers' Journal,* February 18, 1892, pp. 11-12.

27. *United Mine Workers' Journal,* April 26, 1894, p. 4.

28. Powderly, *Thirty Years,* p. 168.

29. Donald B. Robinson, *Spotlight on a Union* (New York, 1948), p. 112.

30. Powderly, *Thirty Years,* p. 168.

31. For the development of this concept see Milton Derber, *The American Idea of Industrial Democracy, 1865-1965* (Urbana, Ill., 1870).

32. Henry White, "A Labor Leader's Own Story," *The World's Work,* 22 (October 1911):14966-67.

33. James Duncan to Elbert Hubbard, February 22, 1906, Mitchell Papers, file 68, Catholic University of America.

34. *United Mine Workers' Journal,* July 11, 1907, p. 2.

35. *United Mine Workers' Journal,* July 26, 1894, p. 4.

36. *Garment Worker,* February 1901, p. 1.

37. Samuel Gompers to E. H. Cherry, February 10, 1892, Gompers' Letterbooks, vol. 7, p. 50, Manuscript Division, Library of Congress.

38. Samuel Gompers, *Seventy Years of Life and Labor,* 2 vols. (New York, 1925), 1:164.

39. American Federation of Labor, *Report of Proceedings of the Thirteenth Annual Convention,* December 11-19, 1893, p. 9.

40. Samuel Gompers to Louis Kemper, January 22, 1904, Gompers' Letterbooks, vol. 84, pp. 173-74, Manuscript Division, Library of Congress.

41. *American Federationist,* May 1910, p. 418.

42. James C. Sylvis, ed., *The Life, Speeches, Labors, and Essays of William H. Sylvis* (Philadelphia, 1872), p. 451.

43. James Duncan to Elbert Hubbard, February 22, 1906, Mitchell Papers, file 68, Catholic University of America.

44. White, pp. 14966-67.

45. Gompers, *Seventy Years,* 2:89.

46. John Mitchell to A. J. Mooreshead, September 7, 1898, Mitchell Papers, file 92, Catholic University of America.

47. Terence Powderly to Charles Howard, July 7, 1884, Powderly Papers, Letter Press Copy Books, vol. 9, p. 204, Catholic University of America.

48. *United Mine Workers' Journal,* January 30, 1896, p. 5.

49. *United Mine Workers' Journal,* March 16, 1893, p. 1.

50. Gompers, *Seventy Years,* p. 31. Such statements were poppycock. In a letter to S. G. Perkins of the Cigar Makers, for instance, Gompers wrote: "If you can show to a number of delegates that in the interest of our cause they ought to vote for me I am sure that you will do so and I shall appreciate your action beyond measure." See Bernard Mandel, *Samuel Gompers, a Biography* (Yellow Springs, Ohio, 1963), p. 158.

51. *United Mine Workers' Journal,* March 16, 1899, p. 7.

52. John Swinton, *Striking for Life* (New York, 1894), pp. 210-12.

53. Powderly, *Thirty Years,* p. 281.

54. *Textile Worker,* July 1916, p. 24.

55. Charles A. and Mary Beard, *Rise of American Civilization,* 2 vols. (New York, 1930), 2:214.

56. *United Mine Workers' Journal,* February 9, 1893, p. 4.

57. *American Federation of Labor: History, Encyclopedia, Reference Book,* compiled by W. C. Roberts (Washington, 1919), p. 179.

58. White, p. 14967.

59. Cited in *United Mine Workers' Journal,* August 15, 1895, p. 2.

60. *United Mine Workers' Journal,* July 6, 1899, p. 4.

61. Sylvis, p. 451.

62. *United Mine Workers' Journal,* December 14, 1916, p. 4.

63. *United Mine Workers' Journal,* March 9, 1893, p. 7.

64. *United Mine Workers' Journal,* March 24, 1904, p. 6.

65. Uriah S. Stephens to R. Griffiths, December 25, 1878, Powderly Papers, Letter Press Copy Books, vol. B, p. 28, Catholic University of America.

66. Terence Powderly to Fred S. Lewis, January 23, 1886, Powderly Papers, Letter Press Copy Books, vol. 15, p. 28, Catholic University of America.

67. Samuel Gompers to M.G. Farnham, March 10, 1892, Gompers' Letterbooks, vol. 7, p. 126, Manuscript Division, Library of Congress.

68. *Typographical Journal,* February 1916, p. 170.

69. William M. Leiserson, *American Trade Union Democracy* (New York, 1959), pp. 75-76.

70. Robert Franklin Hoxie, *Trade Unionism in the United States* (New York, 1919), p. 59.

71. Philip Taft and Philip Ross, "American Labor Violence: Its Causes, Character, and Outcome," *Violence in America,* ed. Hugh David Graham and Ted Robert Gurr (New York, 1969), p. 270.

72. *American Federationist,* May 1910, p. 417.

73. American Federation of Labor, *Report of Proceedings of the Thirteenth Annual Convention,* December 11-19, 1893, p. 9; *United Mine Workers' Journal,* October 27, 1898, p. 4.

74. *Secret Circular,* p. 2.

75. Terence Powderly to U. S. Stephens, May 5, 1879, Powderly

Papers, Letter Press Copy Books, vol. A, pp. 215-16, Catholic University of America.

76. *Textile Worker,* August 1916, p. 13.

77. *American Federationist,* August 1894, p. 117.

78. *Textile Worker,* August 1916, p. 13.

79. *United Mine Workers' Journal,* May 26, 1898, p. 4.

80. *United Mine Workers' Journal,* October 1, 1891, p. 4.

81. *Miners' Magazine,* February 10, 1910, p. 8.

82. *United Mine Workers' Journal,* May 3, 1894, p. 4.

83. *American Federationist,* May 1910, p. 417.

84. Powderly, *Thirty Years,* pp. 175-76.

85. *Typographical Journal,* February 1909, p. 155.

86. *American Federation of Labor: History, Encyclopedia, Reference Book,* p. 227.

87. *Typographical Journal,* January 1913, p. 28; Stevenson, 11-12.

88. Cited in Philip S. Foner, *History of the Labor Movement in the United States* (New York, 1947-65), 4:136.

89. Gompers, *Seventy Years,* 1: 375.

90. Philip Taft, *The AFL in the Time of Gompers* (New York, 1957), p. 233.

91. Joseph G. Rayback, *A History of American Labor* (New York, 1966), pp. 209-12.

92. Frederick M. Heath, "Labor and the Progressive Movement in Connecticut," *Labor History* 12 (Winter 1971):54.

93. Daniel Tobin to G. W. Briggs, June 11, 1909, Teamster Papers,

series 1, State Historical Society of Wisconsin.

94. *Typographical Journal,* January 1913, p. 28.

95. John H. M. Laslett, *Labor and the Left* (New York, 1970).

96. Robert H. Wiebe, *The Search for Order, 1877-1920* (New York, 1967), pp. 145-46; see also Louis Galambos, "AFL's Concept of Big Business: A Quantitative Study of Attitudes toward the Large Corporation, 1894-1931," *Journal of American History* 57 (March 1971): 847-63.

97. *Textile Worker,* August 1916, p. 28.

98. *Garment Worker,* May 1901, p. 7.

99. Daniel Tobin to M. J. Cashal, December 13, 1913, Teamster Papers, series 1, State Historical Society of Wisconsin.

100. Stevenson, p. v.

101. *Miners' Magazine,* February 10, 1910, pp. 7-8; *Typographical Journal,* March 15, 1899, p. 236; *Typographical Journal,* December 1903, pp. 581-82; American Federation of Labor, *Report of Proceedings of the Thirty-Second Annual Convention,* November 11-23, 1912, pp. 162-79.

102. *Typographical Journal,* March 1915, p. 359; *Typographical Journal,* July 1918, pp. 11-13.

103. *American Federation of Labor: History, Encyclopedia, Reference Book,* pp. 183, 309.

104. *United Mine Workers' Journal,* June 4, 1908, p. 2.

105. *United Mine Workers' Journal,* June 26, 1917, p. 4.

106. *Typographical Journal,* October 1906, p. 459.

107. *Typographical Journal,*

May 1, 1900, p. 386.

108. *American Federationist,* September 1895, p. 118.

109. *United Mine Workers' Journal,* February 18, 1892, p. 4.

110. *United Mine Workers' Journal,* January 20, 1910, p. 22.

111. Samuel Gompers to Louis Kemper, January 22, 1904, Gomper's Letterbooks, vol. 84, p. 173, Manuscript Division, Library of Congress.

112. *American Federationist,* July 1908, pp. 522-23.

Chapter 3
Union, Management, and Leadership

1. Emanuel Stein, "The Dilemma of Union Democracy," *Labor: Readings on Major Issues,* ed. Richard A. Lester (New York, 1965), pp. 188-89.

2. Visionaries but not impractical, the leaders of "utopian" unions from the Knights of St. Crispin to the Industrial Workers of the World did not shun the immediate struggle for better hours, wages, and working conditions despite their commitment to the eventual emancipation of labor. See Lloyd Ulman, *The Rise of the National Trade Union* (Cambridge, Mass., 1955), pp. 425-26; Warren R. Van Tine, "Ben Williams: Wobbly Editor" (M.A. thesis, Dept. of History, Northern Illinois University, 1967), pp. 59-60.

3. In the scholarly treatments of the Knights of Labor, one looks in vain for an analysis of union-management relations. Yet in glass manufacturing, mining, railroading, and other industries the Knights had agreements, some of which contained sophisticated features such as profit sharing. An analysis of the Knights' relations with employers, evaluating the extent of agreements, their content, and their fate would be of a great value in reassessing the Noble and Holy Order.

4. Clarence E. Bonnett, *Employers' Associations in the United States* (New York, 1922), pp. 37-97.

5. George Gorham Groat, *An Introduction to the Study of Organized Labor in America* (New York, 1917), p. 168.

6. George Milton Janes, *The Control of Strikes in American Trade Unions* (Baltimore, 1916), p. 11.

7. Philip Taft and Philip Ross, "American Labor Violence: Its Causes, Character, and Outcome," *Violence in America,* ed. Hugh Davis Graham and Ted Robert Gurr (New York, 1969), p. 278.

8. Groat, p. 183.

9. Ibid., p. 177.

10. Ibid., pp. 220-35; Philip Taft, "Collective Bargaining Before the New Deal," *How Collective Bargaining Works* (New York, 1942), p. 875; C. Wilson Randle, *Collective Bargaining: Principles and Practice* (Boston, 1951), pp. 28-29.

11. See Groat, p. 180, for statistics on successful strikes from 1881 to 1905.

12. Stein, pp. 188-89.

13. Robert H. Wiebe, *The Search For Order, 1877-1920* (New York, 1967), pp. 1-10.

14. For the classic discussion of union development see John R. Commons, "American Shoemakers,

1648-1895: A Sketch of Industrial Evolution," *Quarterly Journal of Economics* 24 (November 1909): 53-59.

15. Ulman, p. 236.
16. Ibid., p. 234.
17. Martin Segal, *The Rise of the United Association* (Cambridge, Mass., 1970), pp. 30-33.
18. Ulman, p. 234.
19. Thomas Phillips to John C. Mulryan, May 11, 1890, Thomas Phillips Papers, box 1, U.S. Mss. 12A, State Historical Society of Wisconsin.
20. Chris Evans, ed., *History of the United Mine Workers of America*, 2 vols. (Indianapolis, 1918), 1: 52-53.
21. Janes, pp. 12-15; Robert K. Burns, "Daily Newspapers," *How Collective Bargaining Works* (New York, 1942), pp. 48-49.
22. Cited in Theodore W. Glocker, *The Government of American Trade Unions* (Baltimore, 1913), pp. 172-73.
23. Janes, pp. 12-15.
24. Robert A. Christie, *Empire in Wood* (Ithaca, N.Y., 1956), p. 61; Harold Seidman, *The Labor Czar* (New York, 1938), p. 6; David Brody, "Career Leadership and American Trade Unionism," *The Age of Industrialism in America*, ed. Frederick Cople Jaher (New York, 1968), pp. 292-93.
25. Minutes of Local Assembly 322, Knights of Labor, February 29, 1879, p. 2, Joseph Slight Papers, box 1, folder 1, Ohio Historical Society.
26. Glocker, pp. 109-10.
27. Ibid.
28. Ulman, pp. 223-24.
29. John Mitchell, *Organized Labor* (Philadelphia, 1903), p. 112.
30. Cited in Janes, p. 27.
31. Cited in Ulman, p. 224.
32. Ulman, pp. 223-42.
33. Ibid., pp. 27-32.
34. Ibid., pp. 37-42.
35. Christie, pp. 82, 318.
36. Clarence E. Bonnett, *History of Employers' Associations in the United States* (New York, 1956), pp. 220-56.
37. Taft and Ross, pp. 284-87; Vernon H. Jensen, *Heritage of Conflict* (Ithaca, N.Y., 1950), pp. 25-37.
38. Bonnett, *History*, pp. 413-14.
39. Janes, p. 92.
40. *Cigar Makers' Official Journal*, June 15, 1908, p. 8, cited in David J. Saposs, ed., *Readings in Trade Unionism* (New York, 1927), p. 168.
41. Mitchell, p. 89.
42. Ulman, 194-95.
43. *United Mine Workers' Journal*, June 7, 1894, p. 8.
44. Mitchell, p. 305.
45. Ibid., p. 306.
46. On the fate of Martin Irons see Gerald N. Grob, *Workers and Utopia* (Chicago, 1961), pp. 66-70.
47. John Brophy, *A Miner's Life*, ed. John O. P. Hall (Madison, Wis., 1964), p. 200.
48. *United Mine Workers' Journal*, June 28, 1894, p. 5.
49. *Miners' Magazine*, October 23, 1908, pp. 5-6.
50. Bernard Mandel, *Samuel Gompers, a Biography* (Yellow Springs, Ohio, 1963), pp. 227-32.
51. Cited in Janes, p. 118.
52. John Michael Gowaskie, "John Mitchell: A Study in Leadership" (Ph.D. diss., Catholic University of America, 1968), pp. 238-39.

53. Henry White, "A Labor Leader's Own Story," *The World's Work* 22 (October 1911):14968.

54. Groat, p. 177.

55. Bonnett, *Employers' Associations,* p. 23.

56. Ibid., p. 67.

57. Mitchell, p. 192.

58. Ibid., p. 188.

59. Selig Perlman, *A History of Trade Unionism in the United States* (New York, 1922), p. 145.

60. Randle, pp. 28-29.

61. Taft, "Collective Bargaining Before the New Deal," pp. 885-87.

62. Janes, pp. 35-37.

63. Joseph P. Goldberg, *The Maritime Story* (Cambridge, Mass., 1958), p. 23.

64. Randle, pp. 28-29.

65. Taft, "Collective Bargaining Before the New Deal," p. 881.

66. Bonnett, *Employers' Associations,* pp. 22-23.

67. Cited in James Weinstein, "Gompers and the New Liberalism, 1900-1909," *For a New America,* ed. James Weinstein and David W. Eakins (New York, 1970), p. 105.

68. Cited in Marguerite Green, *The National Civic Federation and the American Labor Movement, 1900-1925* (Washington, 1956),p. 55.

69. Samuel Gompers to C. P. Shea, January 4, 1904, Gompers' Letterbooks, vol. 83, pp. 2-3, Manuscript Division, Library of Congress.

70. *Typographical Journal,* March 15, 1899, p. 236.

71. Bonnett, *Employers' Associations,* p. 18.

72. Cited in Ulman, p. 238 (italics in original).

73. Stevenson, pp. 314-17.

74. William Z. Foster, *Misleaders of Labor* (Chicago, 1927), p. 19.

75. James Weinstein, *The Corporate Ideal in the Liberal State: 1900-1918* (Boston, 1968), p. 22.

76. Milton Derber, "Glass," *How Collective Bargaining Works* (New York, 1942), pp. 700-701.

77. Bonnett, *Employers' Associations,* pp. 70-71.

78. Taft, "Collective Bargaining Before the New Deal," pp. 881-99.

79. Helan Marot, *American Labor Unions* (New York, 1914), p. 27.

80. "List of Plants Operating under National Wage Scale," Joseph Slight Papers, box 7, folder 4, Ohio Historical Society.

81. Bonnett, *Employers' Associations,* p. 49.

82. White, pp. 14967-68.

83. *United Mine Workers' Journal,* March 17, 1910, p. 1.

84. Derber, "Glass," p. 701.

85. Marot, p. 18.

86. Derber, "Glass," pp. 715-16.

87. J. M. Neenan to Members of the Executive Board, November 8, 1910, Joseph Slight Papers, box 2, folder 1, Ohio Historical Society.

88. *Miners' Magazine,* February 17, 1910, p. 3; Foster, pp. 47-48.

89. Segal, pp. 52-53.

90. John Mitchell to Daniel Keefe, March 25, 1901, Mitchell Papers, file 25, Catholic University of America.

91. J. M. Neenan to Officers and Members, July 31, 1909, Joseph Slight Papers, box 2, folder 1, Ohio Historical Society.

92. *Magazine of the International Brotherhood of Teamsters,* October 1904, p. 21.

93. J. B. S. Hardman, "Stakes of Leadership," *American Labor Dynamics,* ed. J. B. S. Hardman (New York, 1928), p. 165.

94. Saposs, *Readings,* p. 223.

95. *The National,* April 1917, p. 5.

96. Waldo E. Fisher, "Bituminous Coal," *How Collective Bargaining Works* (New York, 1942), p. 251.

97. *United Mine Workers' Journal,* May 12, 1904, p. 1.

98. Bonnett, *History,* pp. 443-47.

99. Taft, "Collective Bargaining Before the New Deal," p. 899.

100. Bonnett, *Employers' Associations,* pp. 23-25.

101. Weinstein, *Corporate Ideal,* p. 123.

102. Taft, "Collective Bargaining Before the New Deal," pp. 898-900.

103. Kenneth E. Boulding, *The Organizational Revolution* (New York, 1953), p. 105.

104. Joseph R. Conlin, *Big Bill Haywood and the Radical Union Movement* (Syracuse, N.Y., 1969), p. 77.

105. *Miners' Magazine,* October 12, 1911, p. 3.

106. American Federation of Labor, *Report of Proceedings of the Twenty-Ninth Annual Convention,* November 8-20, 1909, p. 324.

107. Weinstein, *Corporate Ideal,* p. 16.

108. *The National,* May 1917, p. 1.

109. Randle, pp. 58-59.

110. *United Mine Workers' Journal,* July 26, 1917, p. 4.

111. Janes, p. 13.

Chapter 4
Leaders and the Led

1. *American Federationist,* July 1908, p. 522.

2. *Typographical Journal,* August 1, 1898, pp. 102-4.

3. American Federation of Labor, *Report of Proceedings of the Thirty-Second Annual Convention,* November 11-23, 1912, p. 166.

4. *United Mine Workers' Journal,* November 9, 1899, p. 4.

5. Henry White, "A Labor Leader's Own Story," *The World's Work* 22 (October 1911):14966.

6. Abraham Bisno, *Abraham Bisno: Union Pioneer,* ed. Joel Seidman (Madison, Wis., 1967), pp. xi, 158.

7. White, p. 14966.

8. James C. Sylvis, ed., *The Life, Speeches, Labors, and Essays of William H. Sylvis* (Philadelphia, 1872), p. 432.

9. Robert Watchorn, *The Autobiography of Robert Watchorn,* ed. Herbert F. West (Oklahoma City, 1959), p. 18.

10. Ibid., p. 66.

11. Elsie Gluck, *John Mitchell, Miner* (New York, 1929), p. 50.

12. Matthew Josephson, *Union House, Union Bar* (New York, 1956), p. 71.

13. Frank Farrington to John Mitchell, December 12, 1906; Mitchell to Farrington, December 15, 1906, Mitchell Papers, file 323, Catholic University of America.

14. Paul W. Pritchard, "William B. Wilson: The Evolution of a Central Pennsylvania Mine Union Leader" (Ph.D. diss., Dept. of History, University of Pennsylvania, 1942), p. 175.

15. Joseph Michael Gowaskie, "John Mitchell: A Study in Leadership" (Ph.D. diss., Catholic University of America, 1968), p. 213.

16. *Journal of United Labor,* October 22, 1887, p. 2510.

17. Joseph R. Buchanan, *The Story of a Labor Agitator* (New

York, 1903), p. 447.

18.*United Mine Workers' Journal,* November 17, 1898, p. 1.

19.*United Mine Workers' Journal,* February 2, 1899, p. 1.

20.*United Mine Workers' Journal,* July 23, 1908, p. 1.

21. Cited in Lloyd Ulman, *The Rise of the National Trade Union* (Cambridge, Mass., 1955), p. 301.

22. Cited in William Z. Foster, *Misleaders of Labor* (Chicago, 1927), pp. 94-95.

23.*Journal of United Labor,* September 10, 1884, p. 790.

24. Ulman, pp. 3-6, 300-301.

25. Samuel Gompers, *Seventy Years of Life and Labor,* 2 vols. (New York, 1925), 1:166.

26.*Typographical Journal,* June 15, 1902, p. 506.

27.*Miners' Magazine,* February 10, 1910, p. 7.

28. The responding unions followed no consistent form in reporting results. In particular, the percentage of participation was estimated by the leaders. No doubt some leaders, hoping to improve their union's image, reported higher proportions voting than was justified, while leaders opposed to the referendum gave unjustly low returns in order to downgrade the system.

29. American Federation of Labor, *Report of Proceedings of the Thirty-Second Annual Convention,* November 11-23, 1912, pp 162-79.

30.*United Mine Workers' Journal,* January 19, 1893, p. 5.

31. James Hudson Maurer, *It Can Be Done* (New York, 1938), pp. 85-86.

32.*United Mine Workers' Journal,* July 5, 1900, p. 4.

33. John Brophy, *A Miner's Life,* ed. John O. P. Hall (Madison, Wis., 1964), p. 77.

34.*Garment Worker,* April 1893, p. 90.

35.*Garment Worker,* August 1900, pp. 10-11.

36. Josephson, p. 95.

37. Terence Powderly to Edward L. Daley, April 13, 1886, Powderly Papers, Letter Press Copy Books, vol. 17, p. 174, Catholic University of America.

38.*Garment Worker,* February 1895, p. 9.

39. Gompers, 2:138.

40. Victor A. Thompson, *Modern Organization* (New York, 1961), p. 67.

41.*United Mine Workers' Journal,* March 23, 1893, p. 1.

42.*United Mine Worker's Journal,* March 16, 1893, p. 1.

43. Ibid.

44. "Circular from Wm. H. Bailey, NDMW of Miners and Mine Laborers NDA," June 6, 1886, Edward A. Wieck Collection, Archives of Labor History and Urban Affairs, Wayne State University.

45. Robert Michels, *Political Parties,* trans. Eden and Ceder Paul (New York, 1959), p. 53.

46. Gluck, p. 86.

47.*Journal of United Labor,* January 1884, p. 621.

48.*Typographical Journal,* December 1914, p. 770; George James Stevenson, "The Brotherhood of Locomotive Engineers and Its Leaders, 1863-1920" (Ph.D. diss., Vanderbilt University, 1954), p. 119.

49.*New York Times,* July 29, 1948, p. 21.

50.*United Mine Workers' Journal,* July 13, 1899, p. 4; *United*

Mine Workers' Journal, July 29, 1899, p. 2.

51. *United Mine Workers' Journal,* December 24, 1891, p. 4.

52. Gluck, p. 66.

53. Harold Seidman, *The Labor Czars* (New York, 1938), pp. 27-28.

54. Terence V. Powderly, *The Path I Trod,* eds. Harry J. Carman, Henry David, and Paul N. Guthrie, (New York, 1940), p. 35.

55. John Swinton, *Striking for Life* (New York, 1894), p. 150.

56. Jay Rubin and M. J. Obermeier, *Growth of a Union* (New York, 1943), p. 20.

57. Agnes Nestor, *Woman's Labor Leader* (Rockford, Ill., 1954), p. 71.

58. *Journal of United Labor,* January 1884, p. 621.

59. Edward Pinkowski, *John Siney, the Miners' Martyr* (Philadelphia, 1963), p. viii.

60. *United Mine Workers' Journal,* June 9, 1904, p. 4.

61. Pinkowski, p. viii.

62. *Miners' Magazine,* January 23, 1908, p. 14.

63. Ibid.

64. *American Federationist,* September 1904, p. 728.

65. Terence Powderly to C. A. Beatty, November 12, 1886; Powderly to Fisher, November 28, 1886, Powderly Papers, Letter Press Copy Books, vol. 23, Catholic University of America.

66. *Miners' Magazine,* January 23, 1913, p. 7.

67. *United Mine Workers' Journal,* November 16, 1893, p. 2.

68. *United Mine Workers' Journal,* November 10, 1892, p. 8.

69. *Miners' Magazine,* January 23, 1913, p. 7.

70. *Solidarity,* December 28, 1912, p. 3.

71. *United Mine Workers' Journal,* August 15, 1895, p. 7.

72. Marguerite Green, *The National Civic Federation and the American Labor Movement, 1900-1925* (Washington, 1956), p. 87.

73. Pinkowski, p. 224.

74. Robert A. Christie, *Empire in Wood* (Ithaca, N.Y., 1956), pp. 96-105.

75. Melvyn Dubofsky, *We Shall Be All* (Chicago, 1969), pp. 459-60.

76. *United Mine Workers' Journal,* December 13, 1894, p. 1.

77. *American Federationist,* July 1908, pp. 522-23.

78. Pinkowski, p. 244.

79. Powderly, *Path,* pp. 38-39.

80. Samuel Gompers to John F. O'Sullivan, November 28, 1893, Gompers' Letterbooks, vol. 10, p. 87, Manuscript Division, Library of Congress.

81. John Mitchell to W. D. Ryan, May 19, 1902, Mitchell Papers, file 12, Catholic University of America.

82. *United Mine Workers' Journal,* February 14, 1895, p. 1.

83. Gompers, 1:356.

84. Daniel Tobin to George F. Golden, August 7, 1909, Teamster Papers, series 1, State Historical Society of Wisconsin.

85. Samuel Gompers to Julius Friedman, May 12, 1894, Gompers' Letterbooks, vol. 11, pp. 44-45, Manuscript Division, Library of Congress.

86. Richard D. Thomas, "Joseph Barondess: Labor Leader and Humanitarian" (M.A. thesis, Dept. of History, Ohio State University, 1958), p. 14.

87. William J. Duffy to General Executive Board, Knights of Labor, August 7, 1886, Saposs Papers, file 113, State Historical Society of Wisconsin.

88. Powderly, *Path,* p. 106.

89. Jonathan P. Grossman, *William Sylvis: Pioneer of American Labor* (New York, 1945), pp. 90-91.

90. See Thomas L. Hughes to Wm. H. Aston, November 1, 1910, Teamster Papers, series 1, State Historical Society of Wisconsin.

91. *Typographical Journal,* June 1914, p. 762.

92. White, pp. 14968-69.

93. John Gearty to Daniel Tobin, October 14, 1909, Teamster Papers, series 1, State Historical Society of Wisconsin.

94. Robert D. Leiter, *The Teamsters Union* (New York, 1957), p. 43; Josephson, p. 118; *The National,* November 1916, p. 10.

95. *United Mine Workers' Journal,* February 2, 1899, p. 4; *United Mine Workers' Journal,* December 5, 1904, p. 4.

96. *United Mine Workers' Journal,* May 7, 1891, p. 4; *United Mine Workers' Journal,* June 21, 1894, p. 1.

97. *United Mine Workers' Journal,* March 10, 1904, p. 4.

98. *United Mine Workers' Journal,* December 5, 1908, p. 4.

99. Daniel Tobin to Peter Burke, February 19, 1909, Teamster Papers, series 1, State Historical Society of Wisconsin.

100. H. H. Gerth and C. Wright Mills, eds., *From Max Weber* (New York, 1946), pp. 53-54, 262-64, 297.

101. See, for example, *United Mine Workers' Journal,* October 29, 1903, p. 1.

102. *United Mine Workers' Journal,* October 8, 1891, p. 2.

103. *United Mine Workers' Journal,* July 19, 1894, p. 5.

104. *United Mine Workers' Journal,* July 21, 1898, p. 8.

105. *United Mine Workers' Journal,* July 2, 1891, p. 4.

106. *United Mine Workers' Journal,* November 17, 1898, p. 4.

107. *United Mine Workers' Journal,* December 14, 1916, p. 4.

108. *United Mine Workers' Journal,* March 16, 1893, p. 1; *United Mine Workers' Journal,* March 23, 1893, p. 1.

109. *United Mine Workers' Journal,* December 8, 1898, p. 4.

110. *United Mine Workers' Journal,* July 2, 1891, p. 4.

111. *United Mine Workers' Journal,* February 2, 1899, p. 4.

112. *United Mine Workers' Journal,* June 18, 1908, p. 8.

113. Brophy, p. 161.

114. Edmund S. Morgan, *The Puritan Dilemma* (Boston, 1958).

115. *Textile Worker,* July, 1916, p. 28; *United Mine Workers' Journal,* July 19, 1900, p. 7; *Garment Worker,* April 1893, p. 7.

116. Statements taken out of order from Sylvis, pp. 428-34.

117. Grossman, pp. 40-42.

118. *Miners' Magazine,* February 10, 1910, p. 8.

119. *United Mine Workers' Journal,* September 10, 1914, p. 4.

120. *Typographical Journal,* October 15, 1899, p. 318.

121. *United Mine Workers' Journal,* February 8, 1895, p. 1.

122. *United Mine Workers' Journal,* January 24, 1895, p. 1.

123. *United Mine Workers' Journal,* March 7, 1895, p. 5.

124. A. A. Carlton to George E. McNeill, August 1, 1887, Carlton Letter Book, pp. 105-13, State Historical Society of Wisconsin.

125. Terence Powderly to Drew, July 6, 1882, Powderly Papers, Letter Press Copy Books, vol. 1, p. 235, Catholic University of America.

126. *United Mine Workers' Journal,* January 24, 1895, p. 5.

127. H. M. Gitelman, "Adolph Strasser and the Origins of Pure and Simple Unionism," *Labor History* 6 (Winter 1965):80-81.

128. Vincent Joseph Falzone, "Terence V. Powderly, Mayor and Labor Leader, 1849-1893" (Ph.D. diss., Dept. of History, University of Maryland, 1970), p. 272.

129. Terence Powderly to Bob Layton, May 17, 1882, Powderly Papers, Letter Press Copy Books, vol. 1, p. 64, Catholic University of America.

130. Daniel Tobin to George W. Griggs, March 4, 1909, Teamster Papers, series 1, State Historical society of Wisconsin.

131. Daniel Tobin to George Golden, August 11, 1909, Teamster Papers, series 1, State Historical Society of Wisconsin.

132. *United Mine Workers' Journal,* September 9, 1909, p. 1.

133. Sylvia Kopald, *Rebellion in Labor Unions* (New York, 1924), p. 33.

Chapter 5
Mechanisms of Power

1. Will Herberg, "Bureaucracy and Democracy in Labor Unions," *Antioch Review* 3 (September 1943):408-9.

2. Lloyd Ulman, *The Rise of the National Trade Union* (Cambridge, Mass., 1955), p. 4.

3. Ulman, p. 19; Joseph G. Rayback, *A History of American Labor* (New York, 1966), p. 279.

4. International Typographical Union, *Report of the Officers to the 64th Session* (Scranton, Pa., August 12-17, 1918), p. 105; Robert D. Leiter, *The Teamsters Union* (New York, 1957), p. 32.

5. *The National,* September, 1915, p. 24; Theodore W. Glocker, *The Government of American Trade Unions* (Baltimore, 1913), pp. 43-44.

6. Glocker, 126-27; Robert F. Hoxie, *Trade Unionism in the United States* (New York, 1919), p. 120.

7. John Mitchell, *Organized Labor* (Philadelphia, 1903), pp. 75-76.

8. Cited in Glocker, pp. 174-75.

9. Jonathan P. Grossman, *William Sylvis: Pioneer of American Labor* (New York, 1945), pp. 90-91.

10. Thomas L. Hughes to Wm. H. Ashton, November 1, 1910, Teamster Papers, series 1, State Historical Society of Wisconsin (my italics).

11. Cited in Bernard Mandel, *Samuel Gompers, a Biography* (Yellow Springs, Ohio, 1963), pp. 102-3.

12. Ulman, pp. 243-44.

13. Ibid., pp. 213-17.

14. Ibid., pp. 244-51.

15. Cited in William M. Leiserson, *American Trade Union Democracy* (New York, 1959), p. 136.

16. *Typographical Journal,* June 15, 1902, p. 506.

17. Ibid.

18. Matthew Josephson, *Union*

House, Union Bar (New York, 1956), pp. 15-25.

19. Ulman, p. 262.

20. Martin Segal, *The Rise of the United Association* (Cambridge, Mass., 1970), p. 158.

21. American Federation of Labor, *Report of Proceedings of the Thirty-Second Annual Convention*, November 11-23, 1912, pp. 162-79.

22. Segal, pp. 76, 158-59.

23. George Gorham Groat, *An Introduction to the Study of Organized Labor in America* (New York, 1917), p. 103.

24. Joel Seidman, "Some Requirements for Union Democracy," *Labor: Readings on Major Issues*, ed. Richard A. Lester (New York, 1965), p. 168.

25. Ulman, p. 262.

26. Segal, p. 158.

27. Mark Perlman, *The Machinists* (Cambridge, Mass., 1961), pp. 163-65.

28. Glocker, pp. 160-61.

29. Ibid., pp. 168-69.

30. Segal, pp. 39, 43, 82, 151.

31. Leiserson, p. 126.

32. Josephson, p. 35.

33. *Typographical Journal*, March 1915, p. 359.

34. Cited in Leiserson, pp. 132-33.

35. Robert Michels, *Political Parties*, trans. Eden and Ceder Paul (New York, 1915), pp. 24-25.

36. *Typographical Journal*, June 15, 1905, p. 506; Segal, pp. 158-59.

37. *United Mine Workers' Journal*, April 19, 1894, p. 4.

38. Leiserson, pp. 132-33.

39. *Typographical Journal*, March 1915, p. 359.

40. Henry White, "A Labor Leader's Own Story," *The World's Work* 22 (October, 1911):14967.

41. Amalgamated Clothing Workers of America, *Documentary History* (New York, 1914-16), pp. 4-8.

42. John Hayes to A. A. Adams, September 21, 1895, Hayes Papers, box 27, Catholic University of America.

43. T. V. Powderly to John Hayes, July 27, 1887, Hayes Papers, box 36, Catholic University of America; John Mitchell to W. D. Ryan, September 29, 1905, Mitchell Papers, file 12, Catholic University of America.

44. Robert A. Christie, *Empire in Wood* (Ithaca, N.Y., 1956), pp. 137-54; Joseph R. Buchanan, *The Story of a Labor Agitator* (New York, 1903), pp. 359-72; Leiter, p. 29; Josephson, pp. 73-75.

45. T. V. Powderly to John Creamer, September 16, 1886, Powderly Papers, Letter Press Copy Books, vol. 21, Catholic University of America.

46. American Federation of Labor, *Report of Proceedings of the Thirty-Second Annual Convention*, November 11-23, 1912, p. 166.

47. Ibid., p. 171.

48. Fred Greenbaum, "The Social Ideas of Samuel Gompers," *Labor History* 7 (Winter 1966):53-54.

49. Western Federation of Miners, *Proceedings of the Fifteenth Annual Convention*, June–July 3, 1907, pp. 822-23.

50. *United Mine Workers' Journal*, January 14, 1892, p. 1.

51. *United Mine Workers' Journal*, January 6, 1898, p. 4.

52. John Mitchell to Mike Ratchford, September 21, 1898; John Mitchell to William Warner, October 25, 1899, Mitchell Papers, file 92, Catholic University of America,

53. Joseph Michael Gowaskie, "John Mitchell: A Study in Leadership" (Ph.D. diss., Catholic University of America, 1968), pp. 26-32.

54. *Typographical Journal,* December 1, 1898, p. 457.

55. Ibid.; Ulman, pp. 271-74.

56. *Typographical Journal,* December 1, 1898, 457-58.

57. Groat, p. 103.

58. Frederick S. Deibler, *The Amalgamated Wood Workers' International Union of America* (Madison, Wis., 1912), p. 79.

59. *Typographical Journal,* December 1, 1898, p. 458.

60. American Federation of Labor, *Report of Proceedings of the Thirty-Second Annual Convention,* November 11-23, 1912, pp. 162-79.

61. See chapter four, pp. 92-93.

62. *Typographical Journal,* December 1, 1898, p. 457.

63. *Typographical Journal,* January 1, 1901, p. 6.

64. Garth L. Mangum, *The Operating Engineers* (Cambridge, Mass., 1964), p. 32.

65. *Garment Worker,* January 1896, p. 12.

66. American Federation of Labor, *Report of Proceedings of the Thirty-Second Annual Convention,* November 11-23, 1912, p. 168.

67. Perlman, *Machinists,* p. 169.

68. Ulman, p. 276.

69. Ibid., pp. 276-77.

70. Mangum, pp. 28-33.

71. Glocker, pp. 224-25.

72. American Federation of Labor, *Report of Proceedings of the Thirty-Second Annual Convention,* November 11-23, 1912, p. 166.

73. Ibid., p. 167.

74. Mangum, pp. 32-33; see *Typographical Journal,* December 1,

1898, p. 453.

75. Sylvia Kopald, *Rebellion in Labor Unions* (New York, 1924), p. 181.

76. Samuel Gompers to H. S. Mills, May 22, 1897, Gompers' Letterbooks, vol. 20, Manuscript Division, Library of Congress.

77. White, p. 14967.

78. *Typographical Journal,* December 1, 1898, p. 457.

79. Christie, pp. 141-42.

80. *Typographical Journal,* December 1, 1898, pp. 451-54.

81. American Federation of Labor, *Report of Proceedings of the Thirty-Second Annual Convention,* November 11-23, 1912, p. 166.

82. *Typographical Journal,* January 1, 1901, p. 6.

83. Cited in Diebler, pp. 82-84.

84. Glocker, p. 187.

85. Ibid., pp. 186-90; Leiserson, pp. 224-25.

86. Ulman, pp. 286-96; Glocker, p. 195,

87. *United Mine Workers' Journal,* February 1892, p. 2.

88. T. V. Powderly to George S. Boyle, January 25, 1885, Powderly Papers, Letter Press Copy Books, vol. 32, p. 113, Catholic University of America.

89. Leiserson, pp. 224-25.

90. Glocker, p. 118.

91. Christie, pp. 69-78, 142-54.

92. Leiter, pp. 30-31.

93. John Gearty to Daniel Tobin, October 14, 1909, Teamster Papers, series 1, State Historical Society of Wisconsin.

94. Leiserson, p. 227.

95. Vincent J. Falzone, "Terence V. Powderly, Mayor and Labor Leader, 1849-1893" (Ph.D. diss., University of Maryland, 1970),

pp. 286-87.

96. Michael A. Mulcaire, *The International Brotherhood of Electrical Workers* (Washington, 1923), p. 98.

97. Leiserson, p. 227.

98. Ulman, p. 297.

99. *Typographical Journal,* October 1908, p. 393.

100. Leiserson, p. 227.

101. *American Federation of Labor: History, Encyclopedia, Reference Book,* compiled by W. C. Roberts (Washington, 1919), p. 333.

102. *Typographical Journal,* December 1908, p. 646.

103. Glocker, p. 189.

104. Ibid., pp. 176-77.

105. Ibid., pp. 177-78.

106. Ibid., pp. 178-81.

107. American Federation of Labor, *Report of Proceedings of the Fortieth Annual Convention,* June 7-19, 1920, pp. 31-33.

108. United Mine Workers of America, *Report of William Green, International Secretary-Treasurer to the Twenty-Eight Consecutive and Fifth Biennial Convention of the United Mine Workers of America,* Indianapolis, September 20, 1921, pp. 80-85.

109. Glocker, p. 153.

110. *United Mine Workers' Journal,* April 11, 1895, p. 5; *United Mine Workers' Journal,* March 5, 1896, p. 4.

111. Segal, p. 43.

112. *Magazine of the International Brotherhood of Teamsters,* November 1903, p. 11.

113. T. V. Powderly to W. J. Wright, March 4, 1896, Powderly Papers, Letter Press Copy Books, vol. 15, p. 238, Catholic University of America.

114. Norman J. Ware, *The Labor Movement in the United States, 1860-1895* (New York, 1929), p. 91.

115. Knights of Labor, *Proceedings of the General Assembly, First Regular Session,* Reading, Pa., January 1-4, 1878, p. 20.

116. T. V. Powderly to Sharpe, December 9, 1883, Powderly Papers, Letter Press Copy Books, vol. 8, p. 54, Catholic University of America.

117. T. V. Powderly to C. C. Post, August 5, 1894, Powderly Papers, Letter Press Copy Books, vol. 9, p. 364, Catholic University of America.

118. T. V. Powderly to Fred [Turner], March 15, 1886, Powderly Papers, Letter Press Copy Books, vol. 15, p. 296, Catholic University of America.

119. T. V. Powderly to Charles A. Brannon, January 9, 1888, Powderly Papers, Letter Press Copy Books, vol. 32, p. 65, Catholic University of America.

120. T. V. Powderly to W. B. Chapman, July 27, 1886, Powderly Papers, Letter Press Copy Books, vol. 21, p. 2, Catholic University of America.

121. Mulcaire, p. 7.

122. Thomas Phillips to John C. Mulryan, May 11, 1890, Thomas Phillips Papers, box 1, U.S. Mss., 12A, State Historical Society of Wisconsin; Ulman, p. 234.

123. "Sketch of Trevellick," p. 5., Thomas Phillips Papers, box 1, U.S. Mss., 12A, State Historical Society of Wisconsin; Charles E. Killeen, "John Siney: Pioneer in American Industrial Unionism and Industrial Government" (Ph.D. diss., University of Wisconsin, 1942), p. 123;

Grossman, p. 83.

124. "Sketch of Trevellick," p. 5.

125. McAlister Coleman, *Men and Coal* (New York, 1943), p. 44.

126. Killeen, p. 126.

127. Grossman, p. 88.

128. Mangum, pp. 21-25.

129. Ulman, pp. 222-23.

130. Segal, pp. 43-44.

131. Ulman, p. 220.

132. *Typographical Journal*, October 1904, p. 363.

133. *United Mine Workers' Journal*, April 18, 1895, p. 5; ibid., April 25, 1895, p. 8; ibid., December 3, 1896, p. 1.

134. *The National*, August 1916, p. 28.

135. *Typographical Journal*, May 1915, p. 720.

136. Cited in David J. Saposs, ed., *Readings in Trade Unionism* (New York, 1927), p. 153.

137. *Typographical Journal*, August 1907, p. 161.

138. Industrial Workers of the World, *Second I.W.W. Convention*, Chicago, September 17–October 3, 1906, pp. 467-68.

139. Ulman, p. 219.

140. Cited in Saposs, p. 153.

141. *Literary Digest* 64 (January 17, 1920):84-90; American Federation of Labor, *Report of Proceedings of the Eleventh Annual Convention*, December 11-20, 1899, p. 150; American Federation of Labor, *Report of Proceedings of the Fortieth Annual Convention*, June 7-19, 1920, p. 428; International Typographical Union, *Report of the Proceedings of the Forty-Sixth Session*, Milwaukee, August 13-18, 1900, p. 89; Segal, pp. 87-91; Mangum, pp. 22-25, 71-72.

142. American Federation of Labor, *Report of Proceedings of the Thirty-Fourth Annual Convention*, November 9-19, 1914, pp. 376-77.

143. *Typographical Journal*, October 1914, p. 363.

144. *Typographical Journal*, July 1907, p. 31.

145. Joseph P. Goldberg, *The Maritime Story* (Cambridge, Mass., 1958), p. 50.

146. Knights of Labor, *Proceedings of the General Assembly, Sixth Regular Session*, New York, September 5-12, 1882, p. 369.

147. Falzone, pp. 142, 191.

148. Samuel Gompers to Dr. Branch Clark, August 8, 1894, Gompers' Letterbooks, vol. 11, p. 225, Manuscript Division, Library of Congress.

149. Mandel, p. 89; American Federation of Labor, *Report of Proceedings of the Eleventh Annual Convention*, December 11-20, 1899, p. 150; American Federation of Labor, *Report of Proceedings of the Twenty-Seventh Annual Convention*, November 11-23, 1907, pp. 194-95; American Federation of Labor, *Report of Proceedings of the Thirty-Fourth Annual Convention*, November 9-14, 1914, pp. 376-77; American Federation of Labor, *Report of Proceedings of the Thirty-Ninth Annual Convention*, June 9-23, 1919, pp. 435-36.

150. American Federation of Labor, *Report of Proceedings of the Thirty-Fourth Annual Convention*, November 9-14, 1914, pp. 376-77.

151. Gowaskie, p. 80.

152. Amalgamated Clothing Workers of America, *Proceedings of the Third Biennial Convention*, Baltimore, May 13-18, 1919, p. 252; Leiter, p. 32.

153. Daniel J. Keefe to John Mitchell, July 24, 1901, Mitchell Papers, file 28, Catholic University of America.

154. T. V. Powderly to E. H. Perdue, August 17, 1886, Powderly Papers, Letter Press Copy Books, vol. 17, p. 218, Catholic University of America.

155. Samuel Gompers to M. J. Carroll, August 2, 1894, Gompers' Letterbooks, vol. 11, p. 204, Manuscript Division, Library of Congress.

156. *Typographical Journal,* March 1907, p. 309.

157. Victor A. Thompson, *Modern Organization* (New York, 1961), pp. 68-69.

158. Mulcaire, pp. 13-14.

159. Segal, p. 89.

160. *Literary Digest* 64 (January 17, 1920):84-90.

161. *Typographical Journal,* December 1907, p. 280; International Typographical Union, *Report of Officers and Proceedings of the Fifty-Third Session,* August 12-17, 1907, p. 49.

162. American Federation of Labor, *Report of Proceedings of the Thirty-Ninth Annual Convention,* June 9-23, 1919, pp. 33-40.

163. *Literary Digest* 64 (January 17, 1920):90.

164. Scott Nearing, "Earnings in the United States," *The American Labor Yearbook* 2 (New York, 1917-18) :159-61.

165. Christie, p. 139; Segal, p. 89.

166. Cited in Christie, p. 140.

167. John Mitchell to William Warner, October 25, 1899, Mitchell Papers, file 92, Catholic University of America.

168. William Warner to Mitchell, December 1, 1898; Mitchell to War-ner, February 2, 1899; Warner to Mitchell, March 5, 1899; Mitchell to Warner, October 25, 1899, Mitchell Papers, file 92, Catholic University of America.

169. Christie, p. 139.

170. Josephson, p. 74.

171. *American Federation of Labor: History, Encyclopedia, Reference Book,* pp. 306-9; American Federation of Labor, *Report of Proceedings of the Fortieth Annual Convention,* June 7-19, 1920, pp. 31-33.

172. Mandel, p. 101.

173. *Typographical Journal,* August 1909, pp. 137-38; Kopald, p. 192.

174. Mandel, pp. 225-26.

175. John Frey to W. A. Appleton, July 9, 1919, John Frey Papers, box 1, file 3, Manuscript Division, Library of Congress.

176. Josephson, pp. 24-25.

177. Philip Taft, *The AFL in the Time of Gompers* (New York, 1957), p. 112; see Michael Rogin, "Voluntarism: The Political Function of an Anti-Political Doctrine," *Industrial and Labor Relations Review* 15 (July 1962):521-35.

178. Amalgamated Clothing Workers of America, *Documentary History,* pp. 61-62.

179. Ibid.

180. Helen Marot, *American Labor Unions* (New York, 1914), pp. 19-20.

181. Donald B. Robinson, *Spotlight on a Union* (New York, 1948), pp. 81-98.

182. Perlman, *Machinists,* pp. 15-38.

183. *United Mine Workers' Journal,* June 20, 1918, p. 12; *Who Was Who,* 1:721; Solon DeLeon, ed.,

American Labor Who's Who (New York, 1926), p. 23.

184. Kopald, pp. 167-68.

Chapter 6
The New Men of Power

1. "Sketch of Richard Trevellick," p. 7, Thomas Phillips Papers, box 1, U.S. Mss., 12A, State Historical Society of Wisconsin; John Mitchell to William B. Wilson, June 1, 1906, Mitchell Papers, file 99, Catholic University of America.

2. *United Mine Workers' Journal,* April 6, 1893, p. 2.

3. Cited in George James Stevenson, "The Brotherhood of Locomotive Engineers and Its Leaders, 1863-1920" (Ph.D. diss., Vanderbilt University, 1954), pp. 237-38.

4. Bernard Mandel, *Samuel Gompers, a Biography* (Yellow Springs, Ohio, 1963), pp. 171-72.

5. Samuel Gompers, *Seventy Years of Life and Labor,* 2 vols. (New York, 1925), 1:273.

6. *United Mine Workers' Journal,* May 3, 1894, p. 4.

7 *United Mine Workers' Journal,* May 3, 1894, p. 4.

8. *United Mine Workers' Journal,* March 17, 1904, p. 1.

9. *United Mine Workers' Journal,* September 15, 1910, p. 1.

10. *United Mine Workers' Journal,* October 26, 1916, p. 1.

11. Joseph B. Buchanan, *The Story of a Labor Agitator* (New York, 1903), pp. 18, 177-247.

12. *United Mine Workers' Journal,* July 20, 1905, p. 5.

13. *Miners' Magazine,* January 8, 1914, pp. 5-7.

14. *United Mine Workers' Journal,* August 7, 1902, p. 2.

15. Charles E. Killeen, "John Siney: The Pioneer in American Industrial Unionism and Industrial Government" (Ph.D. diss., Dept. of History, University of Wisconsin, 1942), pp. 320-46; Edward Pinkowski, *John Siney, the Miners' Martyr* (Philadelphia, 1963), p. 71; Ray Ginger, *The Bending Cross: A Biography of Eugene Victor Debs* (New Brunswick, N.J., 1949), pp. 162-83; Almonst Lindsey, *The Pullman Strike* (Chicago, 1942, pp. 274-305; Marc Karson, *American Labor Unions and Politics* (Carbondale, Ill., 1958), pp. 50-53; Melvyn Dubofsky, *We Shall Be All* (Chicago, 1969), pp. 96-105, 423-44.

16. Paul W. Pritchard, "William B. Wilson: The Evolution of a Central Pennsylvania Mine Union Leader" (Ph.D. diss., Dept., of History, University of Pennsylvania, 1942), pp. 165-67.

17. *United Mine Workers' Journal,* September 22, 1898, p. 1.

18. *United Mine Workers' Journal,* January 18, 1900, p. 4.

19. *United Mine Workers' Journal,* February 8, 1900, p. 4; ibid., February 22, 1900, p. 4.

20. *United Mine Workers' Journal,* January 17, 1918, p. 8.

21. *United Mine Workers' Journal,* June 4, 1891, p. 8; ibid., June 11, 1891, p. 4.

22. Cited in Richard D. Thomas, "Joseph Barondess: Labor Leader and Humanitarian" (M.A. thesis, Dept. of History, Ohio State University, 1958), p. 60.

23. *United Mine Workers' Journal,* October 14, 1915, p. 11.

24. Robert A. Christie, *Empire in*

Wood (Ithaca, N.Y., 1956), p. 164.

25. Thomas L. Hughes to William H. Ashton, January 2, 1912, Teamster Papers, series 1, State Historical Society of Wisconsin.

26. George Golden to Daniel Tobin, April 2, 1902, Teamster Papers, series 1, State Historical Society of Wisconsin.

27. Samuel Gompers to T. M. Gruelle, May 10, 1894, Gompers' Letterbooks, vol. 11, p. 38, Manuscript Division, Library of Congress.

28. *United Mine Workers' Journal,* February 8, 1895, p. 1; *Typographical Journal,* October 15, 1899, p. 318.

29. Christie, p. 95; John Brophy, *A Miner's Life,* ed. John O. P. Hall (Madison, Wis., 1964), pp. 149-51; Charles A. Madison, *American Labor Leaders,* 2d ed. (New York, 1962), p. 171; Mandel, p. 171.

30. *Magazine of the International Brotherhood of Teamsters*, October 1904, p. 21.

31. *United Mine Workers' Journal,* February 18, 1897, p. 7.

32. *United Mine Workers' Journal,* November 30, 1893, p. 3.

33. *United Mine Workers' Journal,* July 16, 1903, p. 4.

34. *Garment Worker,* May 1901, p. 10.

35. Terence Powderly to John Hayes, July 27, 1887, Hayes Papers, box 36, Catholic University of America.

36. Agnes Nestor, *Woman's Labor Leader* (Rockford, Ill., 1954), p. 154.

37. *United Mine Workers' Journal,* November 3, 1892, p. 4.

38. John Frey to W. A. Appleton, June 30, 1919, Frey Papers, box 1, no. 3; Samuel Gompers to John Frey, February 15, 1917, Frey Papers, box 10, file 138, Manuscript Division, Library of Congress.

39. Maxwell Raddock, *Portrait of an American Labor Leader: William L. Hutcheson* (New York, 1955), p. 65.

40. Mandel, pp. 7-10.

41. Jay Rubin and M. J. Obermeier, *Growth of a Union* (New York, 1943), pp. 27, 31-35.

42. Joseph Slight Papers, Manuscript Division, Ohio Historical Society.

43. Nester, p. 21; Mandel, pp. 8-9; James H. Maurer, *It Can Be Done* (New York, 1938), p. 65; Saul Alinsky, *John L. Lewis* (New York, 1949), pp. 17-18.

44. *United Mine Workers' Journal,* February 6, 1908, p. 1.

45. Raddock, p. 46.

46. Madison, 75-76; Norman Ware, *The Labor Movement in the United States, 1860-1895* (New York, 1929), p. 26.

47. Elsie Gluck, *John Mitchell, Miner,* (New York, 1929), pp. 24-25.

48. *United Mine Workers' Journal,* February 6, 1908, pp. 1, 14; ibid., March 7, 1895, p. 5; ibid., April 16, 1896, p. 4.

49. Alinsky, p. 26.

50. Matthew Josephson, *Union House, Union Bar* (New York, 1956), pp. 74-79; Joseph R. Conlin, *Big Bill Haywood and the Radical Union Movement* (Syracuse, 1969), p. 24; Donald B. Robinson, *Spotlight on a Union* (New York, 1948), pp. 126-27; Garth L. Mangum, *The Operating Engineers* (Cambridge, Mass., 1964), p. 64.

51. Brophy, pp. 149-51.

52. Rubin and Obermeier, pp. 72-

75; Josephson, pp. 70-73.

53. Irving Bernstein, *The Lean Years* (Baltimore, 1960), pp. 111-12; Christie, p. 142.

54. Mangum, p. 64.

55. *National Cyclopedia of American Biography* 26, p. 447; Irving Bernstein, *The Turbulent Years* (Boston, 1969), p. 8.

56. *National Cyclopedia of American Biography* 22:225-26.

57. John Mitchell to W. D. Ryan, September 14, 1899, Mitchell Papers, file 12; John Mitchell to Daniel J. Keefe, January 5, 1902; Daniel Keefe to John Mitchell, January 7, 1902, Mitchell Papers, file 28, Catholic University of America.

58. S. C. Burdett to John Mitchell, March 8, 1904; John Mitchell to S. C. Burdett, March 9, 1904, Mitchell Papers, file 120; M. F. Rafter to John Mitchell, February 5, 1907; John Mitchell to M. F. Rafter, February 7, 1907, Mitchell Papers, file 364, Catholic University of America.

59. John Mitchell to Daniel Keefe, February 27, 1901, Mitchell Papers, file 28, Catholic University o America.

60. John Mitchell to Daniel Keefe, December 22, 1900, Mitchell Papers, file 28, Catholic University of America.

61. John Mitchell to Daniel Keefe, February 16, 1901, Mitchell Papers, file 28, Catholic University of America.

62. Daniel Keefe to John Mitchell, January 2, 1901, Mitchell Papers, file 28, Catholic University of America.

63. John Mitchell to William B. Wilson, August 7, 1903, Mitchell Papers, file 99, Catholic University of America.

64. Christie, p. 67.

65. Mandel, p. 170.

66. Gluck, p. 150.

67. David J. McDonald, *Union Man* (New York, 1969), p. 32.

68. Ibid., p. 35.

69. Cited in C. Wright Mills, *The New Men of Power* (New York, 1948), p. 104.

70. Foster, pp. 23-24; Karson, pp. 160-61.

71. Robert Michels, *Political Parties,* trans. Eden and Ceder Paul (New York, 1959), pp. 310-11.

72. T. V. Powderly to Henry E. Sharpe, July 14, 1884, Powderly Papers, Letter Press Copy Books, vol. 9, p. 224, Catholic University of America.

73. Dubofsky, p. 481.

74. *United Mine Workers' Journal,* March 25, 1897, p. 5.

75. *United Mine Workers' Journal,* June 2, 1892, p. 5.

76. *Typographical Journal,* December 1914, p. 770.

77. Buchanan, pp. 324-25.

78. *United Mine Workers' Journal,* July 6, 1905, p. 2.

79. C. Wright Mills, *The Power Elite* (New York, 1956), pp. 10-11.

80. Ware, p. 83.

81. James Duncan to John Mitchell, March 11, 1904, Mitchell Papers, file 68, Catholic University of America.

82. John Mitchell to James Duncan, March 15, 1904, Mitchell Papers, file 68, Catholic University of America.

83. *United Mine Workers' Journal,* December 5, 1908, p. 4.

84. Solon DeLeon, ed., *American Labor Who's Who* (New York,

1926), pp. 94, 100, 142-43.

85. Lafayette G. Harter, *John R. Commons* (Corvallis, Oreg., 1962), pp. 19-24; Benjamin G. Rader, *The Academic Mind and Reform* (Lexington, Ky., 1960).

86. *Typographical Journal,* April 1915, p. 541.

87. John P. Frey to W. A. Appleton, June 30, 1919, Frey Papers, box 1, Manuscript Division, Library of Congress.

88. Karson, pp. 212-84.

89. George H. Nash, III, "Charles Stelzle: Apostle of Labor," *Labor History* 11 (Spring 1970):151-74.

90. *Textile Worker,* July 1916, p. 9.

91. Ronald Radosh, *American Labor and United States Foreign Policy* (New York, 1969).

92. J. M. Harriman to Earl E. Houck, April 28, 1924, Lewis Papers, State Historical Society of Wisconsin; *Who Was Who,* 2:60.

93. *The National,* April 1917, p. 3.

Bibliography

Primary Sources

Manuscript Materials

Columbus, Ohio. Ohio Historical Society. Joseph Slight Papers.
Detroit, Mich. Wayne State University, Archives of Labor History and Urban Affairs. Edward A. Wieck Collection.
Madison, Wis. State Historical Society of Wisconsin. American Federation of Labor Papers.
Madison, Wis. State Historical Society of Wisconsin. Albert A. Carlton Letter Book.
Madison, Wis. State Historical Society of Wisconsin. International Brother-hood of Teamsters, Chauffeurs, Warehousemen and Helpers Collection.
Madison, Wis. State Historical Society of Wisconsin. John Llewellyn Lewis Papers.
Madison, Wis. State Historical Society of Wisconsin. Thomas Phillips Papers.
Madison, Wis. State Historical Society of Wisconsin. David J. Saposs Papers.
Madison, Wis. State Historical Society of Wisconsin. Robert Schilling Papers.
Madison, Wis. State Historical Society of Wisconsin. Sovereign of Industry Collection.
Washington, D.C. The Catholic University of America, Department of Archives and Manuscripts. John W. Hayes Papers.
Washington, D.C. The Catholic University of America, Department of Archives and Manuscripts. Mary (Mother) Jones Papers.
Washington, D.C. The Catholic University of America, Department of Archives and Manuscripts. John Mitchell Papers.
Washington, D.C. The Catholic University of America, Department of Archives and Manuscripts. Terence V. Powderly Papers.
Washington, D.C. Library of Congress, Manuscript Division. American Federation of Labor: Letter Press Copy Books of Samuel Gompers and William Green, 1883-1924.
Washington, D. C. Library of Congress, Manuscript Division. John P. Frey Papers.

Convention Proceedings

Amalgamated Clothing Workers of America. *Official Convention Proceedings,* in *Documentary History of the Amalgamated Clothing Workers, 1914-1919.*
American Federation of Labor. *Report of the Proceedings of the Annual Conventions, 1881-1920.*
Industrial Workers of the World. *Proceedings of the Annual Conventions, 1905-1906.*
International Typographical Union. *Proceedings of the Sessions, 1898-1918.*
Knights of Labor. *Proceedings of the General Assembly, 1878-1896.*
United Mine Workers of America. *Proceedings of the Conventions, 1891-1919.*
Western Federation of Miners. *Proceedings of the Annual Conventions, 1907-1910.*

Union Journals

Advance.
American Federationist.
Garment Worker.
Magazine of the International Brotherhood of Teamsters.
Journal of the Electrical Workers.
Journal of United Labor. (After December 1889 entitled *Journal of the Knights of Labor.*)
Miners' Magazine.
National.
Stationary Firemen's Journal.
Textile Worker.
Typographical Journal.
United Mine Workers' Journal.

Reminiscences and Autobiographies

Bisno, Abraham. *Abraham Bisno: Union Pioneer.* Edited by Joel Seidman. Madison: University of Wisconsin Press, 1967.
Brophy, John. *A Miner's Life.* Edited and supplemented by John O. P. Hall. Madison: University of Wisconsin Press, 1964.
Buchanan, Joseph R. *The Story of a Labor Agitator.* New York: Outlook Co., 1903.
Chaplin, Ralph. *Wobbly.* Chicago: University of Chicago Press, 1948.

Gompers, Samuel. *Seventy Years of Life and Labor.* 2 vols. New York: E. P. Dutton and Co., 1925.

Haywood, William D. *Bill Haywood's Book.* New York: International Publishers, 1929.

Irons, Martin. "My Experiences in the Labor Movement." *Lippincott's Magazine* 37 (June 1886):618-27.

Jones, Mary H. *Autobiography of Mother Jones.* Edited by Mary Field Parton. Chicago: C. H. Kerr and Co., 1925.

McDonald, David J. *Union Man: The Life of a Labor Statesman.* New York: E. P. Dutton and Co., 1969.

McNeill, George E., ed. *The Labor Movement.* New York: M. W. Hazen Co., 1887.

Maurer, James Hudson. *It Can Be Done.* New York: Rand School Press, 1938.

Mitchell, John. *Organized Labor.* Philadelphia: American Book and Bible House, 1903.

Nester, Agnes. *Woman's Labor Leader: An Autobiography.* Rockford, Ill.: Bellevue Books Publishing Co., 1954.

Powderly, Terence V. *Thirty Years of Labor: 1859 to 1889.* Columbus, Ohio: Excelsior Publishing House, 1890.

_____. *The Path I Trod.* Edited by Harry J. Carman, Henry David, and Paul N. Guthrie. New York: Columbia University Press, 1940.

Swinton, John. *Striking for Life.* New York: American Manufacturing and Publishing Co., 1894.

Sylvis, James C., ed. *The Life, Speeches, Labors, and Essays of William H. Sylvis.* Philadelphia: Claxton, Remsen and Hoffelfinger, 1872.

Watchorn, Robert. *The Autobiography of Robert Watchorn.* Edited by Herbert F. West. Oklahoma City: The Robert Watchorn Charities, 1959.

White, Henry. "A Labor Leader's Own Story." *The World's Work* 22 (September–October 1911):14851-55, 14960-72; 23 (November 1911): 107-114.

Others

Adelphon Kruptos. n.d.

Amalgamated Clothing Workers of America. *Report of the General Executive Board of the Fourth Biennial Convention.* Boston, May 10-15, 1920.

_____. *Documentary History.* 6 vols. New York: Amalgamated Clothing Workers' Union, 1914-16.

American Federation of Labor. *American Federation of Labor: History, Encyclopedia, Reference Book.* Compiled by William Clark Roberts. New York: American Federation of Labor, 1919.

Baker, Ray Stannard. "The Trust's New Tool—The Labor Boss." *McClure's Magazine* 22 (November 1903):30-43.

Brotherhood of Locomotive Firemen and Enginemen. *Constitution, Revised 1913.*

Commons, John R., et al., eds. *A Documentary History of American Industrial Society.* 10 vols. Cleveland: A. H. Clark, 1910-11.

Evans, Chris. *History of the United Mine Workers of America.* 2 vols. Indianapolis: The United Mine Workers of America, 1918.

Granite Cutters' International Association of America. *Constitution, Revised 1921.*

Knights of Labor. *Secret Circular: Explanation of the Signs and Symbols of the Order of the Knights of Labor.* n.d.

United States Bureau of the Census. *Seventh Census Compendium.* 1850.

_____. *Ninth Census Compendium.* 1870.

_____. *Tenth Census Compendium.* 1880.

_____. *Thirteenth Census Compendium.* 1910.

Willey, Day Allen. "The Changed Status of American Labor," *New England Magazine* 29 (September 1903):24-31.

Secondary Sources

Books

Alinsky, Saul. *John L. Lewis: An Unauthorized Biography.* New York: G. P. Putnam's Sons, 1949.

American Labor Year Book. New York: The Rand School of Social Science, 1916-18.

Baker, Elizabeth. *Printers and Technology: A History of the International Printing Pressmen and Assistants' Union.* New York: Columbia University Press, 1957.

Barnett, George. *The Printers: A Study in American Trade Unionism.* Cambridge, Mass.: American Economic Association, 1909.

Bates, Harry C. *Bricklayers' Century of Craftsmanship: A History of the Bricklayers, Masons, and Plasterers International Union of America.* Washington, D.C.: Ransdell, 1955.

Beard, Charles A., and Mary. *Rise of American Civilization.* New York: Macmillan Co., 1930.

Bernstein, Irving. *The Lean Years: A History of the American Worker, 1920-1933.* Baltimore: Penguin Books, 1960.

Beshoar, Barron B. *Out of the Depths: The Story of John R. Lawson, a Labor Leader.* Denver: Colorado Labor Historical Committee of the Denver Trade and Labor Assembly, 1942.

Blau, Peter M. *Bureaucracy in Modern Society.* New York: Random House, 1956.

Bonnett, Clarence E. *Employers' Associations in the United States.* New York: Macmillan Co., 1922.

_____. *History of Employers' Associations in the United States.* New York: Vantage Press, 1956.

Boulding, Kenneth E. *The Organizational Revolution.* New York: Harper and Brothers, 1953.

Brissenden, Paul. *The I.W.W.: A Study of American Syndicalism.* 2d ed. New York: Russell and Russell, 1957.

Brody, David. *Steelworkers in America: The Nonunion Era.* Cambridge, Mass.: Harvard University Press, 1960.

_____. *The Butcher Workmen.* Cambridge, Mass.: Harvard University Press, 1964.

Brooks, Thomas R. *Toil and Trouble.* New York: Dell Publishing Co, 1964.

Calmer, Alan. *Labor Agitator: The Story of Albert R. Parsons.* New York: International Publishers, 1937.

Carsel, Wilfred. *A History of the Chicago Ladies Garment Workers' Union.* Chicago: Normandie House, 1940.

Christie, Robert A. *Empire in Wood: A History of the Carpenters' Union.* Ithaca, N.Y.: Cornell University Press, 1956.

Coleman, McAlister. *Men and Coal.* New York: Farrar and Rinehart, 1943.

Commons, John R., et al. *History of Labour in the United States.* 4 vols. New York: Macmillan Co., 1918-35.

Conlin, Joseph R. *Big Bill Haywood and the Radical Union Movement.* Syracuse, N.Y.: Syracuse University Press, 1969.

Cross, Ira Brown. *History of the Labor Movement in California.* Berkeley, Calif.: University of California Press, 1935.

Danish, Max D. *William Green.* New York: Inter-Allied Publications, 1952.

Deibler, Frederick Shipp. *The Amalgamated Wood Workers' International Union of America.* Madison, Wis.: University of Wisconsin Press, 1912.

DeLeon, Solon, ed. *American Labor Who's Who.* New York: The Rand School of Social Science, 1926.

Derber, Milton. *The American Idea of Industrial Democracy, 1865-1965.* Urbana, Ill.: University of Illinois Press, 1970.

Dubofsky, Melvyn. *When Workers Organize.* Amherst, Mass.: University of Massachusetts Press, 1968.

_____. *We Shall Be All.* Chicago: Quadrangle Books, 1969.

Dulles, Foster Rhea. *Labor in America: A History.* New York: Thomas Y. Crowell, 1949.

Epstein, Melech. *Jewish Labor in U.S.A.: An Industrial, Political and Cultural History of the Jewish Labor Movement, 1882-1914.* New York: Trade Union Sponsoring Committee, 1950.

Flexner, Eleanor. *Century of Struggle: The Women's Rights Movement in the United States.* 1970 ed. New York: Atheneum, 1959.

Foner, Philip S. *History of the Labor Movement in the United States.* 4 vols. New York: International Publishers, 1947-65.

Foster, William Z. *Misleaders of Labor.* Chicago: Chicago Trade Union Educational League, 1927.

Gavett, Thomas W. *Development of the Labor Movement in Milwaukee.* Madison, Wis.: University of Wisconsin Press, 1965.

Gerth, H. H., and Mills, C. Wright, eds. *From Max Weber.* New York: Oxford University Press, 1946.

Ginger, Ray. *The Bending Cross: A Biography of Eugene Victor Debs.* New Brunswick, N.J.: Rutgers University Press, 1949.

Ginsberg, Eli. *The Labor Leader: An Exploratory Study.* New York: Macmillan Co., 1948.

Glocker, Theodore W. *The Government of American Trade Unions.* Baltimore: Johns Hopkins University Press, 1913.

Gluck, Elsie. *John Mitchell, Miner: Labor's Bargain with the Gilded Age.* New York: The John Day Co., 1929.

Goldberg, Joseph P. *The Maritime Story: A Study in Labor Relations.* Cambridge, Mass.: Harvard University Press, 1958.

Gouldner, A. W., ed. *Studies in Leadership.* New York: Harper and Brothers, 1950.

Graham, Hugh Davis, and Gurr, Ted Robert, eds. *Violencee in America.* New York: Signet Books, 1969.

Green, Marguerite. *The National Civic Federation and the American Labor Movement, 1900-1925.* Washington, D.C.: The Catholic University of America Press, 1956.

Groat, George Gorham. *An Introduction to the Study of Organized Labor in America.* New York: Macmillan Co., 1917.

Grob, Gerald N. *Workers and Utopia.* Chicago: Quadrangle Books, 1961.

Grossman, Jonathan P. *William Sylvis: Pioneer of American Labor.* New York: Columbia University Press, 1945.

Hardman, J. B. S., ed. *American Labor Dynamics.* New York: Harcourt, Brace, and Co., 1928.

_____, and Neufeld, Maurice F., eds. *House of Labor: Internal Operations of American Unions.* New York: Prentice-Hall, 1951.

Harter, Lafayette G. *John R. Commons: His Assault on Laissez-Faire.* Corvallis, Oreg.: University of Oregon Press, 1962.

Hays, Samuel P. *The Response to Industrialism.* Chicago: University of Chicago Press, 1957.

Heintz, Albert M., and Whitney, John R. *History of the Massachusetts State Federation of Labor, 1887-1935.* Worcester, Mass.: The Massachusetts State Federation of Labor, 1935.

Henig, Harry. *The Brotherhood of Railway Clerks.* New York: Columbia University Press, 1937.

Henry, Alice. *Women and the Labor Movement.* New York: George H. Doran, 1923.

Hertel, Denver Willard. *History of the Brotherhood of Maintenance of Way Employees: Its Birth and Growth, 1877-1955.* Washington, D.C.: Ransdell, 1955.

Hicks, Obadiah. *The Life of Richard Trevellick, The Labor Orator, or the Harbinger of the Eight-Hour System.* Joliet, Ill.: J. F. Williams and Co.,1896.

Horowitz, Irving Louis, ed. *Power, Politics and People: The Collected Essays of C. Wright Mills.* New York: Oxford University Press, 1963.

Hoxie, Robert Franklin. *Trade Unionism in the United States.* New York: D. Appleton and Co., 1919.

Hutchinson, John. *The Imperfect Union: A History of Corruption in American Trade Unions.* New York: E. P. Dutton and Co., 1970.

Jacobson, Julius, ed. *The Negro and the American Labor Movement.* Garden City, N.J.: Doubleday and Co., Anchor Books, 1968.

Jaher, Frederic Cople, ed. *The Age of Industrialism in America.* New York: Free Press, 1968.

Janes, George Milton. *The Control of Strikes in American Trade Unions.* Baltimore: Johns Hopkins University Press, 1916.

Jensen, Vernon H. *Heritage of Conflict: Labor Relations in the Nonferrous Metal Industry up to 1930.* Ithaca, N.Y.: Cornell University Press, 1950.

Johnson, Allen et al., eds. *Dictionary of American Biography.* 21 vols and supplements. New York: Charles Scribner's Sons, 1928-58.

Josephson, Matthew. *Union House, Union Bar: The History of the Hotel and Restaurant Employees and Bartenders' International Union.* New York: Random House, 1956.

_____. *Sidney Hillman, Statesman of American Labor.* Garden City, N.J.: Doubleday and Co., 1952.

Karson, Marc. *American Labor Unions and Politics.* Carbondale, Ill.: Southern Illinois University Press, 1958.

Kirstein, George C. *Stores and Unions.* New York: Fairchild Publications, 1950.

Kopald, Sylvia. *Rebellion in Labor Unions.* New York: Boni and Liveright, 1924.

Lasch, Christopher. *The Agony of the American Left.* New York: Vintage Books, 1966.

Laslett, John H. M. *Labor and the Left: A Study of Socialist and Radical Influences in the American Labor Movement, 1881-1924.* New York: Basic Books, 1970.

Leiserson, William M. *American Trade Union Democracy.* New York: Columbia University Press, 1959.

Leiter, Robert D. *The Teamsters' Union.* New York: Bookman Associates, 1957.

Lescohier, Don D. *The Knights of St. Crispin, 1967-1874.* Madison, Wis.: University of Wisconsin Press, 1910.

Lester, Richard A. *As Unions Mature.* Princeton, N.J.: Princeton University Press, 1958.

_____. ed. *Labor: Readings on Major Issues.* New York: Random House, 1956.

Lipset, Seymour Martin. *Political Man: The Social Basis of Politics.* Garden City, N.J.: Doubleday and Co., 1959.

_____, Trow, Martin, and Coleman, James. *Union Democracy: The Internal Politics of the International Typographical Union.* New York: Free Press, 1956.

Lombardi, John. *Labor's Voice in the Cabinet: A History of the Department of Labor from Its Origin to 1921*. New York: Columbia University Press, 1942.

Lorwin, Lewis. *The Women's Garment Workers: A History of the International Ladies' Garment Workers' Union*. New York: B. W. Huebasch, 1924.

_____, and Flexner, Jean A. *The American Federation of Labor: History, Policies and Prospects*. Washington, D.C.: Brookings Institution, 1933

Lynch, James M. *Epochal History of the International Typographical Union*. Indianapolis: International Typographical Union, 1925.

McCaleb, Walter F. *Brotherhood of Railroad Trainmen: With Special Reference to the Life of Alexander F. Whitney*. New York: Boni and Liveright, 1936.

McDonald, David J., and Lynch, Edward A. *Coal and Unionism: A History of the American Coal Miners' Unions*. Silver Spring, Md.: Cornelius Printing Co., 1939.

McIsaac, Archibald M. *The Order of Railroad Telegraphers: A Study in Trade Unionism and Collective Bargaining*. Princeton, N.J.: Princeton University Press, 1933.

McMurry, Donald L. *The Great Burlington Strike of 1888*. Cambridge, Mass.: Harvard University Press, 1959.

MacDonald, Lois. *Leadership Dynamics and the Trade-Union Leader*. New York: New York University Press, 1959.

Madison, Charles A. *American Labor Leaders*. 2d ed. New York: Frederick Ungar Publishing Co., 1962.

Mandel, Bernard. *Samuel Gompers, a Biography*. Yellow Springs, Ohio: Antioch Press, 1963.

Mangum, Garth L. *The Operating Engineers*. Cambridge, Mass.: Harvard University Press, 1964.

Mann, Arthur. *Yankee Reformers in the Urban Age*. Cambridge, Mass.: Harvard University Press, 1954.

Marot, Helan. *American Labor Unions*. New York: Henry Holt and Co., 1914.

Mercey, Arch A. *The Laborer's Story, 1903-1952: The First Fifty Years of the International Hod Carriers', Building and Common Laborers' Union of America (AFL)*. Washington, D.C.: Ransdell, 1954.

Michels, Robert. *Political Parties*. Translated by Eden and Ceder Paul. New York: Dover Publications, 1959.

Mills, C. Wright. *The New Men of Power: America's Labor Leaders*. New York: Harcourt, Brace and Co., 1948.

_____. *The Power Elite*. New York: Oxford University Press, 1956.

Minton, Bruce B., and Stuart, John. *Men Who Lead Labor*. New York: Modern Age Books, 1937.

Montgomery, David. *Beyond Equality: Labor and the Radical Republicans, 1862-1872*. New York: Alfred A. Knopf, 1967.

Morgan, Edmund S. *The Puritan Dilemma: The Story of John Winthrop*. Boston: Little, Brown and Co., 1958.

Mulcaire, Michael A. *The International Brotherhood of Electrical Workers: A Study in Trade Union Structure and Function.* Washington, D.C.: The Catholic University of America Press, 1923.

Munson, Fred C. *History of the Lithographers' Union.* Cambridge, Mass.: Harvard University Press, 1963.

National Cyclopedia of American Biography. 50 vols. New York: James T. White Co., 1898-1969.

Perlman, Mark. *The Machinists: A New Study in American Trade Unionism.* Cambridge, Mass.: Harvard University Press, 1961.

Perlman, Selig. *A Theory of the Labor Movement.* New York: Macmillan, 1928.

————, and Taft, Philip. *History of Labor in the United States, 1896-1932.* New York: Macmillan Co., 1935.

Pessen, Edward. *Most Uncommon Jacksonians: The Radical Leaders of the Early Labor Movement.* Albany, N.Y.: State University of New York Press, 1957.

Pinkowski, Edward. *John Siney, The Miners' Martyr.* Philadelphia: Sunshine Press, 1963.

Quint, Howard H. *The Forging of American Socialism.* Columbia, S. C.: University of South Carolina Press, 1953.

Raddock, Maxwell. *Portrait of an American Labor Leader: William L. Hutcheson.* New York: American Institute of Social Science, 1955.

Radosh, Ronald. *American Labor and United States Foreign Policy.* New York: Random House, 1969.

Randle, C. Wilson. *Collective Bargaining: Principles and Practice.* New York: Houghton Mifflin Co., 1951.

Rayback, Joseph G. *A History of American Labor.* Rev. ed. New York: Free Press, 1966.

Renshaw, Patrick. *The Wobblies: The Story of Syndicalism in the United States.* New York: Doubleday and Co., 1967.

Robbins, Edwin C. *Railway Conductors: A Study in Organized Labor.* New York: Columbia University Press, 1914.

Robinson, Donald B. *Spotlight on a Union: A Story of the United Hatters, Cap and Millinery Workers International Union.* New York: Dial Press, 1948.

Rubin, Jay, and Obermeier, M. J. *Growth of a Union: The Life and Times of Edward Flore.* New York: Historical Union Association, 1943.

Russell, Maud. *Men Along the Shore.* New York: Russell and Russell, 1966.

Saposs, David J., ed. *Readings in Trade Unionism.* New York: Macmillan Co., 1927.

Schluter, Hermann. *The Brewing Industry and the Brewery Workers Movement in America.* Cincinnati: International Union of Brewery Workmen of America, 1910.

Scontras, Charles A. *Organized Labor and Labor Politics in Maine, 1880-1890.* Orono, Maine: University of Maine Press, 1966.

Segal, Martin. *The Rise of the United Association: National Unionism in the*

Pipe Trade, 1884-1924. Cambridge, Mass.: Harvard University Press, 1970.

Seidman, Harold. *The Labor Czars.* New York: Boni and Liveright, 1938.

Seidman, Joel. *The Brotherhood of Railroad Trainmen: The Internal Political Life of a National Union.* New York: John Wiley and Sons, 1962.

_____. *The Needle Trades.* New York: Farrar and Rinehart, 1942.

Stevens, George A. *New York Typographical Union No. 6.* Albany, N.Y.: J. B. Lyon Co., 1912.

Stolberg, Benjamin. *Tailor's Progress: The Story of a Famous Union and the Men Who Made It.* Garden City, N.J.: Doubleday and Co., 1944.

Taft, Philip. *The AFL in the Time of Gompers.* New York: Harper, 1957.

_____. *Labor Politics American Style: California Federation of Labor.* Cambridge, Mass.: Harvard University Press, 1968.

_____. *The Structure of Government of Labor Unions.* Cambridge, Mass.: Harvard University Press, 1954.

Thompson, Victor A. *Modern Organization.* New York: Alfred A. Knopf, 1961.

Tingley, Donald F., ed. *Essays in Illinois History in Honor of Glenn Huron Semour.* Carbondale, Ill.: Southern Illinois University Press, 1968.

Todes, Charlotte. *William H. Sylvis and the National Labor Union.* New York: International Publishers, 1942.

Twentieth Century Fund. *How Collective Bargaining Works.* New York: The Twentieth Century Fund, 1942.

Ulman, Lloyd. *The Rise of the National Trade Union.* Cambridge, Mass.: Harvard University Press, 1955.

Ulriksson, Vidkunn. *The Telegraphers.* Washington, D.C.: Public Affairs Press, 1953.

United States Congress. *Biographical Directory of the American Congress, 1774-1961.* Washington, D.C.: Government Printing Office, 1961.

Ware, Norman J. *The Labor Movement in the United States, 1860-1895.* New York: Vintage Books, 1929.

_____. *Labor in Modern Industrial Society.* New York: D. C. Heath, 1935.

Weinstein, James. *The Corporate Ideal in the Liberal State: 1900-1918.* Boston: Beacon Press, 1968.

_____. *The Decline of Socialism in America, 1912-1925.* New York: Vintage Books, 1967.

_____, and Eakins, David W., eds. *For a New America.* New York: Vintage Books, 1970.

Weintraub, Hyman G. *Andrew Furuseth: Emancipator of the Seamen.* Berkeley, Calif.: University of California Press, 1959.

Who Was Who in America. 3 vols. Chicago: A. N. Marquis, 1943-62.

Wiebe, Robert H. *The Search for Order, 1877-1920.* New York: Hill and Wang, 1967.

Wilensky, H. L. *The Intellectual in Labor Unions.* Glencoe, Ill.: Free Press, 1956.

Wolman, Leo. *The Growth of American Trade Unions, 1880-1923.* New York: National Bureau of Economic Research, 1924.

Yearley, Clifton K. *Britons in American Labor*. Baltimore: Johns Hopkins University Press, 1957.

Yellowitz, Irwin, ed. *The Position of the Worker in American Society, 1865-1896*. Englewood Cliffs, N.J.: Prentice-Hall, 1969.

Zieger, Robert H. *Republicans and Labor, 1919-1929*. Lexington, Ky.: University of Kentucky Press, 1969.

Articles

Barnett, George E. "The Dominance of the National Union in American Labor Organization." *The Quarterly Journal of Economics* 27 (May 1913): 455-81.

Carman, Harry J. "Terence Vincent Powderly—An Appraisal." *Journal of Economic History* 1 (May 1941):83-87.

Commons, John R. "American Shoemakers, 1648-1895: A Sketch of Industrial Evolution." *Quarterly Journal of Economics* 24 (November 1909): 53-59.

_____. "Karl Marx and Samuel Gompers," *Political Science Quarterly* (June 1926), pp. 14-27.

Galambos, Louis. "AFL's Concept of Big Business: A Quantitative Study of Attitudes toward the Large Corporation, 1894-1931," *Journal of American History* 57 (March 1971):847-63.

_____. "The Emerging Organizational Synthesis in Modern American History." *Business History Review* 44 (Autumn 1970):279-90.

Gitelman, H. M. "Adolph Strasser and the Origins of Pure and Simple Unionism." *Labor History* 6 (Winter 1965):71:83.

Gouldner, Alvin W. "Attitudes of 'Progressive' Trade-Union Leaders." *American Journal of Sociology* 52 (March 1947):389-92.

Greenbaum, Fred. "The Social Ideas of Samuel Gompers. *Labor History* 7 (Winter 1966):35-61.

Grob, Gerald N. "Terence V. Powderly and the Knights of Labor." *Mid-America* 28 (January 1957):39-55.

Gutman, Herbert. "Protestantism and the Labor Movement: The Christian Spirit in the Gilded Age," *American Historical Review* 62 (October 1966):74-101.

Hardman, J. B. S. "From Job-Consciousness to Power Accumulation." *Proceedings of the Industrial Relations Research Association* 3 (December 1950):146-57.

Heath, Frederick M. "Labor and the Progressive Movement in Connecticut." *Labor History* 12 (Winter 1971):52-67.

Helburn, I. B. "Trade Union Response to Profit-Sharing Plans: 1886-1966," *Labor History* 12 (Winter 1971):68-80.

Herberg, Will. "Bureaucracy and Democracy in Labor Unions." *Antioch Review* 3 (September 1943):405-17.

"Labor Pays Its Leaders Capitalist Wages." *Literary Digest* 64 (January 17, 1920):84-90.

Laslett, John. "Reflections on the Failure of Socialism in the American Federation of Labor." *Mississippi Valley Historical Review* 50 (March 1964):634-51.

Mandel, Bernard. "Gompers and Business Unionism, 1873-1890." *Business History Review* 28 (September 1954):264-75.

Mayer, Thomas. "Some Characteristics of Union Members in the 1880s and 1890s." *Labor History* 5 (Winter 1964):57-66.

Neufeld, Maurice F. "Realms of Thought and Organized Labor in the Age of Jackson." *Labor History* 10 (Winter 1969): 5-43.

Pritchard, Paul W. "William B. Wilson, Master Workman." *Pennsylvania History* 12 (April 1945): 81-108.

Rischin, Moses. "From Gompers to Hillman: Labor Goes Middle Class." *Antioch Review* 12 (June 1953): 191-201.

Rogin, Michael. "Voluntarism: The Politiclal Function of an Anti-Political Doctrine." *Industrial and Labor Relations Review* 15 (July 1962): 521-35.

Seledman, Benjamin M. "Trade Unions—Romance and Reality." *Harvard Business Review* 36 (May-June 1968): 76-90.

Selznick, Philip. "An Approach to the Theory of Bureaucracy." *American Sociological Review* 8 (February 1941): 47-54.

Sorokin, Pitirim. "Leaders of Labor and Radical Movements in the United States and Foreign Countries." *American Journal of Sociology* (November 1927), pp. 382-411.

Stark, Louis. "Problems of Labor Leaders." *The Annals of the American Academy of Political and Social Science* 184 (March 1936): 199-205.

Taft, Philip. "Differences in the Executive Council of the American Federation of Labor." *Labor History* 5 (Winter 1964): 40-56.

_____. "Opposition to Union Officers in Elections." *Quarterly Journal of Economics* 58 (February 1944):246-64.

_____. "On the Origins of Business Unionism." *Industrial and Labor Relations Review* 17 (October 1963): 20-38.

Unpublished Material

Chartener, William Huston. "The Molders' and Foundry Workers' Union: A Study of Union Development." Ph.D. dissertation, Department of Economics, Harvard University, 1952.

Falzone, Vincent Joseph. "Terence V. Powderly, Mayor and Labor Leader, 1849-1893." Ph.D. dissertation, Department of History, University of Maryland, 1970.

Gowaskie, Joseph Michael. "John Mitchell: A Study in Leadership." Ph.D. dissertation, The Catholic University of America, 1968.

Kileen, Charles E. "John Siney: The Pioneer in American Industrial Unionism and Industrial Government." Ph.D. dissertation, Department of History, University of Wisconsin, 1942.

Pritchard, Paul W. "William B. Wilson: The Evolution of a Central Pennsylvania Mine Union Leader." Ph.D. dissertation, Department of History, University of Pennsylvania, 1942.

Stevenson, George James. "The Brotherhood of Locomotive Engineers and Its Leaders, 1863-1920." Ph.D. dissertation, Vanderbilt University, 1954.

Thomas, Richard D. "Joseph Barondess: Labor Leader and Humanitarian." M.A. thesis, Department of History, Ohio State University, 1958.

Van Tine, Warren R. "Ben Williams: Wobbly Editor." M.A. thesis, Department of History, Northern Illinois University, 1967.

Walker, Samuel. "Terence V. Powderly and the Social Context of the Early Labor Movement," Paper read before the Missouri Valley Historical Conference, Omaha, Nebraska, March 9, 1973.

Index

tem, 116-17; and referenda,
126-27; and executive boards,
133-36; 84, 114-15, 139, 143,
150, 161
Lynch, James, 28, 96, 151, 177-
78

McBride, John, 16, 68-69, 100-
101, 110, 164
McBryde, Patrick, 110, 139, 167
McClellan Committee, 111
McDonald, David J., 175
McDonald, Duncan, 77
McGuire, Peter J., 2, 63, 99, 101,
135, 144, 154, 167, 174
Machine Wood Workers' Union,
127
McKinley, William, 171
McLaughlin, Daniel, 7
McNamara, John J., 82
McNulty, Frank J., 26
Madden, Martin B. "Skinny," 97
Madison, Charles, 37
Magidow, Jacob, 102
Mahan, William, 24
Mandel, Bernard, 155-56
Manion, Edward, 25
Marimpietri, Anzuino, 25
Maurer, James, 93, 170
Michels, Robert, 47, 96, 121,
176
Militia of Christ for Social Ser-
vices, 19, 27, 179
Miller, Henry, 143
Mills, C. Wright, 177, 180
Mine Owners' Protective Asso-
ciation, 67
Miners' Association of Western
Pennsylvania, 62
Miners' Magazine, 98-99, 108
Miners' National Association,
14, 62, 64-65, 143-44
Mitchell, John, 25, 43, 44, 65,
69-70, 71, 72-73, 80-83, 89-
90, 96-98, 99, 100, 101, 106,

115, 123, 125-26, 142, 148-
49, 153-54, 162, 166, 167,
171-74, 175, 178
Moffitt, John A., 158
Montgomery, David, 6, 11
Morgan, Edmund, 108
Morrisey, P.H., 79
Morrison, Frank, 21, 82, 147,
157
Moyer, Charles, 82, 98, 165
Mulcaire, Michael, 150
Murray, Philip, 175

National Arbitration and Peace
Congress, 27
National Association of Manu-
facturers, 81-82
National Association of Manu-
facturers of Pressed and
Blown Glassware, 77
National Brotherhood of Opera-
tive Potters, 73
National Citizens Alliance, 18
National Civic Federation, 27,
74-75, 77, 80, 83, 99, 162, 163,
175
National Founders' Association,
58, 72, 77, 81
National Labor Union, 9, 11,
42, 143-45, 162
National War Labor Board, 83
National Window Glass Work-
ers, 78, 79, 80-81, 104, 145,
170
Nearing, Scott, 152
Neenan, J.M., 80, 104
Nester, Agnes, 97, 169-70
new labor leader. See business
unionist
Noonan, James Patrick, 21

O'Connell, James, 158
O'Connor, T.V., 151
old-school labor leader. See
traditional labor leader

Stephens, Uriah S., 35, 37, 40,
46-47, 50, 55, 97, 171
Stereotypers' and Electrotypers'
Union, 74
Stevenson, George James, 76
Stone, Warren, 21, 25, 151,
163, 173
Stove Founders' National De-
fense Association, 58, 67, 73,
78
Strasser, Adolph, 2, 10, 42, 71,
111, 135, 171
Sullivan, Jere L., 104, 154, 171
Swinton, John, 97
Sylvis, William, 5, 42, 46, 65,
88, 103, 108, 115-16, 135,
143-44, 175

Taft, Philip, 2, 74
Talbot, Thomas, 14
Tanner, Charles, 165
temperance movement, 3, 18,
28
Textile Worker, 44, 48, 52
Thompson, Victor, 95, 150
Tobacco Workers' International Union, 92, 119
Tobin, Daniel, 52, 53, 91, 101,
104, 105, 111, 116, 135, 142,
148, 173
traditional labor leader: stereotype of, 2-4, 7-8; average date
of birth, 9; nationality of, 9-12,
19; religious background of,
9-10, 19; residency patterns
of, 12-13, 20-21, 23; occupation of fathers of, 13, 21; education of, 13, 21; business
activities of, 14, 17; age at
attaining office, 14-15, 23;
tenure in office, 15, 24; political activities of, 15-16; membership in social clubs and
reform organizations, 17-18;
compared with business
unionist, 28-31; opposition

from business unionists, 174
Trevellick, Richard, 10, 96,
143-44, 162
Turner, Frederick, J., 14, 35
Typographical Journal, 45, 53,
75, 128, 145, 149

union: as a business, 33, 34, 38,
50-56, 115, 122, 132, 147; as
a democracy, 33, 34, 38, 40-
48, 50, 55-56; as a fraternity,
33, 34, 35-40, 50, 55-56; as an
army, 33, 34, 38, 48-50, 55-56,
115
union recognition, 59, 71-72
union shop, 94-95
United Association of Plumbers,
Gas Fitters, Steam Fitters
and Steam Fitters' Helpers,
26, 79-80
United Brewery Workers, 7, 54,
92
United Brotherhood of Carpenters and Joiners, 26, 63, 66,
67, 131, 134, 135, 144-45, 153,
166, 173, 178
United Cloth Hat and Cap
Makers' Union, 40, 158, 171
United Garment Workers, 21,
41, 42, 45, 71, 78, 87-88, 94,
103, 109, 122-23, 124, 130-31,
157
United Hebrew Trades, 102
United Mine Workers' Journal,
41, 45, 46, 50, 53, 54, 79, 84
90, 93, 96, 98, 99, 104-9, 121,
162, 164, 168, 170, 171, 177
United Mine Workers of America, 7, 16, 17, 25, 26, 43, 51,
68, 72-73, 77, 79, 81, 87, 88,
89, 98, 100, 104-12, 115, 121,
122, 124-26, 134, 138, 139,
145, 153-54, 164, 166, 171-72,
177-78
United Textile Workers, 130,
179